Organizing, Role Enactment, and Disaster

Organizing, Role Enactment, and Disaster

A Structural Theory

Gary A. Kreps
and Susan Lovegren Bosworth
with
Jennifer A. Mooney,
Stephen T. Russell,
and Kristen A. Myers

DELAWARE

Newark: University of Delaware Press
London and Toronto: Associated University Presses

Associated University Presses
440 Forsgate Drive
Cranbury, NJ 08512

Associated University Presses
25 Sicilian Avenue
London WC1A 2QH, England

Associated University Presses
P.O. Box 338, Port Credit
Mississauga, Ontario
Canada L5G 4L8

The paper used in this publication meets the requirements
of the American National Standard for Permanence of Paper
for Printed Library Materials Z39.48-1984.

Library of Congress Cataloging-in-Publication Data

Kreps, Gary A.
    Organizing, role enactment, and disaster : a structural theory /
Gary A. Kreps and Susan Lovegren Bosworth ; with Jennifer A. Mooney,
Stephen T. Russell, and Kristen A. Myers.
        p.   cm.
    Includes bibliographical references (p.   ) and index.
    ISBN 0-87413-468-4 (alk. paper)
    1. Disaster relief—Research.   2. Disasters—Social aspects.
3. Social structure.   I. Bosworth, Susan Lovegren, 1958–
II. Title.
HV553.K73   1994
363.3'4—dc20   92-56767
                                                                      CIP

PRINTED IN THE UNITED STATES OF AMERICA

To our families

Contents

Figures and Tables

Figures

Tables

Foreword

RUSSELL R. DYNES AND E. L. QUARANTELLI

Too many disaster "studies" rest on opportunistic observations by researchers who are unfamiliar with the theoretical literature and whose qualifications rest on being at the wrong place at the right time. Their observations are often cast in terms of the unusual and even the esoteric as they try to capture the drama of the occasion. Disasters, however, are never unique. They are recurrent social situations, and even the dramatic should be firmly rooted in the continuity of social life. That continuity too often is missed. In addition, such "studies" tend to emphasize the trauma, the disruption implicitly suggesting that social structure is irrelevant to the problems at hand and that only heroic individual actions count.

By contrast, this book is firmly rooted in a much more productive tradition. Kreps is one of the few scholars working systematically on theoretical issues relating social structure to disaster. His work and those of his colleagues is solidly based in the sociological tradition, more specifically at the intersection of social organization and collective behavior. He is and has been concerned with the relationship between the persistence of social structure as well as its modification in crisis situations. Here, in his focus on role and role structure, he deals with an issue that recently has received renewed attention in sociological literature—the relationship between micro- and macrolevels of analysis. His work, then, deals with recurrent theoretical issues within sociology.

Especially interesting from our point of view has been his judicious use of secondary materials. When the Disaster Research Center was started in 1963, it was our intent not just to maintain a library but also to establish a data archive. Many considered the idea interesting, but few considered it fundable, especially agencies where results are measured at the end of a calendar year or the end of a specific project. To maintain the richness of our interviews with persons involved in emergency organizations seemed worthwhile, even though our time to utilize those data sources was lim-

13

ited. For many of the graduate students at the center, new data, like new cars, were better, more modern than the files in the library. The excitement for most was out there, not downstairs. Kreps was almost singlehanded and singleminded about the potentialities of the data archives. Much like a prospector looking for treasure, he had been able to base the current analysis on this broad data base. This work is especially pleasing since it validates our decision many years ago that such resources would be valuable in the future.

Equally gratifying is his utilization of the DRC typology as a theoretical guide and his empirical validation of its continued utility. That conceptualization evolved from our initial attempts to deal with our field observations concerning organizational adaptation and our frustration in finding little in the organizational literature to fit our observations. It is still our contention that most organizational theory has difficulty in dealing with emergence and change. Kreps proves instructive in this regard.

One of the more impressive themes in the book is the attempt to understand social structure in crisis situations. In a time when explanations are usually individualistic and in a culture where assumptions are based on psychology, most treatments of crises assume that conventional social structure is irrelevant or an impediment to action. The complexity of the analysis presented here cannot reduce the simplicities of individual behavior. Kreps's analysis underscores the importance of understanding of more routine social occasions. Like all good research, he builds on the efforts of past researchers. The importance of the book is not avoiding the drama but in paying attention to the significant details.

Acknowledgments

The theory building that is summarized in this monograph was influenced in a very direct way by Ralph Turner. We have great respect for his contributions to collective behavior and role theory, and we hope we have built on the foundations provided by them. We also have learned a great deal from his constructive criticisms of the first phase of our archival research on organization and role. The broader program of which that research is a part continues to benefit as well from a host of constructive commentaries provided by twenty-five scholars at a symposium the senior author held in the spring of 1986 (Kreps 1989a).

The specific project reported on here was undertaken by a team composed of the authors and three graduate assistants. The project could not have been completed successfully without the efforts of Jennifer Mooney, Stephen Russell, and Kristen Myers, all of whom were graduate students at the College of William and Mary during various phases of the research. We have listed them as contributors to this volume in special appreciation for all they have done. Thanks also to our colleagues and friends, David Aday and Satoshi Ito, who have been generous with their time and insightful in their comments during all phases of study.

The senior author wishes to thank the College of William and Mary for providing a summer grant, which helped get the project started in 1987; the National Science Foundation for providing necessary funds over a three-year period (1987–90); and the college again for providing a semester leave to work on this monograph. Special thanks also are due our program manager at NSF, William Anderson, for his continued interest in our archival studies. Please note, however, that any opinions, findings, conclusions, and recommendations expressed in this document are those of the authors and do not necessarily reflect the views of the National Science Foundation. Finally, we thank Russell Dynes and Henry Quarantelli for their generous support over the years, for the foundation their own massive research on disasters has provided for everything we have done, and for agreeing to write the Foreword of this book. When the history of disaster research is written, their

15

contributions to this specialty, the discipline of sociology, and the emergency management profession will be among the most important.

This book deals with disaster, organization, and role. Our families made sure that there were few personal emergencies and no disasters to contend with in completing the work on which it is based. We dedicate this book to our spouses, Loretta and Leonard, and to our children, Brad, Bart, Matthew, Landry, and Elizabeth.

GARY A. KREPS and SUSAN L. BOSWORTH

Organizing, Role Enactment, and Disaster

1

Disaster Archives, a Research Program, and Sociological Theory

This book summarizes our attempt to construct a formal sociological theory. By formal theory, we mean one that isolates core concepts, establishes laws of interaction among them, and specifies logical and empirical boundaries for these concepts and laws (Dubin 1978; R. Turner 1980). By sociological theory, we mean one whose core concepts address social structure on its own terms (Durkheim 1938; Warriner 1956, 1970; Mayhew 1980, 1981, 1982). The core structural concepts we address are organization and role. The empirical contexts we examine are the emergency periods of natural disasters. The data we use for this examination are in the archives of the Disaster Research Center (DRC) at the University of Delaware.

In this orienting chapter we summarize initially the history of the research program from which the present study emerged. That history is important for two reasons. First, it necessarily highlights the strengths and limitations (as empirical materials) of the archives we have been examining. Second, it shows how the evolution of the program led to our collaborative efforts. We will then discuss our primary motivation and preliminary approach for studying organizing and role dynamics at the same time. The consequences of that research strategy include an article in the *American Sociological Review* (Bosworth and Kreps 1986), a useful dialogue with Ralph Turner based on this article (reported in Kreps 1989a, 201–13), and finally, the follow-up research summarized in this monograph.

We conclude briefly by providing the rationale for the remaining chapters, each of which is an important step in constructing an explicit theory of disaster, organization, and role. The theory itself is formalized in the last chapter, and a data (research) protocol for testing it appears in Appendix C. The theory can be tested through additional archival studies or, ideally, through primary data collection in the field. The theory and protocol are the natural end-products of the latest phase of our archival studies. They express what we have learned and also our growing appreciation for the contributions of the Disaster Research Center to the discipline of sociology.

History of Kreps's Archival Research Program

Gary Kreps's initial interest in the archives resulted from personal experiences as a field researcher at the Disaster Research Center (1968–71). The DRC was founded in 1963 at the Ohio State University, remained there until 1984, and was moved to the University of Delaware in 1985. The original codirectors (E. L. Quarantelli, Russell Dynes, and J. Eugene Haas) established data archives with the hope that they would expand with each new study undertaken by the DRC. That hope continues to be realized as the center is about to complete the third decade of its existence.

By 1973 the archives contained over three thousand tape-recorded interviews, about twenty-two hundred of which had been transcribed. Several hundred transcribed notes of nonrecorded interviews had been stored along with even larger numbers of after-action reports, disaster plans, organizational logs, newspaper reports, and other documents. About six thousand additional interviews have been tape-recorded since 1973 (see Wenger 1989, 241–44, for an updating), but transcribing was largely abandoned in 1974 because of insufficient funds. From initial work during the summers of 1973 and 1974 to studies funded by the National Science Foundation from 1982 to 1991, Kreps's archival research has been confined to DRC studies of events for which interview transcriptions had been completed earlier. About sixteen hundred of the available twenty-two hundred transcribed interviews have been analyzed one or more times in various projects by ourselves and ten graduate students.

The interviews we have examined are semistructured or unstructured (see Denzin 1989, especially chapter 4). The field instruments were designed originally by DRC researchers to collect data on social responses to disasters as soon as possible after these events occurred. Concepts derived largely from collective behavior and organizational perspectives in sociology were used only as sensitizers for empirical research (Denzin 1989, 13–14); and certainly in the first decade of the DRC's existence, there was no attempt to test any formal theory (Wallace 1971). Key participants were identified in the field, often when the emergency was still in progress. Individuals who agreed to be interviewed were asked to describe, first, their own actions during the immediate emergency period; second, the activities of social units of which they were members; and third, the actions of any other responding units they had observed during the emergency. Interviewees therefore served as respondents *and* informants (Denzin 1989, 173–74). The interviews themselves typically ranged from about one-half hour to two or three hours.

The archives are very difficult to work with. The depth of DRC studies (i.e., numbers of interviews and documents) varies greatly from one event to the next, as does the quantity and quality of information for each event. There is no alternative to tedious spadework because one often does not know where or even if useful data can be found. In his overview of the archives, Wenger summarizes nicely in *Social Structure and Disaster* (Kreps 1989a, 245) the problems we have faced over the years:

> The data are qualitative in nature. The nine thousand interviews are detailed, long narrative accounts. One has to dig, search, and sort through a vast amount of material. For those interviews that have been transcribed, it may mean reading sixty pages of text to find one or two sentences that directly relate to one's interest. In the case of interviews that have not been transcribed (literally thousands), one may have to listen intently to two- or three-hour tape recordings to catch the desired material.

But as our research program over the past several years, we hope, has shown (see Kreps 1989a), the results are worth the required labor-intensive effort. This is because the archives report on what active human beings and social units are doing under emergency conditions and the social contexts in which such action takes place. This makes them very well-suited for empirically grounding the dynamics of organizing and role enactment. While in some sense all research is theory driven, in this case the impact of research on theory has been of equal importance (Merton 1957, 85–120).

Of primary interest to the original DRC field teams were the activities of formal organizations at the local level that had obvious responsibilities immediately prior to, during, or shortly after disaster events. These included police and fire departments, hospitals, utilities, departments of public works, voluntary agencies, and the mass media. The kinds of events studied were primarily earthquakes, tornadoes, floods, and hurricanes. The effort was to determine what was done, either planned or otherwise; the kinds of problems encountered; and how these problems were handled.

The field teams frequently were able to obtain detailed accounts of how formal organizations that were expected to be involved actually responded. The teams sometimes were also able (albeit not always predictably) to record equally useful accounts of the improvisations of groups and organizations that had no predetermined role in an event; and, on more than a few occasions, they discovered social units that did not even exist prior to an event. These latter groups were particularly interesting because even though short-lived, they seemed (analytically, at least) to be comparable to any other organization. The possible parallel between collective behavior and formal organization was therefore an intriguing possibility.

Kreps's interest in working with the archives was the result of sustained puzzling about differences between formal organization and collective behavior (Weller 1969; Weller and Quarantelli 1973); and many very stimulating conversations, debates, and informal brainstorming sessions among colleagues at the DRC about the theoretical value of its research for unraveling those differences (Kreps 1981). It seemed clear to all those involved in discussions at the DRC that purely structural questions are the most interesting and important ones for sociologists to consider. It was also clear that the emergency periods of disasters are strategic research sites for addressing structural questions. This meant that the DRC archives, which were expanding with each disaster studied, ought to be exploited in some fashion. The problem was how systematic analyses of the archives could be accomplished.

Kreps's starting point was a four-fold typology. It had become obvious to DRC researchers after several initial studies that some tool was needed to capture the range of different types of organized responses during the emergency period. That tool, developed during the late 1960s, was the four-fold classification depicted in figure 1.1 (Dynes 1970, 162). All four types had been identified one or more times, but there was no formal counting or cataloguing of them across different kinds of events.

Type I organizations were characterized as *established* because their basic structures exist prior to disasters and much of what they do is predetermined. Examples of established organizations include police and fire departments, utilities, and hospitals.

Type II organizations were characterized as *expanding* because, while much of what they do is predetermined, their basic structure changes from a small cadre of professionals to a much larger struc-

Figure 1.1

Disaster Research Center Typology of
Organized Disaster Responses

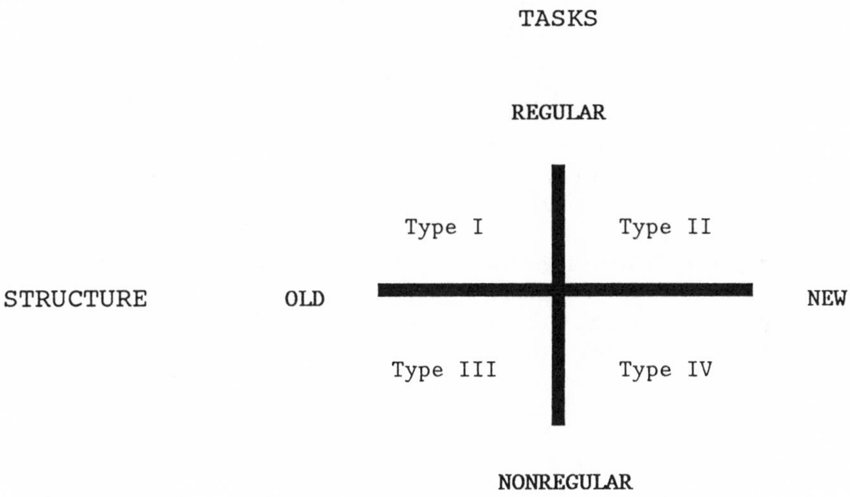

TASKS

REGULAR

		Type I		Type II	
STRUCTURE	OLD				NEW
		Type III		Type IV	

NONREGULAR

Type I: Established organized response
Type II: Expanding organized response
Type III: Extending organized response
Type IV: Emergent organized response

ture composed of formally designated volunteers. Examples of expanding organizations include Red Cross chapters, Salvation Army units, and civil defense agencies.

Type III organizations were characterized as *extending* because, while their basic structures exist prior to disasters, much of what they do is unanticipated. The number of possibilities was assumed to be large, but the most obvious examples are local businesses, purely social groups, churches, and public service organizations.

Finally, Type IV organizations were characterized as *emergent* because, quite simply, their existence generally is confined to the emergency period. While there are numerous possibilities here as well, examples include damage assessment groups, operations groups of various types, and coordination groups.

A concrete example of an emergent organization, one that was reconstructed later by Kreps from the archives, illustrates the type that was of particular interest to him in the early 1970s. The parenthetical letters will be defined below:

A small town on the gulf coast of the United States is impacted severely by a hurricane. Accompanying the physical devastation that follows, streets are inundated with water and communications are severed. Physical movement is minimal and the town is largely isolated for a time. There is little semblance of any organized community response for the next day or so. But by the third day, an official of a nearby national air and space testing facility, who was also a resident of the devastated town, offers the mayor personnel from the testing facility, materials (principally water and fuel), and equipment which are at his disposal. Following the influx of these human and material resources, the mayor calls for a meeting involving the testing facility official, himself, and other civic leaders. The latter includes the director of civil defense, police chief, five town aldermen, and a local doctor. The purpose of the meeting is to determine ways in which these donated resources should be used. A regional telephone company executive offers a meeting site that will later become an emergency operations center (R). With the help of the testing facility official, the mayor organizes what he refers to as the overall civil defense effort involving the above individuals (R-D). Over the next several days, this group responds to various problems dealing with communications, the operations of various evacuation shelters, search and rescue, and assimilation of outside assistance to the community (R-D-A). A task structure emerges rapidly from the momentum created by the group's activities. Major activity areas are formally identified and distinct areas of responsibility are divided among the core members (R-D-A-T).

The above group is improvised rather than planned, thus revealing some of the character of collective behavior (R. Turner 1964; 1989, 207–8). At the same time, its organizational quality can be seen as evolving rather quickly during the emergency period (Thompson 1967, 51–53).

It is a small step from cases such as this one to three very important sociological questions: First, what is an organization? Second, how is organizing similar to and different from collective behavior? And third, are there ways of describing organizing and collective behavior within the same conceptual framework? These questions are analytically critical for the emergency period of disasters because, as the above case reveals, the existence of organization is often an issue rather than a given. Not only do new organizations spontaneously emerge, many existing ones (Type III) undertake nonroutine activities. And even those that are expected to respond (Types I and II) often have to make substantial changes in everyday routines. Finally, many other community organizations temporarily stop operating altogether during the emergency period, suggesting that for analytical purposes they do not exist.

With the above questions in mind, and previous discussions of them by Weller (1969) and Weller and Quarantelli (1973) to guide his effort, Kreps's research with the archives began during the 1973–74 period with some initial reading of two to three hundred interviews. The result was a preliminary statement of what Kreps thought the archives were saying about the commonality of organization and collective behavior as structural concepts (Kreps 1978). The theoretical tool he used to express that commonality was later to become a structural code of domains (D), tasks (T), human and material resources (R), and activities (A). Sustained funding by the National Science Foundation and the College of William and Mary during the 1980s afforded Kreps and later us the opportunity to put that code to work in more detailed analyses of the DRC archives.

With respect to the above three questions, a structural code of domains (D), tasks (T), human and material resources (R), and activities (A) provides one answer to the question: what is an organization? With respect to the above case description, for example, the first thing observed is the presence of resources in the form of the testing facility people and material resources, the local community leaders, and the telephone company facility (R). Resources are defined as *individual capacities and collective technologies of human populations*. The next thing observed is a domain in terms of a formally designated yet totally improvised civil defense effort (R-D). Domains are defined as *collective representations of bounded units and their reasons for being*. The major activities of the operations group are then observed (R-D-A), and from these activities shared understandings emerge quickly about differentiated responsibilities (R-D-A-T). Activities are defined in the code as *conjoined actions of individuals and social units*. Tasks are defined as *collective representations of a division of labor for the enactment of human activities*.

Central to answering the questions above, we argue that domains, tasks, human and material resources, and activities are individually necessary and collectively sufficient for organization to exist. This means that each element observed in time and space is a unique expression of social structure; that their mutual copresence points to the existence of organization; and that no pattern of their emergence is necessarily more frequent, important, or effective than any other. Accordingly, all logically possible combinations and permutations of the elements are expressed taxonomically as forms of association. As noted in table 1.1, a derived sixty-four cell taxonomy includes four one-element forms, twelve two-element forms, twenty-four three-element forms, and twenty-four four-element forms. While only the four-element forms are sufficient for organization to exist, the remaining forty types—all of which describe social structure in process—depict stages in its origins (Kreps 1985a).

The above example of an ad hoc emergency operations group therefore depicts four different structural forms (R, R-D, R-D-A, and R-D-A-T). Notice that when some empirically discernible threshold for any of the four elements has been passed, a structural form exists. As each additional element comes into play, a new form has been created. When all four elements are present, an organization has been socially constructed.

Is collective behavior being observed? Certainly: resources are being mobilized before there is a clear idea of how they are going to be used; and activities are being performed before a division of labor has been worked out. Is formal organization being evidenced? Certainly: nothing happens before the operation is mandated officially; and collective actions are not long sustained in the absence of defined lines of accountability. In this case, the apparent complementarity of collective behavior and formal organizing seems quite appropriate to the circumstances being faced (R. Turner 1964; Thompson 1967).

Observe the subtle differences in the possible ordering of the four elements arrayed in table 1.1. The discrete patterns can be thought of as a continuum: with D-T-R-A or formal organizing at one end and A-R-T-D or collective behavior at the other (Saunders and Kreps 1987). With formal organizing, structural ends (domains and tasks) precede and constrain structural means (resources and activities). With collective behavior, structural means precede and constrain structural ends. A pattern like the above case example (an R-D-A-T form) involves a balancing of the two extremes on the continuum. Formal organizing and collective behavior can therefore be observed as two sides of the same coin (Warriner 1989, 295–304; Kreps 1991).

Referring back to figure 1.1, one might conclude that while a structural code provides a potentially fruitful way of describing the origins of emergent organizations (Type IV), what is to be done with the three other types in the DRC typology? After all, Types I, II, and III already exist and are simply transforming in different

Table 1.1
Taxonomy of Structural Forms

Four-Element Forms: Organization	Three-Element Forms	Two-Element Forms	One-Element Forms
D-T-R-A	D-T-R	D-T	D
D-T-A-R	D-T-A	D-R	T
D-R-A-T	D-R-A	D-A	R
D-R-T-A	D-R-T	T-R	A
D-A-T-R	D-A-T	T-A	——
D-A-R-T	D-A-R	T-D	
T-R-A-D	T-R-A	R-A	
T-R-D-A	T-R-D	R-D	
T-A-D-R	T-A-D	R-T	
T-A-R-D	T-A-R	A-D	
T-D-R-A	T-D-R	A-T	
T-D-A-R	T-D-A	A-R	
R-A-D-T	R-A-D	——	
R-A-T-D	R-A-T		
R-D-T-A	R-D-T		
R-D-A-T	R-D-A		
R-T-D-A	R-T-D		
R-T-A-D	R-T-A		
A-D-T-R	A-D-T		
A-D-R-T	A-D-R		
A-T-D-R	A-T-D		
A-T-R-D	A-T-R		
A-R-D-T	A-R-D		
A-R-T-D	A-R-T		
24 forms	24 forms	12 forms	4 forms

Total Forms = 64

STRUCTURAL CODE

Domains (D) are collective representations of bounded units and their reasons for being.

Tasks (T) are collective representations of a division of labor for the enactment of human activities.

Resources (R) are individual capacities and collective technologies of human populations.

Activities (A) are the conjoined actions of individuals and social units.

ways. Kreps's initial response was that for analytical purposes the life history of any organization can be circumscribed by the event and its immediate aftermath.

Within this time frame, many existing units do not act at all (the absence of structure), or they do unconventional things. The latter is always the case with extending organizations in the DRC typology, and it is often the case with established and expanding ones. In effect, neither involvement of an existing unit nor its precise character can be taken for granted. For purposes of his archival analysis, then, Kreps used the event as a social catalyst (Dubin 1978). In other words, the disaster event served as a catalyst whose presence was necessary for examining structure in process. It is clear from the above example, however, that by invoking the event as a social catalyst, Kreps did not deny the relevance of pre-event conditions for what takes place (Dynes 1970; Quarantelli and Dynes 1977; Stallings 1978; Kreps 1984).

With the structural code in hand, and using the event as social catalyst, Kreps now knew what he was looking for in doing spadework with the archives. Working from late 1981 until early 1983, he completed the first phase of archival analysis. The criteria he used for selecting events previously studied by the DRC were that they could yield interpretable data on organizational enactments; that data production would continue until a sample of three to four hundred enactments was achieved; and that a sufficient number of events would be studied so that organizational form, disaster event, and impacted community differences could be explored.

Kreps's data production stopped with purposive samples of fifteen events, 1,062 interviews, and 423 instances of enacted organization. Twenty-one of the twenty-four organizational forms (all four elements present) arrayed on table 1.1 were documented one or more times, and all but four of the one- to three-element forms were documented one or more times as stages of organizing (Kreps 1989a, 41). Some 65 percent of the organizational forms were enacted by established units, 9 percent by expanding units, 14 percent by extending units, and 12 percent by emergent units.

Even though the original DRC fieldwork emphasized documenting the actions of established and expanding organizations—units whose involvement was expected and sometimes planned before events—only 39 percent of the enactments identified were D-T-R-A forms in the taxonomy. So despite the fact that extending and emergent organizations were documented on a "catch as catch can" basis by DRC researchers, the evidence of collective behavior was quite clear. The D-R-T-A forms and D-R-A-T forms (19 percent of the enactments) pointed to the improvisation of tasks even when a domain is established first. The R-D-T-A and other resources initiated patterns (29 percent of the enactments) suggested that the coexistence of need and available resources can impel organizing in the absence of domains. The clear conclusion was that formal organizing and collective behavior are related in many subtle ways.

The population parameters of organizational enactments for the events studied were (and remain) unknown, and for some events there were usable data on only a few cases. Interestingly enough, feeling that he had overcome the limitations of figure 1.1 for describing collective behavior as organizing in process, Kreps paid no further attention to its continuing potential for theory-building purposes. That was a clear mistake that we have only recently corrected in our studies of role dynamics.

The key requirement Kreps faced in producing a data file from the archives was to describe the presence and sequencing of the four elements for every instance of enacted organization uncovered, regardless of its type in the original DRC classification. Given the focus of the original fieldwork, Kreps assumed that most of the enacting units would be Type I or Type II (established or expanding), but that there would also be plenty of examples of Types III and IV (extending or emergent). The above distribution of enacting units indicates that his assumption was correct.

In completing this history of the research program, it is important to be precise about how Kreps's data file on 423 organizational enactments was produced. For each case selected, Kreps's initial strategy involved locating an enacting unit whose actions were described in enough detail so that he could determine the presence of all four elements of the structural code. This was accomplished in the following way. Unit identifications were not a problem for existing organizations because interviewees were catalogued in terms of their organizational affiliations. Emergent units could be identified also because direct participants or others involved in the emergency usually characterized improvised organizations by specific names. In either case, determining the name of an enacting unit was of critical importance to Kreps for affirming its existence and documenting its domain.

Both domains and tasks were sometimes evidenced in the archives by official declaration or formal planning (often the case for established and expanding organizations), sometimes as written statements, and sometimes only through interpersonal communications between direct participants and legitimating authorities. But in all cases, Kreps's approach was to document domains and

tasks through descriptions of formal or informal communications—
what Mayhew (1980) has termed the organization of information—
as they were relayed to the field interviewers by participants or
informants, recorded in documents, or observed in the field. Thus
Kreps relied on explicit communications and not tacit understandings that may or may not have been operating. His research
strategy was therefore quite conservative. Looking for tacit understandings, Kreps felt, amounted to reading too much into archival accounts.

Kreps documented resources and activities in terms of their content, timing, and location. The archives were far from complete in
all of these regards. Moreover, organizational boundaries were
often difficult to determine when more than one unit was engaged
in the same domain. This meant that identifying discontinuities
in either the timing or location of organizational enactments was
essential for specifying discrete entities in terms of mobilized resources and conjoined action.

Once having located an instance of organization, Kreps's next
problem was to determine the ordering of the four elements at
its origins (i.e., which came first, second, third, and fourth). This
required a reconstruction of what happened from the interviews
and documents. Data on emergent units (fifty-two of them were
found) were generally good—indeed, that is why they could be
identified in the first place—and the sequencing problem was not
too difficult. A similar situation prevailed for existing organizations
(primarily established or expanding) where domains or tasks were
specified prior to the event by formal mandate or planning. Where
sequencing judgments were more uncertain, determining which
element set off the process was less a problem than figuring out
the ordering of the remaining elements. The primary reason for
this latter difficulty was that the quality of the archival data varied
so dramatically. Hundreds of cases were simply dropped because
of inadequate information.

Kreps's research strategy involves feedback between empirical
phenomena (organizational enactments documented in the archives) and combinatory principles (a structural code) that describe them (Sylvan and Glassner 1985, 154-56). The strategy can
be seen as a variant of analytical induction (Denzin 1989, 166-70).
It is a variant of analytical induction because Kreps's objective
has been to describe rather than explain the observed phenomena
(Dubin 1978, 87). The research process began in 1973 with a rough
definition of organization (derived primarily from Weller 1969,
Dynes 1970, and Weller and Quarantelli 1973). After work with

several hundred interviews, the definition made explicit reference to domains, tasks, human and material resources, and activities as individually necessary and collectively sufficient for organization to exist (Kreps 1978). At this point in the process, Kreps assumed that there were many different organizing possibilities, but he had no explicit notion of how many there were. Then, as more detailed work with the archives ensued, these four elements became defined explicitly as a structural code, and the alternative logical possibilities became cells in an empirical taxonomy (Kreps 1985a).

It is obvious that Kreps's research strategy required precise threshold judgments from data of varying quality on very fluid situations (Drabek 1970). Developing precise threshold criteria was and remains an important goal (Kreps 1989a, 186-237). While reliability in the sequencing of the elements is a continuing problem, data on all of the emergent units (fifty-two) and over a hundred of the existing (established, expanding, extending) ones identified originally by Kreps have been reanalyzed one or more times. Attribute judgments, and debates about them, have been part and parcel of this research program. (See Enoch 1988 and Farmer 1989 for discussions of several relevant issues.) One of the major advantages of this structural code for any subsequent taxonomic work is the formal inclusion of counterfactuals. That is to say, there are any number of alternatives for every judgment made about the presence and sequencing of the four elements in the historical happenings that are described.

Archival Studies of Organizing and Role Dynamics

Kreps's initial data production has been followed by a number of analyses and reanalyses of his data file and the creation of several new ones. Among other things, the structural code has been used empirically to describe (1) the origins of emergent units (Type IV in figure 1.1) during disasters (Saunders and Kreps 1987); (2) the restructuring of existing units (Types I, II, and III in figure 1.1) during disasters (Kreps, Crooks, and Linn 1987; Linn and Kreps 1989, 108-35); (3) the formation of dyadic social networks during disasters (Francis and Kreps 1984; Kreps and Bosworth 1987;[1] and (4) the life histories of civil rights organizations (Farmer 1989, 135-66). The code also has been used as a heuristic tool to consider a number of general theoretical issues in sociology, such as the dialectic of social action and social order (Kreps 1989a, 253-78)[2] and the use of structural codes for comparative research (Kreps 1989a,

166-86; 1991, 143-77). The studies of organizing and role dynamics reported on here, therefore, are only one part of a multifaceted research program.

Our collaborative attempt to interrelate the concepts of organization and role began in 1983 when Susan Bosworth was a graduate student in sociology, and they have continued in her subsequent role as a research associate. As noted above, by 1984 Kreps had been working on the development of a structural code for several years. He believed that the commonality of collective behavior and formal organizing during a disaster would be revealed by it. He also believed that structural codes were essential for developing sociological theory in any empirical context. In effect, Kreps sought a basic building block of social structure from which a formal taxonomy could be derived and, ultimately, an explanatory theory of social structure could be produced.

But structural codes of the sort illustrated by Kreps's work are not the only possible basic building blocks of structure. A very obvious alternative, and one that continues to be offered in the vast majority of introductory texts, is the concept of role. We agreed at the outset of our collaboration that it would be very difficult to build a taxonomy of role enactments that might parallel the one on organizational enactments depicted in table 1.1. As Kreps argued later in *Social Structure and Disaster* (1989a, 269):

> Role is profoundly complex because people are. Sociologists have produced thousands of regression equations to document that conclusion. As descriptive concept of structure, role is a morass without good prospect of taxonomic closure. I suspect that is why role theorists (of either positivist or interpretive leaning) give so little attention to classification.

But if we wanted to come up with better descriptions of social structure, the use of role as an additional empirical sensitizer (Denzin 1989, 13-14) might be of enormous value. Indeed, it was obvious that the archives often provided considerable information about role enactments.

Consider the case example presented earlier. Some people, specifically the testing facility official, doctor, and telephone company executive, seem to be creating roles for themselves as the emergency unfolds. But while these individuals are arguably new incumbents, they also seem to have the capacities necessary for expanding their role repertoires. It is also arguable that the roles they perform are as much adopted as they are invented. On the other hand, individuals such as the mayor, police chief, civil defense director, and town aldermen are established incumbents of roles that seem to impel their involvement in the emergency. But the precise nature of their involvement is not predetermined, and it seems quite clear that these people are improvising as they go along.

Thus, regardless of whether one describes this case as organizing or role enactment, an important symmetry is being revealed about structure in process: ostensibly new social arrangements cannot be divorced from already existing social structure; and already existing social structure is always subject to change. Warriner states this symmetry very well in *Social Structure and Disaster* (Kreps 1989a, 302):

> In the study of social phenomena we have often considered change as surprising and requiring explanation. Rather it seems to me that we must be equally surprised at recurrence and we should seek its explanation as assiduously as we seek to explain change.

Thus just as collective behavior and formal organizing are two sides of the same coin, so also are making roles and playing them. The requirements we faced, therefore, were to conceptualize role enactment in terms of role-making *and* role-playing, and then to try to measure this conception as completely as possible with the DRC archives. The end result, we hoped, would be more powerful descriptions of social happenings during the emergency periods of disasters.

Just as with Kreps's previous work on the code, through a process of bouncing sociological ideas about role against archival descriptions of what people are doing, we identified what appeared to be four basic dimensions of role enactment. We believed that each of these dimensions could be wedded with either symbolic interactionist or structuralist conceptions of role (J. Turner 1978; Stryker 1980; R. Turner 1985). Because the former appeared to be more sensitive to role-making and the latter to role-playing, we thought that a merging of these perspectives in our research would be fruitful. The four dimensions are arrayed in figure 1.2.

We termed the first dimension *inconsistency versus consistency of the status/role nexus* to express the extent to which social expectations tied to predisaster positions shape postdisaster role behavior. We termed the second dimension *discontinuity versus continuity of role linkages* to express stability and change with respect to role relationships from pre- to postdisaster time periods.

Figure 1.2

Dimensions of Role Enactment

ROLE-MAKING	◄———————	ENACTMENT	———————►	ROLE-PLAYING
Inconsistent	◄———————	STATUS-ROLE NEXUS	———————►	Consistent
Discontinuous	◄———————	ROLE LINKAGES	———————►	Continuous
Unique role performance	◄———————	ROLE PERFORMANCE	———————►	Role boundary expansion
Homogeneous	◄———————	ROLE DIFFERENTIATION	———————►	Heterogeneous

We termed the third dimension *unique role performance versus role boundary expansion* to express degrees of innovativeness in role performance. Finally, we termed the fourth dimension *homogeneity versus heterogeneity of roles* to express the extent to which postdisaster roles of an organizational enactment become differentiated.

We used the above four dimensions of role enactment to reanalyze a subsample of thirty-nine cases from Kreps's original data file of 423 organizational enactments. The cases were selected because their structural form seemed most likely to represent a balance between collective behavior and formal organization, thereby providing fruitful contexts for preliminary research on the dynamics of role-making and role-playing. Our primary effort was to measure these four dimensions as systematically as possible at each stage of organizing (one, two, three, and four elements in place) for each case. That accomplished, we then wanted to see if the patterns of organizing and role enactment were related in some fashion. One thing was certain: the measurement of role dynamics was not going to be easy.

At each stage of organizing (i.e., one, two, three, and four elements present), ideally some judgment about a pre- to postdisaster status/role nexus would have to be made for all participants. Thus a predisaster occupation or some other central status would have to be identified for each participant, so that this status could serve as the basis for making a judgment about consistent or inconsistent role enactment (first dimension). But often there was no central predisaster status mentioned in the archives for one or more participants.

An ideal measurement plan also would require specifying the number of postdisaster roles for each organized response, as well as the number of incumbents performing each role. Then linkages among all roles would have to be analyzed to determine whether they were established prior to the event (second dimension). But missing information on any incumbent pair or role pair would thwart that data production. Ironically, the dimension of role that seemed most clear to us conceptually at this point in our work would later prove (see chapters 4 and 5) to be the most complicated methodologically.

An ideal measurement plan also would require some assessment of each postdisaster role performance as that related to assumed differences in improvisation (third dimension).[3] The assessment would be based on performance regardless of whether incumbency was established prior to (existing) or during (new) the emergency period. Finally, some judgment would have to be made about the extent to which the overall postdisaster role structure of the organization, regardless of the number of incumbents involved, was differentiated (fourth dimension).

All things considered, we could not hope to implement the above ideal research design, and, quite frankly, we had only the vaguest idea of what it entailed. And while we had confidence that the archives would provide important pieces of the puzzle that intrigued us (certainly enough to sustain the work), we were very much aware that missing information was going to be inevitable. We thought that organizational enactments like the earlier example might be manageable because they are small, central predisaster statuses are identified for core members, and the number of postdisaster roles is fairly circumscribed. But as will be shown in the chapters to follow, neither we nor the reviewers of our work realized—even for cases such as these—the subtleties of role enactment that we were trying to measure.

The concept would prove to be every bit as elusive as collective behavior and formal organization. Moreover, the size of the social unit was going to be critical: the larger it was, the greater the measurement demands were going to be, and the more likely was there to be missing information. As a result, the findings we reported from our initial study represented, in every sense, only the first step toward a more adequate conception and measurement of role. In the final analysis, we have come to believe that the ideal research design can only be implemented through primary data collection.

Our preliminary findings were detailed in an article that was published in the *American Sociological Review* (Bosworth and Kreps 1986). That article is reprinted as the next chapter of this monograph. Very briefly adumbrating what is to follow, our central findings were that both role-making and role-playing are evidenced as organizing begins, that role-playing increases progressively as organizing unfolds, and that its progressive character is embedded with improvisation and role-making. We concluded that a perspective on organizing during a disaster becomes more powerful by adding the concept of role to it. But we had only scratched the surface in figuring out how and why that is so.

A Preview of Remaining Chapters

As noted above, chapter 2 is the original publication from our research on organizing and role. It is reprinted here primarily for reasons of efficiency. The essay provides a concise statement of the first phase of our work and, in so doing, describes what we did and its connections with disaster research and role theory. The article also summarizes some exploratory modeling that includes a large number of independent variables that we have continued to use. In effect, chapter 2 is the essential baseline from which we will then show how our conception and measurement of role evolved over time. Not only have we made important revisions in these regards, but in making these revisions it has become necessary to change our unit of analysis from the organizational to the individual. Why we have done so will become clear in chapters 4 and 5. Finally, the formal theory we present in the last chapter will be bounded to the circumstances of disaster (Dubin 1978). However, we think it need not be for reasons that we hope were well-stated in the original article.

Chapter 3 follows with a summary of a dialogue with Ralph Turner on the American Sociological Review (ASR) article. Turner critiqued the article at a symposium Kreps held in 1986, and both his critique and our response are reprinted from *Social Structure and Disaster* (Kreps 1989a, 207-18). Chapter 3 concludes with a detailed addendum that provides a transition from the first phase of our work to that which is summarized in the remainder of the monograph. A key step in the process of theory building, our dialogue with Turner and our subsequent consideration of his own theorizing about role (R. Turner 1980) have been both fruitful and very exciting. Not only does his work offer useful suggestions that we needed to consider, the dialogue has stimulated links between his and our respective conceptions of role enactment that we think even he might not have anticipated. In part quite serendipitously, then, the exchange with Turner has given us a deeper awareness of the theoretical problem we are endeavoring to solve.

Chapters 4 and 5 summarize the revised conception and measurement of role that has resulted from the exchange with Turner. They report on the major difficulties Jennifer Mooney, Stephen Russell, Kristen Myers, and we have faced, the necessary transition we have made from the organizational to the individual unit of analysis, and our findings on role enactment for both of these levels. Recall that interviewees in the original DRC field studies were considered to be respondents *and* informants. For most of the short history of this research program, we have treated interviewees as informants on organizational enactments. But we did not appreciate fully until quite late that they could serve more effectively as respondents reporting on their own role enactments. It also has become clear that Kreps's previously collected data on organizational enactments remain very important sources of contextual variables for modeling these individual role enactments.

That modeling is summarized in chapter 6. Here we identify correlates of role enactments that are the empirical foundation of the formal theory developed in chapter 7. Ironically, a key correlate turns out to be the same DRC typology of organized disaster responses that stimulated this research program many years ago. In constructing the formal theory in the final chapter, we have benefitted from Dubin's (1978) heuristic approach to theorizing generally, and Ralph Turner's (1980) more focused strategy for developing an integrated role theory. The book closes with a data (research) protocol that we think can be used to test the theory, either through additional work with the DRC archives or, ideally, through primary data collection.

Theory building is a process, the precise directions of which are often hard to predict (Wallace 1971, 17-19). Accordingly, we firmly believe that it is as important to document theorizing in process as it is to present any product that results from it. Much can be learned from such a documentation. We offer this chapter as well as this entire book with that theme in mind.

2

Structure as Process: Organization and Role

Organization, Role, and Social Structure

Organization and role are conventional sociological concepts. Despite their heavy use as explicit expressions of social structure, both remain underdeveloped. Each, in its own way, represents structure as problem of action *and* problem of order. The problem of action is one of determining how social units are created and sustained by individual thoughts and behaviors. The problem of order is one of determining how individual thoughts and behaviors are shaped and controlled by social units (Parsons 1938; 1950). So defined, these problems are unique yet reducible to one another (Alexander 1982; Collins 1985; Shalin 1986). Interpreted as social action, structure is in a constant state of becoming something else (Berger and Luckmann 1966). But the new can never be divorced from what is already there (Warriner 1970). Interpreted as social order, structure is an ever-present force, one analyzed on its own terms (Mayhew 1980, 1982). But what is always there is constantly transforming (Strauss 1978; Giddens 1979).

Expressed as either action or order, then, social structure is an unrelenting paradox. This paradox is best analyzed as a dialectical process (Rossi 1983; Sylvan and Glassner 1985; Shalin 1986). The various dimensions of that process are revealed by streams of events (Stinchcombe 1978; Collins 1981; Mayhew 1982; Wallace 1983). If organization and role are to serve as expressions of structure—indeed if they are to be seen as coterminous with it—their conception and measurement must be informed by dialectical reasoning. That is what is attempted here. Specifically, we examine these two concepts as interrelated processes in the structural drama of disaster. A developmental theory of organization is sum-

This chapter is a slightly revised version of an article published in *American Sociological Review* 51:699–716 (1986).

marized initially (Kreps 1983; 1985a; 1985b; 1987), followed by a multidimensional conception and measurement of role-making and role-playing at the origins of organization. The dialectic of role-making and role-playing is then modeled illustratively with data on thirty-eight instances of organization that took place during the emergency period of natural disasters (Kreps 1984). We close with a summary of key points; and an argument for form of association as an essential bridge between individual and social unit.

Organization and Social Structure

In disaster or any other setting, structure is form of association that is conditioned by content of historical events (Wolff 1950 on Simmel). Such a conception is impelled by the empirical reality of organization as process. Four elements—domains, tasks, resources, and activities—are individually necessary and collectively sufficient for organization to exist (Weller 1969; Kreps 1978). Domains (D) and tasks (T) are structural ends of organization. Resources (R) and activities (A) are structural means. Means-ends relationships involving (D), (T), (R), and (A) reveal organization as ever emerging and changing (Merton 1957). The four elements depict Parsons's idea of analytical realism, and their empirical patterning illustrates Weber's notion of historical ideal types (Weber 1949; Adriaansens 1980). The indicated parenthetical letters serve as a structural code, which can be used taxonomically to distinguish organization from other classes of social structure (Kreps 1985a).

The Structural Code

Domains (D) are collective representations of bounded units and their reasons for being (Durkheim 1938). In the circumstance of disaster, domains translate actual or threatened impacts as spheres of collective action that distinguish direct participants from all others. Stated or written in communications at the boundaries of those spheres of action, domains identify organization as open system that has power and external legitimacy (Thompson 1967).[1] *Tasks (T) are collective representations of a division of labor for the enactment of human activities* (Durkheim 1933). As such, they are vocabularies of collective action that give it focus and interdependence (March and Simon 1958). Stated or written in communications of those who enact them, tasks identify organization as closed system that has power and internal legitimacy (Thompson 1967). As things, domains and tasks are independent and may precede or follow each other in the unfolding of organization.

Resources (R) are individual capacities and collective technologies of human populations (Durkheim 1933; Weber 1968; Lenski and Lenski 1982). Widely varying in both kind and quantity, resources provide objective and subjective requisites of collective action (McCarthy and Zald 1977; Gamson, Fireman, and Rytina 1982). Their presence in a process as things comes to be defined with reference to domains and tasks. However, their mobilization may precede or follow either of them. *Activities (A) are the conjoined actions of individuals and social units* (Alihan 1938; Hawley 1950). As things, activities both enable and are constrained by domains, tasks, and resources. Accordingly, they are no more or less important than the remaining elements. The term *conjoined* rather than *interdependent* is used advisedly (Wallace 1983). We argue that all means-ends relationships should be grounded empirically in the flow of communications (Mayhew 1980). To respond that there are always tacit understandings operating is only to beg questions about what they are and how they come into being (Garfinkel 1967; Goffman 1981; Collins 1985).

Central to the theory, each element is analytically distinct from the others and relates equally with structure as unit and as process. This means that all elements are unique expressions of social structure; their copresence establishes the existence of organization; and no pattern in their arrangement can be assumed. Accordingly, all logically possible combinations and permutations of the elements are expressed taxonomically as forms of association (Kreps 1985a). A derived sixty-four-cell taxonomy includes four one-element forms, twelve two-element forms, twenty-four three-element forms, and twenty-four four-element forms. While only the four-element forms are sufficient for organization to exist, the remaining forty types represent stages in its origins.[2]

The following examples illustrate the grounding of the theory in case studies of organizing in the aftermath of disaster. In table 2.1 we summarize purposive samples of events, transcribed interviews, and organized responses that we have developed from spadework with the archives of the Disaster Research Center.[3] Also included is a subsample of cases we have selected for more detailed analysis of role-making and role-playing. The rationale for the selection of the latter cases is spelled out in the next section.

The first example is one of many types that can be positioned in the taxonomy as one of twenty-four organizational forms. It is

Table 2.1
Events, Interviews, and Organized Responses:
Total Sample and Role Analysis Subsample

Event	Total Sample		Role Analysis Subsample	
	Interviews	Instances	Interviews	Instances
Alaska Region Earthquake, 1964	250	92	13	7
New Orleans, La. Hurricane Betsy, 1965	128	36	7	4
St. Paul, Minn. Floods, 1965	50	6	2	1
Minneapolis, Minn. Tornadoes, 1965	30	7	-	-
Central South Colorado Floods, 1965	58	33	3	3
Mankato, Minn. Flood, 1965	22	4	3	1
Topeka, Kansas Tornado, 1966	143	64	14	7
Belmond, Iowa Tornado, 1966	13	7	1	1
Jackson, Miss. Tornado, 1966	50	8	-	-
Fairbanks, Alaska Flood, 1967	98	55	13	5
Oak Lawn, Chicago, Ill. Tornado, 1967	59	18	4	3
Jonesboro, Ark. Tornado, 1968	35	22	5	1
Gulf Coast Hurricane Camille, 1969	70	36	9	4
Minot, N.D. Flood, 1969	37	16	2	1
Fargo, N.D. Flood, 1969	19	19	1	1
Total	1,062	423	77	39

1 earthquake: 250 interviews, 92 organized responses
2 hurricanes: 198 interviews, 72 organized responses
6 tornadoes: 330 interviews, 126 organized responses
6 floods: 284 interviews, 133 organized responses

described as an A-R-T-D form, with the four letters of the structural code representing each of the four stages of organizing.

A, A-R, A-R-T, A-R-T-D

An organization of search and rescue emerges following an earthquake. The event takes place without forewarning, is regional in scope, destructive in magnitude, and its prompt and secondary physical impacts are over within minutes to several hours. The central business district and a large residential area of a major city are seriously damaged. Immediately following impact many individuals who happen to be in or near these areas engage in joint actions related to search and rescue of victims (Activities). A few of these early responders have search and rescue training. Within an hour many search and rescue teams converge on the impacted areas. Both formal and informal, they come from city agencies, other municipalities, the military, and several voluntary search and rescue groups (Activities-Resources). A task structure emerges among some of these disparate groups within several hours after impact, with prominent roles played by members of a mountain rescue group and members of an emergent "damage control" group (Activities-Resources-Tasks). The legitimacy of an integrated search and rescue operation is not officially recognized by city government officials until about twelve hours after impact (Activities-Resources-Tasks-Domain). By then it is operating, now formally, out of the city's public safety building. Formal search and rescue actions continue for another twenty-four to thirty hours.

This example suggests a sequencing of the code that begins with activities (A), followed by the mobilization of key resources (A-R), which then leads to the development of a division of labor (A-R-T), and finally to the establishment of a domain that is officially recognized and legitimated within the impacted community (A-R-T-D). People are observed creating social structure when routines have been disrupted (social action). Still, there is no denying the importance of existing structure for what is happening. Both established and emergent units are evidenced and can be described (sui generis) as maintaining collective life when it is threatened (social order). But although these units can be observed as fixed entities or things, they are being changed by human beings. The dialectic of action and order is symmetrical in the sense that the contradiction of each is the conduit to the other.

The performance of search and rescue suggests that social action compels social order because things are happening before there are collective representations of what is going on. However, there are many different paths to the achievement of organization. A domain may be established (D) and tasks socially defined (D-T) prior to the mobilization of resources (D-T-R) and performance of activities (D-T-R-A). In this circumstance social order compels social action because collective representations of what is to be done, and how, constrain what takes place. A second example from the data file illustrates just such an arrangement of the four elements. The domain in this case is evacuation during a flood.

D, D-T, D-T-R, D-T-R-A

Evacuation of a potential flood plain is enacted by a fire department prior to impact. A river runs through a large metropolitan area. A state police unit wires the city fire department with information that the river is at flood level, that flood waters are causing considerable damage upstream, and that flood conditions are expected to reach the city within several hours. A fire department communications operator contacts the fire chief, who then puts the fire department on standby alert. The fire department is schooled in evacuation procedures through predisaster preparedness activities. After being notified by the operator, the fire chief goes to the site of the initial city police command post and informs police personnel of his intention to evacuate low lying manufacturing and residential areas of the city. Following this discussion there is agreement that the fire department will handle the evacuation of selected low lying areas (Domain). Upon receiving additional information from the police and water departments, the chief decides to divide the fire department's equipment and personnel into two sections, one on each side of the river, to ensure an adequate distribution of resources for both evacuation and fire protection. Working through the normal chain of command, he orders fire personnel to mobilize and relocate people and possessions below one thousand feet from the bank on each side of the river (Domain-Tasks). Fire department personnel and equipment are then deployed according to the chief's dictates (Domain-Tasks-Resources). While the threatened population already has been warned of flooding by the mass media, fire department personnel move door to door in order to evacuate all residents in the selected lowland areas. There is sufficient time prior to flooding to both evacuate those threatened and to recheck the areas covered (Domain-Tasks-Resources-Activities). Several threatened individuals choose to remain anyway, arguing that they must protect or secure their property. Some of those who remain are stranded. The evacuation of those stranded by high water is then accomplished by using fire department boats. As conditions become more severe, larger boats are requested by the fire department and several are volunteered. The evacuation is terminated shortly after impact when all those stranded have been successfully evacuated. In the face of considerable property damage, there are no deaths or serious injuries resulting from the flood.

The range of forms of organization implied by these two examples can be conceived of as a continuum: with D-T-R-A or social order at one extreme and A-R-T-D or social action at the other. Pure social order is Weber's substantively rational actor and formally rational unit (Kalberg 1980). Pure social action is Durkheim's innovative individual and constraining moral order (Durkheim 1933). Thus both extremes capture human being and social unit as object and subject of each other (Rossi 1983; Sylvan and Glassner 1985; Shalin 1986). The 423 organized responses identified through archival analysis fall at various points on this continuum. Critical for the methodology, even though most of the cases (all but fifty-two) were enacted by established units of various types (i.e., they existed before the disaster event), existence is not assumed for purposes of observing organizing processes. In effect, the disaster event serves as a social catalyst for studying the origins of organization (Dubin 1978). With respect to theory building, then, the life history of organization is circumscribed by the event and its immediate aftermath. Within this time frame, many existing units do not act at all or do unconventional things. Thus, neither involvement nor its precise character can be taken for granted. By invoking the event as social catalyst, we do not deny the relevance of pre-event conditions for what takes place.

We have summarized the distribution of the data file in table 2.2. While there is greater evidence of order-driven forms, it is in large part related to the original data collection strategy of the Disaster Research Center.[4] Despite that data collection bias, the relevance of improvisation comes through dramatically. The D-R-T-A and D-R-A-T types point to the flexible nature of task performance, even when domain is enacted first. The R-D-T-A and other resources initiated patterns suggest that the coexistence of need and available resources can initiate organization in the absence of a domain. And all of the non-D-T-R-A and non-A-R-T-D forms (59 percent) indicate that social order and social action are related in some rather subtle ways. Such subtleties appear to be most pointed for those thirty-nine cases in the sample that fall at the precise midpoint of what we term a social order-social action metric (Kreps 1985a).[5] Here

Table 2.2
Organizational Forms:
Social Order — Social Action Metric for Total Sample

Organizational Forms	Logical Metric	Number of Forms	Number of Units: Total Sample	
D-T-R-A	6 (+3)	(1)	167	(167)
D-T-A-R			5	
D-R-T-A	5 (+2)	(3)	53	(59)
T-D-R-A			1	
D-R-A-T			27	
D-A-T-R			2	
T-R-D-A	4 (+1)	(5)	4	(100)
T-D-A-R			-	
R-D-T-A			67	
D-A-R-T			1	
T-R-A-D			21	
T-A-D-R	3 (0)	(6)	-	(39)
R-D-A-T			12	
R-T-D-A			4	
A-D-T-R			1	
T-A-R-D			-	
R-A-D-T			15	
R-T-A-D	2 (-1)	(5)	13	(31)
A-D-R-T			1	
A-T-D-R			2	
R-A-T-D			13	
A-T-R-D	1 (-2)	(3)	4	(22)
A-R-D-T			5	
A-R-T-D	0 (-3)	(1)	5	(5)
	Totals	(24)	423	(423)

no simple judgment can be made about whether the six types so located are either action-driven or order-driven. The forces of action and order are in a state of complementarity or perhaps mutual tension. The following example illustrates one of these six types.

T, T-R, T-R-A, T-R-A-D

Material resources are mobilized by residents of one community and provided to the victims of another. An entire region is impacted by a major earthquake. Although several communities suffer serious damage, some are spared. Considerable concern is expressed by residents and leaders of one unimpacted city about the adequacy of assistance being provided to a small and isolated town that was devastated by tsunamis (giant waves) that followed the earthquake. A joint meeting involving representatives from the un-impacted city's chamber of commerce, city government, and the trucking industry takes place on the fourth day following the event. A chairman is appointed and food, communications, and transportation committees are set up (Tasks). At least fifty people are mobilized for the collection of food and other commodities in the unimpacted city (Tasks-Resources). Enough supplies for three trucks and one other vehicle are collected over the next few days. A core group consisting of the unimpacted city's public works director, engineer, and building inspector, as well as a privately employed architectural engineer then transport the supplies to the impacted town, which is some distance away. Leaders and residents of the devastated town have no knowledge of this assistance until it arrives on site. The core group meets with some members of the impacted community's town council and offers the assistance (Tasks-Resources-Activities). The following day the town council meets and formally requests the core group to take over the distribution of its own resources as well as perform other community functions (Tasks-Resources-Activities-Domain).

This third example of origins involves the development of a division of labor (T), the mobilization of a critical mass of individuals (T-R), the presence of conjoined actions relating to that division of labor (T-R-A), and, finally, the legitimation of what is taking place by officials of the devastated town (T-R-A-D). Unlike the first two cases, neither ends nor means predominate. Tasks and domains independently express the entity quality of organization. Observe the discontinuity between them, for example, activities could have been delayed until an on-site domain was established (a T-R-D-A form)—yet the continuity of both with predisaster routines. The process described reflects the elusive relationship between action and order in structure. This relationship can be described more fully by adding the concept of role to the above processual approach to organization. To be precise, much can be learned about the interrelationships of organizing, role-making, and role-playing from further analysis of the thirty-nine cases at the midpoint of the metric depicted in table 2.2. That analysis follows.

Role and Social Structure

In benchmark studies of helping behavior, Barton (1969) and Taylor, Zurcher, and Key (1970) anticipated the relationship between organization and role presented here. They argued, as have many others since, that disasters are strategic research sites for comparative studies of social structure (Quarantelli and Dynes 1977). Questions about how social structure is created and maintained remain central to the field (Kreps 1984). The above three examples of organizing, as well as a host of others, document the necessity of improvisations when communities are disrupted by the unexpected. The more severe the disaster, the more important are these improvisations for meeting the needs of victims. At the same time, response to disaster shows how critical community routines are for what occurs; achieving organization is impossible without them. The mutual reinforcement of the old and the new makes an interesting puzzle.

Role is an important piece in the solution of that puzzle. Just like organization, meaningful conceptualization of role calls for dialectical reasoning. Drawing on the traditions of symbolic interactionism and structuralism, J. Turner (1978), Stryker (1980), and R. Turner (1985) nicely summarize action and order perspectives on role. In so doing, they show the need for a multidimensional approach to its conception and measurement. Those role theorists taking an action perspective emphasize the individual and role-making. Those taking an order perspective emphasize the unit and role-playing. Combining action and order perspectives, the concept of role implies at least the following: social expectations of behavior, action as defined within the traditions of voluntarism, and forms of association in which actions and expectations in some manner interrelate. While the Meadian "self" and "taking the role of the other" (as opposed to role-taking) are relevant to all of the above (R. Turner 1962, 1976, 1978), the emphasis here is on structural manifestations of person-role linkages (Weinstein and Tanur 1976; Weinstein 1977; Stryker 1980).

Because the thirty-nine cases at the midpoint of the metric point to balance or tension between action and order, they provide potentially fruitful contexts for preliminary investigations of role-making and role-playing. Each enactment of organization is analyzed below as a four-stage process (one, two, three, and four structural elements enacted). The relative presence of role-making and role-playing is assessed independently at each stage. That determined, role dynamics at progressive stages then serve as dependent variables with respect to physical, temporal, and social characteristics of their occurrence.

Conceptualizing Role-making and Role-playing

A set of four explicit dimensions has been developed in order to make judgments about role-making and role-playing as each element of organization is enacted. The first dimension is termed inconsistency versus consistency of status/role nexus. Its focus is perhaps the most conventional structural conception of role (Linton 1936; Handel 1979). Status is a socially recognized category of actors. As such it serves as a constraint on individual behavior. To some degree, therefore, social expectations shape the actions of and toward positionally labeled individuals. These expectations are referred to as roles. The consistency of the status/role nexus across pre- and postdisaster time periods is at issue with this dimension. Inconsistency implies a redefinition of appropriate behavior (role-making dominates), while consistency suggests an understood status/role connection (role-playing dominates). A college student directing faculty during an evacuation is an example of the former. A faculty member directing students in this same effort is an example of the latter. A mixture of both role-making and role-playing indicates some redefining of expectations, but also a degree of stability from pre- to postdisaster time periods.

The second dimension is discontinuity versus continuity of role linkages. This dimension gives pointed attention to the relational dimension of role (Mead 1934; Strauss 1978). When multiple roles of a postimpact response are not connected before the event (they would be with the student-faculty example), new role relationships must be created by the participants. Role-making is being evidenced in this circumstance. On the other hand, role-playing dominates where predisaster linkages among roles are mirrored following impact. Discontinuity is exemplified by volunteer station wagon owners providing ambulance service as directed by trained medical personnel. Continuity is evidenced by experienced ambulance drivers providing the same service. Neither role-making nor role-playing dominates when there is a mixture of discontinuous and continuous role relationships.

The third dimension is unique role performance versus role boundary expansion. This dimension gives pointed attention to human agency, or what has been termed voluntarism (Parsons 1938; Blumer 1969; Giddens 1979; Alexander 1982; Shalin 1986). Role-making dominates when no collective representation of role enactment exists at a given stage. An example would be spontaneous search and rescue by individuals who happen to be in or near a heavily damaged area. Role-playing dominates when such representation does exist. An example would be search and rescue at this same site by anyone having relevant training. Both unique role performance and role boundary expansion imply a contradiction. The latter may involve innovativeness (R. Turner 1980), but expectations of action give it focus. The former is the purer form of creativity, yet it is driven by ultimate values (e.g., altruism). Evidence of both unique role performance and role boundary expansion indicates that neither role-making nor role-playing dominates.

The final dimension is homogeneity versus heterogeneity of roles. This dimension makes an explicit connection between role performance and organizing (Thompson 1967; Barton 1969; Taylor, Zurcher, and Key 1970; Dynes 1970, 1987). Specifically, it indicates whether role enactments are homogeneous, heterogeneous with a defined task structure, or heterogeneous with an undefined task structure. The first possibility suggests that roles are undifferentiated and still in the process of being defined. For instance, volunteers are providing sandwiches for victims. Each participant is involved in the entire process of preparing the food and each develops his or her own technique for doing so. Role-making dominates in this circumstance. With increased specialization and a defined task structure, roles are established and behavior dictated by social control. Thus, as a production line for preparing sandwiches is developed, there is a shared understanding of appropriate role enactment at each step along the line. Here role-playing dominates and there is continuity of role performance as volunteers come and go. When roles are heterogeneous, but a task structure is not well defined, there is a mixture of role-making and role-playing. Such is the case when some sandwich makers are developing a rudimentary production line while others are not.

Measurement of Role-making and Role-playing

The archival materials for each of the thirty-nine cases falling at the midpoint of the social order–social action metric have been reexamined for purposes of measuring role-making and role-playing. Each dimension in the set has been scored in the following way:

Inconsistency versus consistency of pre- and postdisaster status/role nexus:
  1 = inconsistency of pre- and postdisaster status/role nexus, role-making dominates
  2 = mix of inconsistent and consistent pre- and postdisaster status/role nexus
  3 = consistency of pre- and postdisaster status/role nexus, role-playing dominates
  9 = uncertain

Discontinuity versus continuity of pre- and postdisaster role linkages:

    1 = discontinuity of pre- and postdisaster role linkages, role-making dominates

    2 = mix of discontinuity and continuity of pre- and postdisaster role linkages

    3 = continuity of pre- and postdisaster role linkages, role-playing dominates

    9 = uncertain

Unique role performance versus role boundary expansion:

    1 = unique role performance, role-making dominates

    2 = mix of unique role performance and role boundary expansion

    3 = role boundary expansion, role-playing dominates

    9 = uncertain

Homogeneity versus heterogeneity of roles

    1 = roles homogeneous, role-making dominates

    2 = roles heterogeneous with undefined task structure

    3 = roles heterogeneous with defined task structure, role-playing dominates

    9 = uncertain

As outlined above, a score of 1 for any particular dimension at a given stage indicates role-making. A score of 3 suggests role-playing. A mix of role-making and role-playing is given a score of 2 as the midpoint between the two extremes. By then adding the scores across all four dimensions, the totals range from 4 (1 point on each of the four dimensions: role-making dominates) to 8 (2 points on each of the four dimensions: mix of role-making and role-playing) to 12 (3 points on each of the four dimensions: role-playing dominates) for each stage of origins. Archival data were insufficient for role analysis in one of the thirty-nine midpoint cases. With four dimensions at each of four stages of organizing for the remaining thirty-eight cases, a total of 608 judgments about role enactments had to be made. The attempt with all dimensions was to make clean empirical distinctions.[6]

To illustrate the measurement of role, we use the previously described T-R-A-D form. Tasks (T) set off organization. Active involvement of local officials is evidenced, suggesting consistency of the status/role nexus for these participants. However, other community members (e.g., trucking personnel) also influence the establishment of committees, indicating inconsistency of the status/role nexus for them. The first dimension is therefore scored 2 or a mix of role-making and role-playing. Similarly, while local officials, in particular, exhibit continuity of pre- and postdisaster role linkages, there was little or no continuity for many of those involved in setting up a task structure (e.g., an architectural engineer and truckers). A score of 2 on the second dimension indicates that neither role-making nor role-playing dominates. With respect to the third dimension, while familiar roles are being expanded by those involved in the city government and the chamber of commerce, other participants are enacting unique roles related to the emergency. For example, a bank president and an employee of an electrical firm are members of a core group that establishes committee subdivisions. The score is again 2 or mixed role-making and role-playing. With respect to the fourth dimension, the evidence indicates that a wide variety of roles are part and parcel of an emergent division of labor. Roles are being differentiated and are well defined, pointing to a score of 3 or role-playing. The aggregate score across the four dimensions is 9 for the first stage of organizing, which indicates that both role-making and role-playing are in effect.

At the second stage a task structure exists and precedes the mobilization of personnel and equipment to carry it out (T-R). As in the first stage, there is a mix (score of 2) of inconsistent and consistent status/role nexus. The former is evidenced by mobilizing volunteers to obtain food, fuel, and medical supplies at no charge from local vendors. The latter is documented by the city manager requisitioning several city-owned trucks for picking up supplies and equipment. More people are now becoming involved in the response. The resulting mix (score of 2) of discontinuous and continuous role linkages is more apparent but less precise at this second stage as a sheer function of the number of participants mobilized to obtain commodities. Some unique role performance continues to take place because confusion remains about precisely what the impacted community will need and how to get it. There is no evidence of attempts to contact officials from the devastated coastal town. Thus notwithstanding the presence of a division of labor, many people are enacting new roles and improvising to do so. Others are operating within the constraints of roles defined at stage 1 (score of 2). Finally, a differentiated and well-defined task structure remains intact and viable at stage 2 (score of 3). The aggregate score across the four dimensions is 9, again indicating a mix of role-making and role-playing.

To conserve space we will truncate stages 3 and 4 of this case. As the commodities are being collected and transported to the disaster site (T-R-A), role-playing tied to the response becomes increasingly important. Much of what is happening is impelled by prior improvisation as well as shared values related to helping the devastated community. Continued role-making relates to contacts between a core group, the military, and an acting mayor. The aggregate score across the four dimensions is 9 for stage 3. Role-playing predominates at stage 4 (aggregate score of 12). The key boundary spanning roles here link government officials of impacted to assisting communities. There is both consistency of status/role nexus and continuity of role relationships. There is no evidence of unique role performance at this point. Predefined tasks related to the distribution of commodities are now being implemented.

We are dealing with organization as a crescive chain of events. Accordingly, the contexts for judgments about role-making and role-playing change as each additional element comes into play. Pivotal, of course, is establishing spatial and temporal discontinuity in the emergence of the four elements (Wallace 1983). Certainly the greater the number of participants and the more circumscribed the emergence of organization in time and space, the more difficult it is to make diachronic distinctions. Yet all forms of association have life histories. It is important to grapple with defining precisely what these forms are and how they come into being (McKelvey 1982). The theory presented here is apropos of Stinchcombe's (1968) distinction between the origins of systems and their maintenance. His focus is on the latter and reciprocal causation (Faia 1986). Our focus is on the former and stages of development (Kimberly and Miles 1980).

Illustrative Modeling of Role-making and Role-playing

This section summarizes the results of exploratory modeling that informs a better understanding of the dynamics of organization and role. Role-making and role-playing at the origins of organization serve as dependent variables in a series of bivariate and multivariate analyses. Marginal distributions of composite role scores are first summarized and then followed by a discussion of possible correlates of role that have been measured from the archives. We then present statistical relationships between role scores and their correlates.

Marginal Distributions of Role-making and Role-playing

As measured above, role can be expressed as a continuum, with lower scores indicating greater degrees of role-making and higher scores indicating greater degrees of role-playing.[7] Composite scores, by element stage, for the thirty-eight cases reported on in this chapter appear in table 2.3. A score of 4 represents role-making in pure form; a score of 8 does the same for mixed role-making and role-playing; and a score of 12 indicates uniformity of role-playing. The marginals point to the increasing momentum of role-playing as organization is enacted. Notice the wider distribution of scores at the first stage (one-element form). In spite of the bias of the primary data collection (see note 4), 18 percent of the cases give evidence of considerable role-making (scores of 6 or less); and 39 percent give evidence of a substantial mix of role-making and role-playing (scores of 7 to 10). All role-playing at stage 1 involves an extension of predisaster routines. However, subsequent role-playing (stages 2, 3, and 4) may have little to do with these routines for dimension 3 (role boundary expansion versus unique role performance) and 4 (homogeneity-heterogeneity of roles of key participants). Here it is possible for role-playing to be completely circumscribed by the response and the event.

Role-playing increases as organization comes into being. Yet interestingly enough, what might be termed "perfect role-making" (a score of 4) is documented twice during the second stage (two elements present). The organizational forms of the two cases having scores of 4 are the same (R-D-A-T). Neither unit existed prior to the event, and both evidenced role-making at stage one (scores of 5 in both cases). This was followed by an increase in role-making associated with crystallization of domain. In one case, role-making resulted from public announcement of a domain before it was internally defined and legitimated. In the other case, a group of volunteers created a domain that was then endorsed externally. These and many other examples point to the rapidly changing circumstances of the emergency period. It is because each stage is examined independently of the others—and scores judged only in terms of those elements present—that the fluid nature of role dynamics can be captured.

It is possible for role-playing to dominate early in the process, while role-making comes into play later on. As is suggested in later findings, much of this appears to be related to problems associated with the emergence of the elements. Notwithstanding that, the marked movement toward role-playing from the first to second stages, and at each subsequent stage, is associated with residual role-making. The blending of socially expected and improvised role performance is indicated by the considerable mixing of role-making and role-playing (scores of 8–10) at both the second (39 percent)

Table 2.3
Role-making to Role-playing Distribution by Stage of Origins

Role-making and Role-playing Scores	Element Stages			
	1	2	3	4
4	-	2	-	-
5	5	-	-	-
6	2	-	1	-
7	4	-	-	-
8	4	2	2	1
9	2	5	6	-
10	5	8	10	3
11	4	9	9	12
12	12	12	10	22
Total	38	38	38	38

and third (47 percent) stages. Thus even as collective representations of what is happening become more clearly articulated in the flow of communications (Mayhew 1980), circumstances continue to call for flexibility and improvisation. By the final stage, when all four elements of organization are in place, role-playing takes over.

Given the major skewness in the data, continuum scores at each of the first 3 stages are recoded as trichotomies for stages 1 and 2, and a dichotomy for stage 3. At stage 1 scores are collapsed into three ordinal categories: those below the midpoint (scores of 4, 5, 6, 7) evidence greater to decreasing role-making and an increasing mix of role-making and role-playing (recoded 1, N = 11); scores of 8, 9, and 10 evidence greater to decreasing mix and increasing role-playing (recoded 2, N = 11); and scores of 11 and 12 evidence greater to complete role-playing (recoded 3, N = 16). The higher the score, the greater the degree of role-playing. The same procedure is followed for stage 2 recoding (N's of 2, 15, and 21, respectively). Stage 3 has only one score evidencing role-making. That score and mixed role-making and role-playing (scores of 6, 8–10, N = 19) are separated dichotomously from role-playing scores (11 and 12, N = 19). The predominantly mixed scores are recoded 2, and the role-playing scores are recoded 3. The above recoding procedure creates reasonable marginal splits while still retaining the substantive integrity of the continuum (see note 7). Because of the small sample and dominance of role-playing at stage 4, no statistical analysis of the final stage is reported below.

Correlates of Role-making and Role-playing

In table 2.4 is a summary of correlates of role and their measurement from the archives. The three general types are characteristics of organizational elements, enacting units, and disaster events. While the list includes many variables, it is by no means exhaustive. We have listed only what the Disaster Research Center archives have yielded thus far. Some correlates derive directly from the organizational theory proposed earlier, while others are informed by mainstream disaster and organizational research. The archives are very uneven and difficult to work with. Often crude ordinal ranges are the best that can be extracted from the available materials. What is involved throughout, therefore, is preliminary theory building and not hypothesis testing. Correlations among the eighteen potential correlates are in Appendix A. Their relationships with role scores are discussed in the next section. We precede that with a brief examination of table 2.4 and our reasons for selecting the variables arrayed there.

Table 2.4
Correlates of Role-making and Role-playing

Correlate Type	Measurement
ELEMENT CHARACTERISTIC	
First appearing element	R or A=0 (N=17); D or T=1 (N=21)
Timing of first element	Hours from impact: 1-2=1 (N=12); 3-24=2 (N=10); 25-72=3 (N=11); more than 72=4 (N=5)
Domain problem	No=1 (N=20); Yes, maintenance=2 (N=9); Yes, origins=3 (N=9)
Task problem	No=1 (N=20); Yes, maintenance=2 (N=7); Yes, origins=3 (N=11)
Resource problem	No=1 (N=25); Yes, maintenance=2 (N=9); Yes, origins=3 (N=4)
Activities problem	No=1 (N=12); Yes, maintenance=2 (N=7); Yes, origins=3 (N=19)
ENACTING UNIT CHARACTERISTIC	
Type of enacting unit	Nonemergency=0 (N=20); Emergency=1 (N=18)
Size of unit	Number of participants: 9 or fewer=1 (N=6); 10-20=2 (N=11); 21-50=3 (N=10); Over 50=4 (N=11)
Preparedness	No formal preparedness=1 (N=24); Formal preparedness=2 (N=14)
Complexity of response	4 or fewer tasks=1 (N=17); more than 4 tasks=2 (N=21)
Concern for victims	Not expressed in communications=0 (N=15); Expressed in communications=1 (N=23)
Social network relevance	Links: local, state, or national=0 (N=25); Self-contained at initiation=1 (N=13)
Number of network links	None=0 (N=13); 1-3=1 (N=19); more than 3=2 (N=6)
Time network established	Established prior to event=0 (N=21); Specific to the event=1 (N=17)
Community type	Metropolitan: No=0 (N=14); Yes=1 (N=24)
Disaster experience	No disaster experience, few threats=1 (N=6); No disaster experience, several threats=2 (N=21); One or more disasters=3 (N=11)
EVENT CHARACTERISTIC	
Length of forewarning	Earthquakes=1 (N=7); Tornadoes=2 (N=11); Floods=3 (N=12); Hurricanes=4 (N=8)
Magnitude-scope of impact	Severity: Low=0 (N=12); High=1 (N=26)

Element characteristics include the sequencing of ends (D, T) and means (R, A) of organization, the timing of the first appearing element relative to impact, and any element problems occurring during the course of the response. With respect to sequencing, we felt that forms initiated by ends would evidence greater degrees of role-playing, and forms initiated by means would evidence greater degrees of role-making. Such relationships are consistent with the logic of action and order developed earlier. With respect to timing, disasters are nonroutine events. Responses to them necessarily will be nonroutine to some extent, regardless of when they occur relative to impact. We suspected that those responses beginning immediately before or after impact might reveal different role enactment as a simple function of the constraints of time. Finally, problems related to the four elements were recorded for the entire life histories of the thirty-eight cases examined.[8] The archives do not always provide sufficient information to pinpoint whether the problem took place at the four stages of origins or sometime later. The scoring therefore tries to capture both the presence of a problem and the increasing likelihood that it occurred at origins. Organizational problems call for innovativeness. Perhaps the latter is revealed by role-making.

Enacting unit characteristics provide profiles of the units themselves, their social networks, and the communities that surround them. The type of enacting unit (see note 4), size, disaster preparedness, and complexity of tasks depict organization as closed system of collective action (Thompson 1967; Perrow 1979). Size is a standard measure in organizational research (Hall 1982). Preparedness was documented by written disaster plans or formal training but did not have to be tied to the type of event that struck the community. We thought that regardless of how vague preparedness was, its very exercise might increase role-playing during the emergency. The cut point on complexity (tasks) is arbitrary and reflects the fact that beyond the identification of four tasks, precision about outside parameters breaks down. The resulting distinction obviously is very crude. As can be seen from the earlier case descriptions, more general yet distinct tasks are represented in the archives. This is in keeping with Durkheim's (1938) notion of collective representations as vocabularies of action (March and Simon 1958).

Participant concerns for victims and the relevance, number, and timing of social networks represent the enacting unit as open system of collective action (Thompson 1967; Aldrich 1979). Concern for victims is a normative factor used to sustain interaction among participants (Barton 1969; Dynes 1970). The archives document such concern in both formal and informal communications for some of the cases. We felt that altruism—as ultimate value—might be related to role-making. Any instance of organization may be linked in various ways to a broader network of social units. Three possibilities were examined. First, we determined whether the response was largely self-contained at origins or linked with other local, state, or national units. Second, we measured the number of network linkages, with precision about outside parameters breaking down at scores higher than 3. Third, those cases where the networks were uniformly established after the event were distinguished from those where some to all linkages were established prior to the event. All three measures point to differences in the complexity of the social environment. We suspected that enactments within extant, larger, and new networks would exhibit some strain toward role-making.

Finally, we sought to distinguish differences in the type and disaster experience of the impacted community in which organizing took place. The distinction between metropolitan and nonmetropolitan communities measures differences in their human and material resources. Disaster experience represents differences in cultural heritage as that relates at least generally to the circumstances of the event. Both measures point to advantages in dealing with unusual circumstances of disaster (Wright and Rossi 1981). We felt that the presence of those advantages might be reflected in role performance: role-playing because of a reduced need to improvise; role-making because of physical, social, and cultural wherewithal to do so if necessary.

Event characteristics highlight temporal, physical, and spatial dimensions of impact (Dynes 1970; Perry 1982; Kreps 1984). Length of forewarning measures increasing time to get ready. Earthquakes, tornadoes, floods, and hurricanes have progressively longer time lags between threat cues and impact. Our suspicion was that time might provide an opportunity for innovation and role-making. Magnitude and scope of impact measure the severity of the event. Five of the events we studied were more massive in terms of their physical magnitude (deaths, injuries, and damages) and/or geographic scope of impact than the others. Cases associated with these events were distinguished from all others. Our thought here was that role-making would be impelled by the degree of physical and social disruption (Fritz 1961; Kreps 1984).

Patterns of Association Between Role-making, Role-playing and Their Correlates

Role-making to role-playing at the origins of organization serves as the dependent variable in a series of correlation and regression analyses, broken down by stages 1–3 of organizing. To repeat, relative absence of variance precludes analysis of stage 4. We present the findings in table 2.5. First, we array all bivariate correlations that are statistically significant at the .10 level by stage. Positive signs reveal a strain toward role-playing. Of eighteen potential correlates of role-making and role-playing, fourteen operate at one or more stages of origins. Those that do not (domain problem, resources problem, type of enacting unit, and magnitude-scope of impact) are indicated by broken lines. We then present partial standardized regression coefficients for a second subset of correlates that meet a .10 significance criterion for adding variables to equations. The majority of coefficients identified are at the .05 level or better. While we are exploring rather than predicting, the data reduction approach is reasonable given the relatively small number of cases (thirty-eight) in the sample. In particular, we used stepwise techniques in regression analyses to lower the ratio of variables to cases in equations. In effect, we tried to balance the search for insights with concern about Type I error. Finally, the variance explained by the subset of statistically significant partials is included for each stage.

Stage 1 findings indicate that if the first element initiated is D or T (the latter for all but one of twenty-one cases), there is a much greater degree of role-playing. This suggests that the early presence of a collectively represented division of labor—or what might be termed shared communications of how a response is being enacted—provides a strong indication of the extent to which predisaster routines guide behavior during the emergency. Additional evidence of role-playing is associated with disaster preparedness; when the response is largely self-contained as opposed to linked with a broader social network at origins, and when the response takes place in metropolitan as opposed to nonmetropolitan communities.

Disaster preparedness points to predefined role obligations that are called forth by the occurrence of something unusual. It appears that at this earliest stage of organizing, the increased clarity of role demands resulting from preparedness decreases the probability of role-making. Still, it does not preclude the possibility of flexibility when unanticipated circumstances arise later on. Participants in self-contained responses have fewer opportunities to redefine appropriate behavior. Thus, they are more likely to respond on the basis of established practices. Finally, the ratio of disaster impacts to remaining resources tends to be lower in metropolitan communities. Here routines are less severely disrupted and emergency response is more likely to take place with reference to these routines.

The findings also point clearly to the dynamics of role-making

Table 2.5
Correlation and Regression Analysis: Role-making and Role-playing Continuum

Correlate	Stage 1		Stage 2		Stage 3	
	r	b	r	b	r	b
Role stage 1			.72	.59***	.41	
Role stage 2					.49	.55***
ELEMENT CHARACTERISTIC						
First appearing element	.65	.65***	.40		.26	
Timing of first element					-.38	-.40***
Domain problem	----------------		----------------		----------------	
Task problem	-.28		-.28		-.27	
Resource problem	----------------		----------------		----------------	
Activities problem					-.33	-.22*
ENACTING UNIT CHARACTERISTIC						
Type of enacting unit	----------------		----------------		----------------	
Size of unit					.39	.32***
Preparedness	.27				-.22	-.23*
Complexity of response	-.28		-.22			
Concern for victims			-.32	-.22**		
Social network relevance	.35		.23			
Number of network links	-.37					
Time network established	-.40		-.49	-.24**		
Community type	.25				.22	
Disaster experience	-.22					
EVENT CHARACTERISTIC						
Length of forewarning					-.23	
Magnitude-scope of impact	----------------		----------------		----------------	
Constant		1.53		1.88		1.99
R^2 (stepwise)		.42		.61		.66
N=38						

* P< .10   ** P< .05   *** P< .01

at stage 1. As we note in table 2.5, the greater the likelihood of task contingencies at origins, the greater the evidence of role-making. The correlation implies elemental attempts to improvise a division of labor in the face of unusual demands. A similar strain toward role-making occurs when the task structure is more complex, when the social network of the enacting unit is emergent or larger, and when the broader community has been threatened or directly impacted before. The latter finding is perhaps the most interesting. Notice in Appendix A that communities with more experience tend to have more severe events ($r = .31$). We conclude that while preparedness increases clarity about what is to be done (role-playing), experience serves as tacit cultural resource that enhances flexibility (role-making). There is no question that both clarity and flexibility are needed during the emergency period.

Obviously much has been made of largely low to moderate bivariate correlations. We think that approach is justified—particularly at this first stage in the process—in our attempt to empirically relate organizing with role. The key finding is the presence of ends (T or D) as first appearing element. It alone accounts for over 40 percent of the variance in role; no other variable meets the minimum requirement for inclusion in the regression equation. At least at this first stage, then, the apparent result of ends as first element is enhanced clarity about what is happening. This same variable is positively related with type of unit (emergency-relevant), preparedness, and self-contained response (see Appendix A). The underlying pattern in such relationships is social order and role-playing. Ends (T or D) as first appearing element is also inversely related with a number of variables that at this or later stages of origins seem to enhance innovation (complexity of tasks, length of forewarning, timing of first element, the size and newness of social networks, and community disaster experience). The underlying pattern in such relationships is social action and role-making.

Stage 2 findings indicate that role-playing at stage 1 relates strongly to its counterpart as the second element of organization comes into play. This is documented at both bivariate and multivariate levels. Recall from the marginals that role-playing is increasing at the second stage. The forces of order are building momentum. Of interest is the fact that the presence of ends as first appearing element continues to show a positive association with role-playing. But it is far less powerful and does not make the regression equation. Preparedness and occurrence of the response in a metropolitan community are no longer significantly correlated with role-playing. Only self-contained responses continue to show a residual positive correlation (not statistically significant in the regression equation). These findings suggest that predisaster routines remain important but their control weakens as organization unfolds. We conclude that these routines become less relevant as the unique demands of the situation call for new forms of social action. Recall the substantial remaining mix of role-making and role-playing at the second stage. What is now implied is an intriguing admixture of routine practices, emergent constraints, and continuing attempts to innovate.

With regard to attempts to innovate, there is also consistency of role-making findings from stage 1 to stage 2. Specifically, while task contingencies, more complex task structures and emergent social networks continue to be associated with role-making; only the latter makes the regression equation. And while the number of social network linkages is no longer a statistically significant correlation, the direction of its relationship is consistent with that found in stage 1 (see Appendix A). These findings again point to elemental attempts to improvise a course of action. What appears to be developing, however, is a facilitating mix of the old and the new as the response unfolds. In addition, participant concern for victims is newly associated with role-making in both correlation and regression analyses. This finding recalls Durkheim's discussion of the moral order: disaster disrupts the rational character of social routines and reveals their foundation in the nonrational social bond. The results are innovative attempts at organized altruism that are consistent with ultimate values.

By stage 3 role-playing is becoming more and more evident. However, much of it is specific to the response and not tied to predisaster routines. As noted in table 2.5, the continuity of role-playing between stages 1 and 2 is sustained for stage 3, which is evidenced in both correlation and regression analyses. With regard to the latter, stage 1 role scores are dropped to eliminate problems of multicolinearity. Ends (T or D) as first appearing element is again associated with role-playing, but the relationship weakens further. The findings lend additional support for the conclusion drawn earlier, namely that predisaster routines are enmeshed with new structural constraints and continuing improvisations.

Two other variables—type of community and size of enacting unit—are also associated with role-playing. The finding for the former is consistent with stage 1. Our interpretation there, that disasters are less disruptive of routines in metropolitan communities because of lower impact ratios, is sustained. Size of enacting unit newly appears in both correlation and regression findings. In one sense, this is not surprising. The greater the number of participants, the greater the need to predict what they are doing. But what is surprising is the delayed appearance of what has become a standard variable in organizational research. Most studies of organization simply assume its existence, but our research illustrates how size impels organization developmentally as an instrument of control.

Other variables, some appearing earlier and some only now, help to unravel residual role-making at stage 3. Greater length of forewarning, task problems, activities problems, and greater time difference between impact and first appearing element are associated with role-making. The latter two variables also make the regression equation. These findings suggest that there is a continuing need to improvise as organization is enacted, and that time is a scarce resource for doing so. Notice also that preparedness is now associated with role-making in both correlation and regression analyses. At stage 1 it had been associated with role-playing. This finding supports the idea that preparedness has dual value. First, it increases clarity about what to do early in the process. Second, it is a resource for flexibility as organization unfolds. In the latter sense, preparedness operates as a tacit cultural advantage, in a manner similar to disaster experience. In Weberian terms, perhaps preparedness supports the requirements of both formal and substantive rationality.

Although not grounded in the nomenclature of role, this is precisely the argument made in an earlier monograph by Dynes and his coauthors (1972). They noted, with confirmation by several others (e.g., Rossi, Wright, and Weber-Burdin 1982; Drabek, Mushkatel, and Kilijanek 1983), that sensitivity to hazards is generally low at state and particularly at local levels in the United States—until there is an emergency. The preparedness that takes place generally is not substantial, mainly because of the infrequency of events, the absence of resources and constituencies to promote hazard awareness and mitigation, and considerable uncertainty about how much of either is actually needed. Our findings suggest that a modicum of preparedness and experience can make a difference in the aftermath of the unlikely. It is possible that too much of either breeds false confidence. Comparative studies of response to a variety of hazards appear to be necessary since such studies imply an important contribution of sociological theory to public policy (Perrow 1984; Short 1984).

Summary and Final Comments

We have argued that dialectical reasoning informs an interrelated theory of organization and role. Organization is defined as a structural code having four elements: domains (D), tasks (T), resources (R), and activities (A). An empirically grounded taxonomy specifies the origins of organization as falling on a continuum of order-driven to action-driven forms of association (D-T-R-A to A-R-T-D). Four dimensions then represent a multidimensional approach to role as organization emerges (one to four elements present). These dimensions are empirically grounded for thirty-eight instances of organization that point to balance or tension between action and order. Marginal distributions of role-making and role-playing evidence an increase in the latter as each additional element of organization is enacted. However, the progressive character of role-playing is embedded with improvisation and role-making.

Role has been analyzed on its own terms and as it relates to a variety of correlates. The statistical analyses show that role-making and role-playing are both unique and reducible to one another. Their respective uniqueness is most sharply demarcated when the first element of organization is enacted. The unusual circumstances of disaster disrupt social routines and require new definitions of appropriate behavior. The role-making that results is associated with task contingencies, a more complex division of labor, greater disaster experience in the impacted community, and larger or emergent social networks. However, such role-making does not preclude early reliance on community routines. Even as structure is being created to meet the unique demands of disaster, much role-playing is being evidenced as an external force that molds the actions of participants. This is especially apparent when the first element of organization is T or D, when the response is self-contained rather than boundary spanning, when there has been formal preparedness, and when the broader community has ample resources with which to respond.

Role-playing increases just as role-making continues with the unfolding of organization at stages 2, 3, and 4. Several relevant variables at stage 1 continue to operate at subsequent stages, and new variables come into play. Most notable of the new correlates are participant concerns for victims (role-making), the timing of the first element (role-making), activities problems (role-making), and the size of the enacting unit (role-playing). Finally, while preparedness had been associated with role-playing early in the process, it later shows some connection with role-making. This dual role of preparedness—one that is captured developmentally—smacks of a balancing of formal and substantive rationality.

We have presented an exercise in conceptualizing and measuring structure (Blalock 1979). Our work suggests that a developmental theory of organization becomes more powerful by adding the concept of role to it. Whether the focus is organization or role, the requirement is conceiving and observing social process. Neither concept is more important than the other, and neither concept is necessarily micro or macro. In the end, all sociological concepts require descriptions and explanations of the forces of action and order. Therein lies the puzzle of social structure (Alexander 1982).

Social structure is no more or less than streams of events. Any description or explanation of such events calls forth three unique yet reducible realities. The first is the human being, which is a convenient place to start, but not a more basic building block than the others. The second is the social unit, which enables and is conditioned by the actions of human beings in time and space. The third is the form of association, which is the linking mechanism between human being and social unit. Omit the human being and there can be no social unit. Omit the social unit and there can be no human being. Remove the form of association and there is no way to observe the paradox of the separate existence and mutual reduction of human being and social unit. It makes no difference whether the paradox is expressed as conflict or solidarity—both are omnipresent. Exploiting the paradox can lead to better understandings of what the world is like. Our modest directive is simply this: describe forms of association to capture the paradox of structure. Once described, explain these forms with reference to characteristics of human beings and social units who enact them.

3

A Dialogue on Disaster, Organization, and Role

Aspects of Role Improvisation

RALPH H. TURNER

Susan Bosworth and Gary Kreps have taken on an ambitious and interesting task in studying the emergence of social organization in response to community disasters. Their focus on the process through which organization emerges carries us well beyond simple organizational correlate research. Their systematic attention to the different orders in which essential components of organization may appear, and the consequences of this variation, are important refinements over fixed stage approaches. Their attention to improvisation versus continuity in early postdisaster roles addresses one of the perennial concerns of disaster research, bringing it into a theoretical context that extends beyond the study of disasters. And their principal goal, to relate a role spontaneity dimension to the pattern by which organization develops, makes one think about the entire process of emergent or reemergent organization and the patterning of social roles. Finally, they briefly titillate us by suggesting their research can be understood as a step toward addressing the higher abstraction of the paradox of order and action.

Most of my comments here relate to their conceptualization and operationalization of social organization, and their dichotomy of role-making versus role-playing. I will also comment briefly on the relationship between the two and on their reference to the paradox of order versus action.

This is a considerably expanded version of an exchange found in chapter 8, "Commentaries on the Research Program of Kreps's Group," of *Social Structure and Disaster* (Kreps 1989a, 207–19).

Critical in evaluating and interpreting this chapter is a comfortable understanding of the four essential components of organization. I found the expositions in the chapter too brief to give me confidence that I could have applied them in the way intended. So I returned to Kreps's 1978 essay entitled "The Organization of Disaster Response," in which the components seem to be defined more concretely. In both statements there is something of a continuum from domain as the most general and abstract to activity as the most specific and concrete. There is a clear logical parallel to Smelser's (1962) rendering of Parsons's components of social action as a continuum from values to norms, to mobilization into organized roles, to situational facilities. For Smelser the ordering becomes a matter of rationality, and departure from appropriate ordering is short-circuiting, while Bosworth and Kreps think of a dimension of organization. By identifying domains and tasks as ends and resources and activities as means, they do import a similar implication of rationality, which they do not explore.

In Kreps's earlier statement domain is, "The generalized image of the organized social action held by both participants and relevant others in any instance of organized disaster response, providing an overall orienting definition of the legitimate purposes of the behavior" (Kreps 1978, 68). Domain in this sense is quite similar to Turner and Killian's ([1957] 1972) value orientation, as an integration of the goals and ideology of a social movement. We read further that "tasks are social definitions of how a specified domain of organized response is to be accomplished. . . . For example, the domain of debris clearance may require prior search and rescue efforts, inspections of buildings, blocking of streets, passage of emergency ordinances and many other tasks. . . ." (Kreps 1978, 69). We skip over "resources" as sufficiently clear, except that the availability of resources is a matter of degree: the level of resources is almost never either 0 or 100 percent, so there must be some arbitrariness in deciding when to classify a case as meeting the criteria for the resources component. Furthermore, if people are resources, how can one have activity without people? Activities, then, "represent observable organized response behavior during disaster situations. Activities may or may not conform to task definitions. . . ." (Kreps 1978, 70).

In this earlier statement of the components, three points seem relatively clear. First, when the domain is identified, tasks are means rather than ends, as they are classified in Bosworth and Kreps (1986) and chapter 2 above. Even as defined there, how can a "division of labor for the enactment of human activities" be an

end rather than a means? Second, domain, task, and activity constitute a continuum of generality and abstractness, and can probably
only be distinguished in relative terms. For example, if feeding
disaster victims is a domain (Kreps 1978) in one situation, it can
also be one of the tasks in a more inclusive domain of caring for
the immediate needs of victims. How does the investigator decide
that a social unit has tasks but as yet no domain? If there is mutual
agreement on tasks in a group, is that not their domain? Third,
classification as domain, task, or activity depends upon how
broadly the participants or other relevant bodies think about the
context and purpose of activity in the situation. How is this to be
determined? Surely not by probing the depths of individual
psyches!

The answer to this last question lies in the authors' conception
of organization. The components are applied on the basis of some
agreement as to what a social unit is doing. But agreement can be
at different levels. An ad hoc crew of volunteer emergency workers
like those described in Louis Zurcher (1983) can develop their own
consensus, with only vague awareness of what they are doing in
the larger community. But from the examples that Bosworth and
Kreps present, the establishment of a domain seems to depend
more on the decision of some higher body representing the whole
community—perhaps even a body whose authority predates the
disaster. Yet from the A-R-T-D example in Bosworth and Kreps
(1986) and chapter 2 above, it appears that a division of labor
(tasks) can be established by informal agreements among those
engaged in activity. Why should domain have to be legitimated at
a higher community level than tasks?

Some of my difficulty in thinking with the Bosworth-Kreps
framework relates to early indoctrination into the idea of informal
organization, recognizing that the essential processes that make an
organization work follow patterns at variance from those formalized into organizational charts and rules. There seems to be an
unclarified shifting between thinking of orgnaization as formal and
as informal organization.

I raise these questions because I don't yet feel that I fully understand what the authors mean by organization. I think I understand
disorganization: when activities or tasks occur at cross purposes
(e.g., in a brush fire, someone advises homeowners to wet down
their roofs with garden hoses while fire fighters are unable to fight
fires effectively because of lowered water pressure in the mains).
And I understand a simple absence of organization: when different
people and units act on their own with no coordination, though

not necessarily at cross purposes. But it is not entirely clear how organization, identified by agreement at some level on domain, tasks, resources, and activities relates to these states.

The other essential variable is a continuum from role-making to role-taking. When first introduced, the conception was not of a dichotomy between role-playing and role-making, but of role-making as a normal component of role-playing (R. Turner 1962). The point was that we do not play roles uncomprehendingly by rote, but that we take the role of relevant others and improvise role details so as to interact effectively with them, within the broad and often vague guidelines that constitute role prescriptions. To this we should add that every situation we encounter is unique in some respects and requires at least a modicum of improvisation. As a corollary, when people describe or explain roles, they typically do so more in terms of goals, values, styles, and sentiments than by offering precise behavioral catalogs.

If this distinction matters for the current project, it is because it highlights a difference between what might be called ordinary implementative role-making and a more radically innovative role-making when it is necessary to invent a role for an unprecedented situation or to reformulate a role drastically—for example, when firemen must allow fires to burn without interference.

Some might see this as nit-picking, because there are important differences between situations in which roles can be functionally adequate or tenable (R. Turner 1980) on the basis of established rules or customary practices and situations that require more improvisation. Granting this point, can the distinction be appropriately thought of as individual versus collective? In two respects, improvisation or role-making is not strictly an individual process. First, I find it useful to distinguish between formal role conceptions and informal or working role conceptions. The latter are improvisations that have been informally negotiated among role incumbents so as to fill gaps in formal prescriptions, make roles more effective, or render them tenable. For the most part role-making is not so much an individual matter as it is a turning to others who are not legitimate role definers for consensus in enacting a role. Ad hoc disaster rescue crews, for example, quickly seek consensus on priorities and conceptions of reasonable versus unreasonable risk. Second, when a situation calls for a role that does not exist as part of the potential incumbent's role repertoire, a role is typically formulated in good part by a process of role prototyping. The volunteer in an ill-defined disaster emergency situation becomes the nurse, the social worker, the policeman, the fireman, the paramedic, or some other familiar prototype role incumbent. Both the reconceptualization of role-making into the antithesis of role-playing and the identification of role-making as an individual rather than collective phenomenon relate to the hypothesis that altruism is related to role-making. Does this imply either that role-playing is intrinsically self-interested, or that role-playing is mindless? Are not motives and sentiments built into role? Is the role of mother comprehensible apart from the sentiment of mother love? Is not altruism an integral part of some of the key institutionalized roles that bear on search and rescue and disaster relief? Could the possible empirical correlation be a consequence of a bias not to credit activity to altruism when the self-sacrificing behavior is expected in an institutional role?

As I examine the criteria for distinguishing between role-making and role-playing, I believe that some clarification could render the analysis more precise. I believe it would be more consistent with the logic behind the theory of roles to distinguish between role-making and role reallocation. By role allocation (R. Turner 1968) I mean the assignment of particular individuals or categories of persons to particular roles. The authors include the allocation of roles to persons who would not customarily play those roles as one kind of role-making. But a crucial justification for use of the concept of role is that a role can be played as recognizably the same by different incumbents. When a role traditionally limited to males is opened up to females, this fact of reallocation should be kept analytically separate from the question of whether the role undergoes change in goals, values, styles, sentiments, strategies, or tactics as a consequence. This is important for the theoretical purity of the concept of role. Every definition of role makes the ultimate referent behavior, whether it be actual behavior (Davis 1948), modal or customary behavior (Goffman 1961), expected behavior, or appreciated behavior (R. Turner 1985). This distinction is important because of the phenomenon of role appropriation (S. Perry, Silber, and Bloch 1956). First observed and named in disaster behavior when a child unexpectedly enacts in exemplary fashion an adult role when available adults are unable to do so, the phenomenon of someone rising to the occasion is widespread. The theoretical importance of this concept in relation to a situation calling forth a system of roles is obvious. The distinction is also important because of the interchangeability of redifferentiation and reallocation as solutions to the problem of an ill-functioning or untenable role system. Elsewhere I have offered the beginning of a theory concerning the circumstances under which differentiation (transformative role-making) or reallocation will be favored as the solution (R. Turner 1980). I think the circumstance in which amateurs fight fire the best they can with garden hoses, using whatever familiarity they have with the role of fireman for guidance, until the "real" firemen come along should be distinguished from the situation in which genuinely novel or unfamiliar problems require improvisation in the absence of a prior role conception or substantial deviation from the customary patterns of role performance.

What these disparate observations about role theory add up to is to question the usefulness of lumping into a single index of role-taking-to-role-making so heterogeneous a set of differentiations, except as a first stage of analysis. Correlations such as those reported in the latter portion of the article (chapter 2) are intrinsically difficult to interpret when several kinds of differences are merged into a single dimension. Furthermore, such merging makes it impossible to search for tautological effects, such as a possible identity between the organization component of task (division of labor) and the role homogeneity criterion of role-making (roles are undifferentiated).

The analysis might also profit from comparison with Charles Powers's (1981) attempt to specify the conditions under which role-imposition or role-improvisation prevails, emphasizing such variables as power distribution, routinization, privacy, interpersonal dependence, and continuity of personnel.

Perhaps it is hardly surprising that role improvisation as the authors have defined it declines as organization proceeds, or that there is less opportunity for role improvisation when authorities can size up and define the situation from the start. More interesting is the possibility that some kind of improvisation may be initially fostered by the establishment of domain before the rest of the components are established. Such deviations from linearity warrant special attention.

I was troubled by a possible ambiguity over whether the authors' conception of organization incorporates a conservative bias, or whether it is equally applicable to emergent as well as continuing or reestablished organization. For the most part I believe their criteria of organization give full credit to emergent organization, except in two respects. First, I do not know exactly how they apply Durkheim's concept of collective representation. Can a collective representation be a short-term emergent, or does it imply continuity over time, like the concept of culture? Second, if domain must be defined by some legitimate authority, a bias toward continuity rather than emergence is introduced. In the dimension of role-making-role-taking, on the other hand, there does seem to be a substantial bias toward identifying role-playing with continuity. If, then, the conceptualization of organization allows for emergence as well as continuity, but only continuity can be classified as role-playing, what is the meaning of any observed relationships between the two? Would not a correlation in which both variables either allows for or excluded emergence be theoretically more meaningful?

In their admirable effort to show how middle-level theorizing fits into a higher level of theorizing, the authors pose the paradox of order versus action, and propose that it be analyzed dialectically. But is there a paradox of order versus action, or is this a pseudo problem? Empirically we see universally a world in which there is a very loose patterning and coordination of behavior, just as there is only a weak patterning of individual behavior. But why should we formulate this as a paradox? It becomes a paradox only when we create two ideal types of order and spontaneity that are logically incompatible as polar types. The paradox lies in the empirical coexistence of approximations to the two logically incompatible ideal types. But why approach the analysis in terms of two imaginary systems in the first place? What I am suggesting is that the paradox is a reification that may detract from effective analysis of social phenomena rather than offering a meaningful formulation through which light can be shed on social behavior.

The reference to dialectical process is also puzzling. Dialectic has a rather precise meaning: first there is a thesis, which then generates its antithesis; thesis and antithesis engage in struggle in the course of which both are replaced by a synthesis; the synthesis becomes the new thesis and a new round of the process ensues. But I see no such process in Bosworth and Kreps's analysis, but rather a governing strain toward order that is interrupted from time to time by disruptive events. I have already suggested that I find the conceptualization of role-playing and role-making as thesis and antithesis the creation of a false separation in terms of which role-playing and organized behavior are conceived as mindless behavior. In short, I am asking whether the escalation of intrinsically interesting and practical middle-level problems to the level of superabstraction in the form of ideal types is a constructive enterprise. My tentative answer is no.

If the escalation were to abstract principles of sufficient precision that they could be manipulated through syllogistic or other precise logic and empirical referents identified with certainty, I could only applaud the effort. But when—as in most higher-level sociological theorizing—the escalation is to ideal types that create imaginary problems through the logical incompatibility of the theorist's own creations, and when those types are so imprecise that they must be manipulated more by intuition than by logic, I suggest that the enterprise is counterproductive.

I conclude by hoping that the authors will continue what they have begun in this article (chapter 2), while further clarifying or refining the components of organization and by treating their role spontaneity dimension in a more differentiated fashion, rooted in a more sophisticated conception of social role dynamics.

Response to Commentary of Ralph Turner

GARY A. KREPS AND SUSAN LOVEGREN BOSWORTH

Ralph Turner's positive comments on our research are encouraging, and his criticisms are instructive. With regard to the latter, Turner points initially to the need to refine our notion of organization. At issue here is the analytical power of the four elements and the structural code derived from them. The skeptical reader must be convinced that they are useful tools for determining what organization is, how it comes into being, and how it is sustained or lost in disaster and (perhaps) other settings. We are in complete agreement with Turner on the need for continuous fine tuning. Other chapters in part 1 of *Social Structure and Disaster* (Kreps 1989a) indicate that conceptual refinements have been central preoccupations of our work. Still, there has been obvious continuity over time in our definitions of D, T, R, and A. We seek a theory of organizing that is simple and compelling. The elements and code must be analytically precise, yet flexible with respect to contextual differences in the enactment of organization (Dubin 1978; Blumer 1969).

Turner's helpful pondering about the four elements communicates nicely our concerns of the past several years, as we grapple with differences between disorganization, the simple absence of organization, and its existence. We think the theory has descriptive potential, in part because it is consistent with the way people think about organizing, and also because it provides common ground for theories of formal organization and collective behavior. We feel the same way about notions of role-playing and role-making as complementary expressions of social structure. Certainly a more elaborate definition of organization can be developed by increasing the number of elements included. We use four that we think together capture organizing in its most elemental sense and, in so doing, subsume most of the correlates that organizational theorists associate with the concept. Similar to R. Turner's (1985) admonition about role, we think that social scientists must be sensitive to the fact that those who enact organization interpret what they do as gestalts (wholes) rather than detailed structural inventories.

The relative presence and absence of organization is expressed theoretically as one- to four-element forms of association. Our findings on the origins of organization illustrate what we have in mind in this regard. And although we have a long way to go, we are beginning to show that disorganization can be interpreted as problems in the emergence or restructuring of the elements. Granted, there is no question that we have consciously avoided use of the term *disorganization* in presentation of findings. Such a term implies normative judgments that we think are premature until we better understand where, when, and how organization is enacted. More to the point of Turner's uncertainty with our definition of organization, we ask (with him) why is it so hard to pin down something that is so obvious to so many?

Would not students of collective and organizational behavior agree that organization necessitates, at some point, external recognition and legitimacy of a purposive and bounded entity (D)? Would they not agree that organization requires internal clarity about a division of labor (T)? Can organization be contemplated without reference to human and material resources (R) or the conjoined actions of individuals or social units in time and space (A)? In effect, we are trying to build on what is basic (and obvious) about organization by theorizing about how it works. What is basic is also commonly shared by social scientists and the people they study. Interestingly enough, however, the concreteness and uniqueness of the elements seem readily apparent only if organization is assumed to exist. When that assumption is questioned, as we do in studies of origins, then the important subtleties Turner raises become critical.

Why is this the case? We think it is because, in the end, the existence of organization is based on agreement among direct participants, legitimating authorities, and outside observers that it is there (Giddens 1976). We have played the role of outside observers in our archival studies of disaster response. As the last link in a consensus chain, we have searched for instances of organization, and then tried to reconstruct how they took place. Keeping this methodological point in mind, Kreps's chapter 7, "Reflections on D, T, R, A," in *Social Structure and Disaster* (1989a, 186–96) anticipates some of the questions about the elements posed by Turner.

Nevertheless at least three concerns merit special attention. First, why should domains have to be legitimated at some higher community level than tasks? As implied above, organizing does not take place in a vacuum. Regardless of how it unfolds, a necessary condition of viability is some threshold of outside awareness and acceptance of an entity and what it is doing. The important point here is that organization is boundary spanning. Building on Thompson's (1967) useful distinction between domains and tasks, we have argued that the former reflects the open system character of organization and the latter its closed system character. What we have not done, and need to do, is pay greater attention to boundary spanning roles.

Second, when domain is identified, must not tasks become means rather than ends? Not at all. As collective representations, domains and tasks both are appropriately called ends because they involve individual understandings and unit symbolizations of purpose. It is only when one assumes that domains are somehow more general and inclusive as goals, sentiments, or values that tasks are accorded the status of means. As noted below, we argue against that assumption. It is important to add that we are not proposing causal relationships among the elements. Each one is proposed as a unique dimension of organizing and used, first and foremost as a tool of description. The closest Kreps comes to an explanatory argument is the complementarity thesis found in chapter 6, "Social Structure: Paradox, Form, and Complementarity," of *Social Structure and Disaster* (1989a, 166–85). Even there it is only connected very loosely with evolutionary theory.

Third, do not activities, tasks, and domains constitute a continuum of increasing generality and inclusiveness that can only be distinguished analytically rather than empirically? As for generality, the answer is no. Turner implies that individual actions and perhaps meanings are less abstract and more observable than collective representations. We disagree. The latter are not just ideas; they are parts of the material culture (such as written and verbal communications) that can be recorded just as readily as physical behaviors and psychic states. Until convinced otherwise, we conclude that all of the elements are equally concrete or abstract.

As for inclusiveness, we think that Turner highlights perhaps the most interesting puzzle of social science: bridging micro- and macrolevels of analysis. At this point we have no clear image of this puzzle, only what can be gleaned from working with D, T, R, and A. In a very preliminary way, we have suggested that one- to four-element forms of association may be hierarchically arranged (Wallace 1983). This means that first, each element must reflect increasing levels of inclusiveness on its own terms; and second, increasing levels of inclusiveness across the four elements must be related as one- to four-element forms of association. It is relatively easy to illustrate that such presumed levels of organizing as tribes, cities, empires, nation states, and world systems are connected in some hierarchical fashion. It is very difficult, however, to describe and explain how this happens. Concepts are needed, and so are strategies for life history studies of the above entities.

Turner then raises a concern about our use of a continuum of role-playing to role-making. He argues that we imply a distinction between rote response (role-playing) and innovativeness (role-making) that is not in keeping with conceptions of role coming from interactionist (as opposed to structuralist) traditions (Stryker 1980; Mayhew 1980; R. Turner 1985; Stryker and Statham 1985). He then (and later) critiques our use of dialectical reasoning. If we understand him correctly, Turner believes that we are proposing a false dichotomy of individual and unit: one that we express, respectively, as action versus order and role-making versus role-playing. The issue Turner raises is important for assessing (in Turner's terms) "how middle-level theorizing fits into a higher level of theorizing." He asks "whether the escalation of intrinsically interesting and practical middle-level problems to the level of superabstraction in the form of ideal types is a constructive enterprise." His tentative answer is no. Because our tentative answer is yes, we will try to restate our reasoning as clearly as possible.

We do make explicit a dialectic of individual and unit. This means that each is thesis and antithesis to the other. As synthesis, form of association serves as a bridge that allows observation of individual and unit at the same time. The action and order that can then be observed at any level of form (a new thesis) is always being undermined in a continuous dialectic of means (R, A) and ends (D,T). Thus, contrary to Turner's assertion, role-playing does not affirm the unit and deny the individual. Nor does role-making affirm the individual and deny the unit. Just as with action versus order, individual and unit are affirmed at both ends of the continuum. The false dichotomy that troubles Turner is precisely what we are trying to overcome with our descriptions of structure. Our use of ideal types involves an appeal to pragmatism, not superabstraction.

We fully agree with Turner's assertion of a universal reality in which individual behavior and collective action are, at best, loosely patterned. He sees a tension between imaginary systems (reifications) and the empirically given. So do we. Our goal is to measure structure in a way that makes sense. As we have argued throughout, our conceptual and empirical sense of structure is that individual and unit are symmetrical dimensions of form. Sacrifice one for the other analytically and the result is less descriptive power of structural theory. It seems to us that this conclusion is grounded equally well in structuralist and interactionist traditions in sociology (Warriner 1956, 1970).

Anticipating that Turner will remain unconvinced, it is important to assess why a meeting of the minds on the need for or value of dialectical reasoning is so difficult to achieve. Paradigm disputes are certainly relevant. Turner's own work on collective behavior and role involves an attempt to imbue any conception of social structure with interactionist principles. For him, structure is a process where intelligent individuals always take the vantage points of others into account, and improvise as they go along (R. Turner 1985). The reality of the individual is affirmed, and so is the indivisibility of what we have termed action and order. Maybe that is why Turner concludes that we have constructed a false dichotomy. We affirm the reality of the individual as well. But we also point to a parallel reality of the unit in our attempt to be resolutely multidimensional about process (Alexander 1982; Rossi 1983).

Perhaps it comes down to this: Turner sees interactionism overcoming both psychological and sociological reductionism. With the same goal in mind, our effort is to make the dialectic of action and order work by exploiting an analytical triangle of individual, unit, and form of association. We see that triangle as a possible tool in Turner's own effort to overcome still another false dichotomy: interactionism versus structuralism (Shalin 1986). Our debate with Turner, if there is one, will not be resolved at the philosophical level. It will be resolved through substantive inquiry, as we all try to come up with more powerful descriptions and explanations of what the world is like. To that end, the remainder of Turner's commentary offers a number of constructive suggestions for expanding our conception of role.

While Turner sees our measurement of role as a potentially useful departure from static approaches, he pushes us to go beyond this first stage by refining our conception of role-making and role-playing. Turner sees us coming at role from the structuralist position, which, for him, is inherently limiting if the individual is sacrificed analytically. He approaches role as an interactionist, which, for us, is inherently limiting if the unit is sacrificed analytically. Our common ground is structure as process. We agree that our reported research is only a first stage. We want to be pushed in the interactionist direction because greater balance is needed. We think that Turner offers some useful direction for second-stage work.

Turner seems to be saying that both role-making and role-playing need to be refined. He specifically suggests that the collective as well as individual sides of role-making are revealed by distinguishing between implementative (role prototyping) and radically innovative (role appropriation) role enactments. The former involves taking on a role that already exists (is collectively understood) but is not a part of the individual's current repertoire. For the latter an individual must invent a new role or radically reformulate an existing one to meet unusual circumstances. Turner suggests also that the individual, as well as collective sides of role-playing, is revealed by distinguishing between working (informally negotiated) and formal (officially imposed) role enactments. The former directly involves improvisation. The latter involves responding on the basis of established rules, procedures, and power arrangements (Powers 1981).

We think these kinds of distinctions are interesting, important, and can be measured through further work with the archives or primary data collection on disaster responses. While we remain convinced that a continuum of role-playing to role-making is useful, the dialectic of individual and unit will assume greater descriptive power with the refinements suggested by Turner. Studies of process remain the essential bridge between organization and role. From the perspective of role, the question is, how do role allocation and reallocation processes lead to a system of differentiated roles? From the perspective of organization, the problem becomes how individually necessary conditions of existence (D, T, R, A) become four-element forms of association? What Turner then calls the functional adequacy or tenability of the system of roles being created or transformed (R. Turner 1980), we call the survivability of the entity until the reason for organizing has ended.

Turner seems to agree that, for the most part, our conception of the four elements gives full credit to both established and emergent organization. We answer his final questions about organization and role, as a close to our response to his commentary. First, can collective representations be short-term and emergent as well as longer-term and established before the emergency? The answer is yes. Second, if domain requires external legitimacy by some authority, does this not create a bias toward continuity? The answer is no because the legitimating authority(ies) may be emergent as well as established. Third, does the role continuum not exhibit a bias toward identifying role-playing with continuity and role-making with change? The answer is yes for two of the four criteria (inconsistency versus consistency of the status/role nexus and discontinuity versus continuity of role linkages) at all stages of organizing. The answer is yes for the remaining two criteria (unique role performance versus role boundary expansion and homogeneity versus heterogeneity of roles), but only at the first stage of organization (one element present). All subsequent role-playing for these criteria may be completely circumscribed by the response and the event. We add that the organizing to which role relates may itself be emergent. The sample of thirty-nine cases at the midpoint of the action-order metric includes both established and emergent units.

Turner's last, two-part question is the most intriguing of all of his questions. We have interpreted (and rephrased) it in a way that makes sense to us. If organizing is emergent as well as established, but some role-playing is biased toward established routines, what is the meaning of any observed relationships between organizing and role-playing? Would not a strategy in which both concepts either allowed for or excluded continuity with established routines be theoretically more meaningful? Our response to the initial part of the question is that the role-playing that occurs may reflect continuity with established practices or emergent improvisations, depending on the stage of organizing and which of the four criteria are at issue. Our response to the last part of the question is that we should discuss it more as we get on with the work. It may have been a mistake to begin our role studies on a sample of both established and emergent organizations. It will be possible in the future to create subsamples of only established or emergent organizations, and then to compare correlations of organizing and role-playing across the two samples. This would partially respond to Turner's position and could provide new insights about organization and role. We could also analyze the current and any subsequent role criteria separately, with the aim of calibrating each in terms of a continuity criterion.

But as we have said in several different ways, the new can never be divorced from what is already there, and what is already there is constantly transforming. This is the basic dialectical assumption that underlies all that we do. As we refine our measurement of role-making and role-playing along the lines suggested by Turner, we hope that we can convince him of the utility of that assumption.

Addendum

Turner's critique, as well as our response, can be divided into two parts. The first one focuses on Kreps's conception and measurement of organizing, and the second addresses our treatment of role. With respect to the conception of organizing, our formal response to Turner's critique, much related discussion in *Social Structure and Disaster* (Kreps 1989a, 186–237), one subsequent paper (Kreps 1991), and the first chapter of this book represent our best efforts to clarify how the structural code has been applied to disaster archives. At least for now, therefore, we are content to rest our case. We also suggest that there are at least two possibilities for further research with this particular code.

One path is continued work with Kreps's taxonomy (table 1.1) to refine the code and assess its reliability. As noted in chapter 1, the fact that the taxonomy has built-in counterfactuals is an important asset in these regards. A second path is to apply an alternative conception of organizing to the same archival data. One such alternative was offered by Walter Wallace in *Social Structure and Disaster* (Kreps 1989a, 219–37), and it would be interesting to determine its relative descriptive power. Either of the above paths would be encouraging because, in our judgment, the development of some kind of structural code is important for disaster research and sociology generally.

Notwithstanding that arguable position, it is the second part of the above exchange with Turner that stimulated our expanded archival research on role. At various stages of the ensuing study, we have reached substantial agreement with Turner on several key matters. The foundation of these agreements are the exchange itself and also some of Turner's own theoretical work on role. Of greatest value to us has been his article titled "Strategy for Developing an Integrated Role Theory" (R. Turner 1980). In that article Turner highlights three processes (what are called observed tendencies) that he believes must be taken into account in any theorizing about role. These are termed *role differentiation and accretion, role allocation,* and *role complementarity.* In the following discussion, we will define these processes from Turner's work and link them directly to our original conception of role enactment. Therein lies what we see as an emerging consensus with Turner, one that serves as the foundation of our refined measurement of role enactment.

Our first area of consensus is probably the most basic. We have agreed with Turner since the beginning of our new work that regardless of one's view about the value of dialectical reasoning, paradoxical reasoning, or superabstraction in sociology, every definition of role must make human behavior analytically central. In referencing behavior, then, the theorist must never treat role-playing and role-making as a dichotomy. There are two reasons for this requirement: First, role-making is a normal component of role-playing. This means that while "existing" incumbents always take the role of others into account (Mead 1934, 253–57), the fact that they improvise as they go along makes it clear that role-playing is as much an individual as it is a structural phenomenon. Second, role-playing is a normal component of role-making. This means that because "new" incumbents take the role of others into account also, their improvisation is as much a structural as it is an individual phenomenon.

The symmetry of role-playing and role-making is nicely illustrated by our third dimension of role enactment (role performance). Role boundary expansion implies an existing incumbent who improvises to varying degrees. Turner refers to lower degrees of improvisation as formal role enactment and higher degrees as working role enactment. Both structure and the individual are affirmed. Unique role performance implies a new incumbent who improvises to varying degrees as well. Turner refers to lower degrees of improvisation here as role prototyping. Thus, while the role is not a part of the individual's predisaster repertoire, expectations attached to it are well established, and the individual conforms to them as a new incumbent. Turner refers to higher degrees of improvisation as role appropriation (or what we feel is better termed role redefinition). We interpret that to mean that the new incumbent, perhaps because of a lack of knowledge of role expectations, or because of the unusual demands of the situation, deviates from conventional patterns of role performance. Once again, both structure and the individual are affirmed.

Fundamental to any discussion of role performance is Turner's conception of *role differentiation and accretion* (1980, 126). By that he means (as we interpret him) that in any situation where people interact there is a natural tendency for their behaviors, sentiments, and motives to become distinguishable as discrete entities called roles. Presumably the more people involved, the greater the potential for discrete roles to emerge. In any event, once roles become differentiated, it logically follows that the behavior, sentiments, and motives that appear subsequently in similar situations will become patterned (i.e., they will become assigned to now existing roles).

With reference to our third dimension of role enactment, what Turner calls formal role enactment by an existing incumbent and role prototyping by a new incumbent are analytically comparable in the sense that role differentiation has already happened. Working role enactment by an existing incumbent or role redefinition by a new incumbent are analytically comparable also, but now in the sense that differentiation is still in process. Turner refers to the latter as *redifferentiation*. But the critical thing to keep in mind here is the analytical importance of both stability and change in thinking about incumbency, regardless of whether it is existing or new.

Our second area of agreement relates also to what Turner calls role differentiation and accretion, but in a way that makes more than one level of analysis explicit. To be specific, we agree that the actual performance of a given role must be distinguished from the broader system of roles of which it is a part (Bates and Harvey 1975, 83–128). We clearly had tried to capture that distinction with the fourth dimension of role enactment (role differentiation) by connecting it explicitly with Kreps's previous definition of organizing. As Turner implies in his critique as well as the above conception of differentiation, asking how an organization has come into being necessarily involves asking how certain roles have become differentiated from others.

Answering the question about how roles are differentiated requires a clear statement about the division of labor in any social system. Kreps makes that division of labor explicit definitionally with the tasks (T) element in his structural code. In his critique, however, Turner cautions us that our conception of the fourth role dimension creates a possible tautology in correlating any composite role score by stage of organizing. He is quite right. We therefore decided to drop the fourth criterion, as we have conceived it originally, with the hope that systemic role differentiation could be measured independently and more precisely in subsequent work. Specifically, we had already used the number of tasks as an independent variable to represent organizational complexity. We hoped now to produce analytically parallel measures of role complexity such as the total number of roles performed in an organized response.

As Turner (1980, 128–29) has noted, sociological principles of functionality and tenability of a role system are part and parcel of role differentiation. With respect to functionality, the question becomes how efficiently and effectively is the role system working. While certainly efficiency and effectiveness can be measured in many different ways, the focus seems to be on structure sui generis. With respect to tenability, the question becomes how personally rewarding is a role system for respective role incumbents. Measurement of the extent to which a system is personally rewarding is also multifaceted, but now the focus appears to be at the individual level of analysis.

Our third area of agreement extends directly from the second, and it relates once again to Turner's reference to a role system. In speaking about a system of roles, Turner highlights his two remaining fundamental processes, *role allocation* and *role complementarity*. We think they inform, respectively, our two remaining dimensions of role enactment. However, the issue now becomes how one system of roles (in our studies, an organized disaster response) relates to a more inclusive system of roles (in our studies, the impacted community and broader society) of which it is a part (Bates and Harvey 1975, 208–20). We will summarize Turner's thoughts about role allocation and role complementarity separately and, in so doing, show how we think each of them connects to role enactment during a disaster.

Turner (1980, 126, and in his formal critique) refers to role allocation as the assignment of particular persons or categories of people to particular roles. While precisely how or why this allocation occurs remains unclear, Turner (1980, 129–30) offers a number of possible explanations. What he sees as a useful but superficial explanation (because it only shows *how* allocation occurs) is that the assignment is based on either ascription (e.g., gender, race, age) or achievement (e.g., skill, motivation, training). But what he sees as more powerful explanations (because they show *why* allocation occurs) relate to connections between desirability and power on the one hand, and the fit between role characteristics and the individual on the other. With regard to the former, because roles demonstrably differ in their desirability (with respect to extrinsic and intrinsic rewards), Turner argues (from the tenability principle primarily) that the most desirable roles will tend to be allocated to the most powerful individuals or categories of individuals. With regard to the latter, Turner argues (from both tenability and functionality principles) that roles are sorted out in such a way so that there is a fit between individual dispositions (attitudes, preferences, skills, aptitudes) and essential role requirements.

This conception of role allocation reinforces nicely our first dimension of role enactment (status-role nexus). The reason for this is quite straightforward. Regardless of how or why roles become allocated in a community or society prior to a disaster, they shape the behaviors of and toward positionally labeled individuals. Thus, any time there is consistency in what we have termed the status-role nexus from pre- to postdisaster time periods, for Turner the systemic allocation of roles has remained stable (functional and tenable) in the face of nonroutine circumstances. However, any time there is inconsistency in the status-role nexus, the systemic allocation of roles has been changed in response to these same circumstances. Turner refers to the latter as reallocation. Here functionality and tenability principles are at issue.

Similar to role allocation, Turner argues (as we interpret him) that some conception of a role system must be assumed in discussing what he terms *role complementarity* (R. Turner 1980, 126). By role complementarity Turner means that every role in a system is formed in such a way that it is interdependent with at least one other (alter) role (Bates and Harvey 1975, 94–99). This suggests that any time we find continuity in what we have termed a role linkage, for Turner the complementarity of the role system from pre- to postdisaster time periods has remained stable. However, any time we find discontinuity in role linkages, the complementarity of the role system has been changed in response to these same circumstances. Just as with role differentiation and role allocation, Turner argues that patterns of role complementarity have important implications for the functionality and tenability of the role system. His joint appeal to social structure and the individual is therefore evidenced throughout.

Our fourth and final area of agreement with Turner, in a very real sense, summarizes chapters 1–3 of this monograph. The agreement is fundamental and it can be stated in the following way: Regardless of whether the enacting social unit is established, expanding, extending, or emergent (from the original DRC typology); regardless of whether the form of association evidences formal organizing or collective behavior (D-T-R-A to A-R-T-D); and regardless of whether role enactment evidences role-making or role-playing; any conception of social structure during a disaster must not be biased in terms of either stability or change of predisaster social arrangements.

In closing this chapter, we restate our unequivocal acceptance of the coequal reality of social structure and the individual. We do so not as an unnecessary diversion to superabstraction, but as an intense appeal to philosophical pragmatism (Collins 1985, 180–91). Simply put, we believe that if the theorist wants to describe and explain how the world works with respect to organizational and role dynamics during a disaster, then she or he must take as given that neither individual nor structure is more real than the other (Warriner 1956).

Despite our possible disagreement about the importance of that point, we think Turner would concur that giving structure and the individual equal attention in any given theory or piece of research is very difficult and perhaps, on pragmatic grounds at least, unnecessary. With that in mind, at least one of Turner's major theoretical interests has not been addressed systematically in our work: namely, the relationship between role and the self concept (R. Turner 1976; 1978; 1980). But that neglect speaks more to the limitations of the archives and the current boundaries of our theorizing (which includes the behavior of individuals while excluding sentiments and motives) than it does to any preference on our part. Social structure is what we are trying to explain. While pyschic states of human beings are part of the explanation of structure, thus far we have not been able to measure them in our research. Simply put, people have to be asked pointedly about their sentiments and motives.

4

Role Dynamics and Emergent Organizations: Conception and Measurement

This chapter summarizes the second phase of our conception and measurement of role dynamics. As noted in the last chapter, we equate the first dimension, status-role nexus, with stability and change of role allocation *from* the community and society *to* the organized disaster response. We equate the second dimension, role linkages, with stability and change of role complementarity *from* the community and society *to* the organized disaster response. We equate the third dimension, role performance, with stability and change of role differentiation *from* the community and society *to* the organized disaster response. The final dimension, which previously allowed for examining role differentiation within the organized response itself, has been dropped from the analysis to avoid a possible tautology with the (T) element of the structural code. However, the complexity of role enactment will be addressed later as a possible explanatory variable.

Implementing the expanded role analysis with the organized response as unit of analysis required substantial amounts of information on each case selected. Where earlier (Bosworth and Kreps 1986) we had characterized cases as being mixed role-playing and role-making whenever one or the other did not predominate, now we wished to show the precise proportions of participants role-playing and role-making on each of the three dimensions. This meant that we had to identify and label a central predisaster status and postdisaster role for every participant in order to make proportional judgments about the consistency or inconsistency of the status-role nexus (first dimension). Once all postdisaster roles had been identified, we also had to isolate all role and incumbent pairs

This chapter is based on our collaborative research with Jennifer Mooney. The study is summarized in Mooney's master's thesis, "Organization and Role: Conception and Measurement" (1989).

to make proportional judgments about stability and change of role complementarity (second dimension). Finally, for each post-disaster role performance, we had to make judgments about the extent to which incumbents (existing or new) were improvising during role enactment (third dimension).

Two preliminary decisions were central for the research that followed: First, we decided that it would be impossible to measure role dynamics at every stage of organizing (one, two, three, and four elements present). The expanded data needs were simply too great. We took as given, therefore, that all organizations studied were in process, and that the actual pattern of origins (formal organizing to collective behavior) would be examined later as an independent variable. Second, we felt that the fifty-two emergent organizations previously identified by Kreps would be the most manageable because of their generally smaller size (48 percent had fifty or less participants, and 38 percent had twenty or less). Small size was no guarantee, however, of sufficient data. The case highlighted in the first chapter, for example, proved to be unworkable for the third dimension of role enactment. While organizational tasks are identified in the archives, there is no clear information in them about who is doing what once the emergent organization is ongoing.

Our major objectives in this chapter are to walk the reader through the research design and then to summarize major descriptive findings on emergent organizations. The first section of the chapter restates our revised conceptions of the three dimensions and how we sought to measure them. The second section of the chapter provides two cases that detail how our research design was implemented. The major difficulties we faced in working with the archives will be highlighted in these two sections. The third section of the chapter summarizes findings on twenty-nine emergent organizations for which adequate data were available. The conclusion of the chapter provides a brief but necessary transition to the third and final phase of data production, which is reported on in chapter 5.

Conception of Role Dynamics

Status-role nexus, role linkages, and role performance will be discussed separately as unique dimensions of role enactment. While role is complex and multidimensional, we agree with Ralph Turner that the three dimensions isolated below are among the most important ones. They address what people are doing and the relevance of their actions for stability and change of social structure.

Status-Role Nexus: Role Allocation

A status is a social position that has expectations of human behavior attached to it. These expectations are referred to as roles. The question being addressed with this dimension is as follows: Is allocation of a postdisaster role to a given person expected given one or more positions in that individual's predisaster status set? Where allocation is expected, there is consistency of the status-role nexus; where it is not expected, there is inconsistency (Merton 1957, 368–70).

Accordingly, for each participant in an organized disaster response we initially had to identify and label a primary postdisaster role. We accomplished this by *naming* a role as closely as possible to what an individual was actually doing (e.g., search and rescue leader as opposed to search and rescue worker). We then searched the archives for information on the incumbent's predisaster status set to identify that individual's *occupation*. Next we had to determine whether the postdisaster role would be expected of someone having that occupation (e.g., a county sheriff serving as a search and rescue leader in a rural area). Because often more than one participant in an organized response was performing the same postdisaster role (e.g., search and rescue workers), we hoped to derive two proportions for the status-role nexus, one relating to postdisaster role incumbents and the other relating to the roles themselves.

Obviously occupation is only one of many social positions in any individual's status-role set, but we focused on it for several compelling reasons. First, there was no question that occupation is a major status for the kinds of people chronicled in the archives. It was equally clear that such occupations linked these individuals pointedly to at least a broader community role allocation system. Second, while the archives virtually never provide a complete accounting of an individual's status set, they very regularly include information on type of employment or job title. The potential to standardize measurement was therefore high. Third, if a participant in an organized response was not gainfully employed, we often were able to identify another, analytically comparable primary status (e.g., student, housewife) that would allow for some judgment about consistency or inconsistency of the status-role nexus. Absent data on either postdisaster role or predisaster status (occupation in the vast majority of cases), the case would be considered uncertain on this dimension for a given participant.

Suppose, hypothetically, that three postdisaster roles have been identified for an emergent organization of twenty-five people and that there is one incumbent performing the first role, three incumbents performing the second one, and twenty-one incumbents performing the third one. Suppose also that specific occupations have been recorded for all twenty-five people as the primary predisaster status that will be used to determine consistency or inconsistency of the status-role nexus. Measuring this dimension can be accomplished in the following way. An initial judgment about the status-role nexus must be made for each of the twenty-five incumbents so that the proportions of them judged consistent and inconsistent can be quantified. Postdisaster roles can then be analyzed on their own terms. In this hypothetical case, the first role will be either consistent or inconsistent because there is only one incumbent. The second and third roles will be consistent or inconsistent depending upon how the majorities of their respective incumbents (three and twenty-one) are judged initially. The proportion of roles consistent and inconsistent can then be quantified.[1]

Other than missing data, which were a chronic problem, the major difficulty we faced was how to handle formal volunteers (e.g., for the Red Cross, Salvation Army, hospitals, and police and fire departments) whose predisaster occupations were unknown or irrelevant to the disaster, but whose formal status as volunteers often predicated their postdisaster roles. In such cases we still judged their status-role nexus to be inconsistent (or uncertain), using occupation as our sole referent. While in subsequent data production (see chapter 5) we would note the possibility of role allocation being based on a status other than occupation, we continue to believe that it is essential to measure this dimension as uniformly as possible. Standardization is achieved, and the broader status set of any participant necessarily comes into play in determining incumbency for the third dimension (role performance, discussed below).

Another major problem was that even assuming there was information on occupation or some other equivalent status, our judgments about consistency/inconsistency might simply be wrong (e.g., would you expect a pathologist to be providing medical treatment?). Where respondents did not provide their own assessments of status-role expectations, or when face validity did not appear to be obvious, we contacted local people having the same occupational titles as the participants and asked them if the given postdisaster role we had observed would be expected of them. Interestingly enough, the kind of problem we faced with the archives could be largely overcome in the field by simply asking incumbents the same direct questions. As we will try to show at the end of this monograph, knowing what you are looking for can lead to highly structured research protocols.

Role Linkages: Role Complementarity

This dimension captures what Bosworth and Kreps (1986) term (from George Herbert Mead) the *relational dimension* of status-role. It parallels also what Ralph Turner (1980) terms (again from Mead) *role complementarity*. If multiple roles of an organized response are linked prior to a disaster, then these role links are continuous and role complementarity is stable. If multiple roles are not linked prior to a disaster, then these role links are discontinuous, and the basis of role complementarity is changing. While this conception of role complementarity can be stated concisely, measuring it requires a rather elaborate procedure, one that is very sensitive to the size of an organized response.

Having identified and labeled postdisaster roles and predisaster statuses for all participants in an organized response (first dimension above), our task now was documenting the composite of postdisaster role relationships that were operating. To that end, we assumed that all roles of an organized response were related *directly* in some fashion. We considered this to be a reasonable assumption, given the generally small emergent units we were studying. While it was certain that some incumbent relationships would involve people who were performing the same roles, we decided to focus only on *inter-role* relationships. To simplify matters further, we decided that only inter-role relationships *within* the organized response would be documented. This meant that, at this stage at least, we were indifferent about role links that were boundary spanning (i.e., inter-role relationships that connected an emergent organization to a broader response system).

Suppose, hypothetically, that five postdisaster roles have been identified for an emergent organization. This means (by the formula for combinations of *n* things taken two at a time) that there are ten possible inter-role pairs that have to be judged for purposes of describing the extent to which role relationships are continuous or discontinuous. Suppose also that the organized response has fifteen people; that there are three incumbents performing each of the five roles; and that occupation is being used uniformly as the primary predisaster status for purposes of comparing pre- and postdisaster structural arrangements.

To describe the continuity/discontinuity of the ten possible inter-*role* pairs in this hypothetical example, judgments must first be made about the continuity/discontinuity among all associated *incumbent* pairs. This means that each of the three incumbents performing one disaster role must be paired, respectively, with each of three incumbents performing a second role, for a total of nine judgments about continuity/discontinuity. The same procedure must be repeated for each of the ten inter-role pairs, yielding a total of ninety judgments about incumbent relationships within the emergent organization.

Each of these ninety possible incumbent pairs must then be examined to determine whether the relationship is continuous (e.g., a doctor and a nurse) or discontinuous (e.g., a college professor and a meat inspector). It does not matter whether there is evidence in the archives that people know each other personally or not. The judgment about role complementarity is based strictly on whether predisaster occupational statuses are or are not linked routinely in everyday circumstances. When all of the ninety possible incumbent pairs have been judged in this way, the proportions of them that are continuous and discontinuous can be quantified.

Once all of the above is accomplished, it is then possible to derive the proportions of the ten possible inter-*role* pairs that are continuous and discontinuous with predisaster structural arrangements. In this hypothetical example, if more than four of nine incumbent pairs are continuous or discontinuous for any of the ten possible role pairs, then that particular role pair evidences either a relatively stable or a changing pattern of role complementarity. The resulting proportions of inter-role pairs that are continuous and discontinuous can then be quantified as the last step in the measurement of this dimension.[2]

Role Performance: Role Differentiation

The focus of this dimension is the actual performance of postdisaster roles by specific individuals, which is quite different from the allocation of roles to particular statuses (status-role nexus). As implied from our earlier discussions (see pages 80–83, in particular), role differentiation is perhaps the most basic social process, and one that relates equally with role-playing and role-making. Two issues must be addressed in measuring postdisaster role performance: *incumbency,* which can be either existing or new; and *improvisation,* which can vary from low to high for either existing or new incumbents. Incumbency is established initially: if the post-disaster role is represented anywhere in the person's current predi-saster status set (e.g., a formal Salvation Army volunteer staffing a food kitchen), incumbency is termed existing; but if it is not represented anywhere (e.g., a merchant next door dropping in and providing the same service), incumbency is termed new. That determined, as detailed below some judgment is then made about the level of improvising.

We next developed the six-fold typology depicted on figure 4.1 for purposes of examining role performance. The three types on the left side of the figure depict varying degrees of improvising by an existing incumbent. The three types on the right side of the figure depict parallel degrees of improvising by a new incumbent. Social structure and role invention are exhibited as the twin foundations of both role-playing and role-making as we have conceptualized them. The six types are specified as follows:

(first level of improvising)

Formal Role Enactment: existing incumbent, conventional performance.
Role Prototyping: new incumbent, conventional performance

(second level of improvising)

Working Role Enactment: existing incumbent, improvised performance.
Role Redefinition: new incumbent, improvised performance

(third level of improvising)

Radical Role Transformation: existing incumbent, fundamental change in performance
Radical Role Redefinition: new incumbent, fundamental change in role performance

The lowest level of improvising is represented by formal role enactment (role-playing) and role prototyping (role-making). Both types are characterized by familiarity with role expectations and conformity to them during the disaster. The middle level of improvising is represented by working role enactment (role-playing) and

Figure 4.1

Types of Role Performance in Emergent Organized Responses

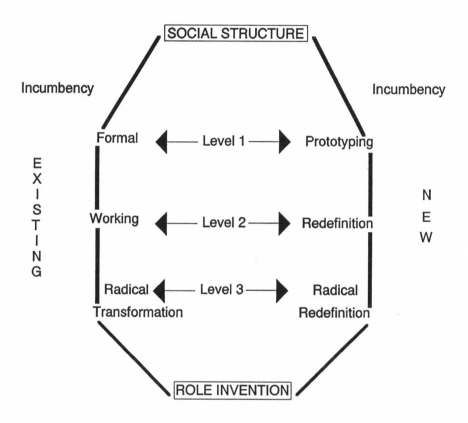

role redefinition (role-making). Both types are characterized by some deviation from the conventional enactment of an existing role that is based on incumbent interpretations of the role or the special circumstances in which it is being enacted. The highest level of improvising is represented by radical role transformation (role-playing) and radical role redefinition (role-making). Both types are characterized by major deviation from the conventional enactment of a given role that is based, once again, on incumbent interpretations of the role or the circumstances in which it is being enacted.

Basic to the typology depicted on figure 4.1 is an assumption that while *no* role performance takes place in a social vacuum, *all* role performance involves some degree of improvising. Both social structure (order) and role invention (action) are thereby affirmed (Alexander 1982). One might then ask: If role-playing and role-making are two sides of the same coin, why reference either of them in conceiving and measuring this or any other dimension of role dynamics. The justification can only be based on semantic grounds.[3]

As might be anticipated, isolating conventional (first level) from improvised role performance was far less a problem than separating modest (second-level) from extreme (third-level) forms of improvising. Relatively few cases of the latter were identified and, as we will show in chapters 5 and 6, we decided to collapse the second and third levels in all subsequent data production in order to increase reliability. Still, we think that a major reason for this measurement problem is the fact that most of the events studied by the DRC had impacts that were far from massive in terms of either physical damage or social disruption. The greater the impact of disaster, the more important are varying levels of improvising for meeting unusual demands on people and the social system.

In closing this section, it is important to note that the above three dimensions capture very different properties of role. The uniqueness of role linkages from status-role nexus and role performance, respectively, is quite clear and requires no further comment. However, the uniqueness of status-role nexus and role performance with respect to the latter's incumbency component reveals an interesting subtlety that we think is important to keep in mind. That subtlety is revealed by the four-fold property space depicted in figure 4.2, where status-role nexus categories are cross-classified with postdisaster role incumbency categories. In reviewing the figure, it seems quite clear that cells 1 and 4 are both logical and empirical possibilities. In other words, it is quite likely for someone with a consistent status-role nexus to be an existing postdisaster role incumbent (e.g., a doctor providing emergency medical care), and someone with an inconsistent status-role nexus to be a new incumbent (e.g., a college professor directing an emergency shelter).

But one must also be able to show that it is empirically possible for someone with a consistent status-role nexus to be a new incumbent (cell 2), and for someone with an inconsistent status-role nexus to be an existing incumbent (cell 3). We have found many

Figure 4.2

Property Space for Status-Role Nexus
by Postdisaster Role Incumbency

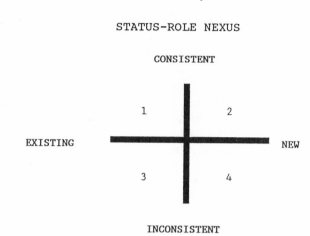

STATUS-ROLE NEXUS

CONSISTENT

POSTDISASTER   EXISTING   NEW
ROLE INCUMBENCY

1   2

3   4

INCONSISTENT

1: Consistent status-role nexus, existing incumbent
2: Consistent status-role nexus, new incumbent
3: Inconsistent status-role nexus, existing incumbent
4: Inconsistent status-role nexus, new incumbent

examples of cell 3 in the archives. They occur whenever a position other than occupation in someone's status set (most often when someone is a predesignated volunteer) includes expected performance of a postdisaster role (e.g., a police reserve officer directing traffic). And while we have found few examples of cell 2, they do occur (e.g., a civil defense director from one county prior to a disaster becomes the CD coordinator for two adjacent jurisdictions following a regional disaster). Cell 2 cases are perhaps the most intriguing possibilities of all with respect to role differentiation.

In summary, we attempted to capture empirically three basic and unique dimensions of role. The conception and measurement challenges we faced were difficult, but not impossible. The research involved collaborative efforts, which followed cooperative exchanges of ideas among many people, but most importantly with Ralph Turner. Successful in the end or not, this kind of process is precisely what Blalock (1979, 893-94) suggested in his presidential appeal to fellow sociologists. In the sections that follow we will summarize the implementation of the above research design.

Case Illustrations on Role Dynamics

Two case studies are described in some detail, first, to show how our research design was implemented and, second, to communicate some sense of the range of variation in role dynamics for the emergent organizations we were able to document. The first case describes a temporary morgue and the second one describes a damage control crew that was working under the auspices of a much larger volunteer center.

Case Illustration I: Temporary Morgue

This case was described previously by Kreps (1989, 38) as a D-R-A-T form of organizing:

A temporary morgue is set up following a tornado. The county coroner is not a doctor but a local funeral director. He has no coroner's office, no staff, and no morgue. He usually simply signs autopsies after they are completed by hospital pathologists. After the tornado, representatives for the only local hospital say their staff cannot handle those killed (thirty or more) by the event. A discussion by the coroner and two pathologists at the hospital leads to a decision to set up a temporary morgue. The coroner requests use of the local YMCA facility for the morgue. The YMCA director (who is a personal friend of the coroner's) accedes to the request (Domain). The coroner, the two pathologists, a licensed embalmer (also a personal friend of the coroner), and a marine recruiter go to the YMCA. The YMCA director opens the facility and provides several rooms and a couple of staff (Domain-Resources). Concurrently, ambulances start bringing bodies to the morgue; people come to the morgue concerned about the missing; bodies start to be identified (no autopsies are done, and none is intended); and several ministers who stop by or come with concerned residents start attending to the needs of the bereaved (Domain-Resources-Activities). The need for "organization" is expressed by the key participants. The identified and unidentified dead are physically separated, with the two pathologists attending to them. The licensed embalmer, a marine recruiter, and a volunteer college student take on paperwork tasks. The coroner acts as director of the morgue, files official death certificates, and maintains liaison with the hospital, funeral homes, and next of kin. Two or more ministers are asked to remain and attend to the needs of the bereaved at another location in the building (Domain-Resources-Activities-Tasks). The morgue closes about twenty-four to thirty hours after it opens.

I. STATUS-ROLE NEXUS

The relevant data are summarized in table 4.1. There are at least nine incumbents and five postdisaster roles specifically identified in the data. The primary issues to be concerned about, of course, are the validity and reliability of the judgments that we made. Recall that current occupation (or some analytical equivalent) was the only status in the broader predisaster set that we used to make judgments about status-role nexus. Other statuses could only come into play in terms of the incumbency component of role performance (third dimension).

The decisions were very clear-cut for the two ministers, two pathologists, and the YMCA director because their respective status-roles remain the same from pre- to postdisaster. It also seemed clear that the actual substance of what the clerical workers are doing would not normally be expected of marine recruiters, college students, and embalmers. But what about the director of the temporary morgue? He holds two occupations, coroner and funeral director, and the archives are not clear on which is the primary one. But because both statuses are employment related, and both involve handling the deceased, consistency seemed to be the correct choice.

The findings suggest that there is substantial consistency in the status-role nexus overall, both in terms of incumbency and in terms of the postdisaster roles themselves.[4] With respect to role allocation from the community and society to this emergent organization, therefore, the evidence on this dimension points primarily to stability rather than change. Is the process functional (efficient and effective)? It appears that a needed service is being provided quickly and appropriately. Is the process tenable (personally rewarding)? There is no way of knowing for sure from the archives how participants feel about issues of power and fit, but the opportunity for intrinsic rewards certainly exists. Finally, do the respective organizational and role analyses reinforce each other? We think most

Table 4.1
Status-Role Nexus, Temporary Morgue

Postdisaster Role	Predisaster Status	Consistent Nexus (Incumbent)	Consistent Nexus (Role)
1=Morgue director	Coroner/Funeral director	yes	yes
2=Clerical A	Marine recruiter	no	
Clerical B	Embalmer	no	no
Clerical C	College student	no	
3=Minister A	Minister A	yes	yes
Minister B	Minister B	yes	
4=Pathologist A	Pathologist A	yes	yes
Pathologist B	Pathologist B	yes	
5=YMCA director	YMCA director	yes	yes

Number of postdisaster incumbents: N=9
Number of postdisaster roles: N=5

	Incumbents		Roles	
Proportion consistent:	67%	(6)	80%	(4)
Proportion inconsistent:	33%	(3)	20%	(1)
Proportion perfectly mixed:	-----		0%	(0)
	100%	(9)	100%	(5)

certainly, in the sense that both stability and change are being documented.

2. ROLE LINKAGES

Recall that all logically possible inter-role pairs must be identified initially—in this case there are five roles and therefore ten inter-role pairs. That determined, each inter-role pair must be examined separately with respect to all possible incumbent pairs subsumed by it. The worksheet represented in table 4.2 summarizes the necessary incumbent pairs and role pairs that must be examined for the temporary morgue. Each postdisaster role is given a number (morgue director = 1, clerical = 2, minister = 3, pathologist = 4, and YMCA director = 5); and beginning with role 1, all possible incumbent and role pairs are arrayed along with judgments (yes or no) about continuity. The resulting proportions are presented at the bottom of the table. Remember that a perfect mix of continuous and discontinuous relationships is possible only when there is an even number of incumbent or role pairs (see note 2). Both incumbent and role pair proportions are needed to give a complete picture of what is happening.[5]

Possible problems of validity and reliability remain very important. Because the morgue director has two occupations, coroner and funeral director, there are two chances of continuity for every relationship involving him. We concluded that all judgments represented in table 4.2 were fairly clear-cut (we were uncertain about the YMCA director/minister link until we checked) except possibly for the link between college student and minister. Here we argue against continuity because of the lack of uniformity in the relationships between the clergy and a host of social statuses. Broadly or narrowly defined, the contact may be routine, but it very well may not be.

Another problem relates to the relevance of statuses other than occupation for role complementarity. The obvious example in this case was that predisaster friendships were relevant in two instances for the morgue director. Thus it was clear that by using occupation as the sole referent for examining role linkages, we ran the risk of underrepresenting continuity, perhaps to a substantial degree. Accordingly, we decided that in all subsequent data production (see chapters 5 and 6) we would note instances of continuous links based on the entire status sets of individuals. Unfortunately, the archives are woefully inadequate in providing information that could easily be collected through primary data collection.

Measurement problems aside, the findings on this dimension are very different from those on the first one. Where substantial consistency with predisaster structural arrangements is evidenced for status-role nexus, substantial discontinuity is evidenced for role linkages. With respect to role complementarity from the community and society to this emergent organization, then, the pattern primarily is one of change rather than stability. But at the same time, the earlier conclusion that role allocation has been functional and tenable can be sustained for role complementarity. Finally, the findings for this case suggest that role linkages are more sensitive to change than are status-roles, particularly for the kinds of disasters (generally low impact events in highly industrialized societies) chronicled in the DRC archives (Kreps 1984). In events with

Table 4.2
Role Linkages, Temporary Morgue

Postdisaster Role	Predisaster Role Pair	Continuous Pair (Incumbent)	Continuous Pair (Role)
1=Morgue dir.	Cor/Fun'l dir →2=Recruiter	no	
	Cor/Fun'l dir →2=Embalmer	yes	no
	Cor/Fun'l dir →2=Student	no	
	Cor/Fun'l dir →3=Minister A	yes	yes
	Cor/Fun'l dir →3=Minister B	yes	
	Cor/Fun'l dir →4=Pathologist A	yes	yes
	Cor/Fun'l dir →4=Pathologist B	yes	
	Cor/Fun'l dir →5=YMCA Director	no	no
2=Clerical	Recruiter →3=Minister A	no	
	Recruiter →3=Minister B	no	
	Embalmer →3=Minister A	no	no
	Embalmer →3=Minister B	no	
	Student →3=Minister A	no	
	Student →3=Minister B	no	
	Recruiter →4=Pathologist A	no	
	Recruiter →4=Pathologist B	no	
	Embalmer →4=Pathologist A	yes	no
	Embalmer →4=Pathologist B	yes	
	Student →4=Pathologist A	no	
	Student →4=Pathologist B	no	
	Recruiter →5=YMCA Director	no	
	Embalmer →5=YMCA Director	no	no
	Student →5=YMCA Director	no	
3=Minister	Minister A →4=Pathologist A	no	
	Minister A →4=Pathologist B	no	no
	Minister B →4=Pathologist A	no	
	Minister B →4=Pathologist B	no	
	Minister A →5=YMCA Director	yes	yes
	Minister B →5=YMCA Director	yes	
4=Pathologist	Pathologist A →5=YMCA Director	no	no
	Pathologist B →5=YMCA Dirctor	no	
		(31)	(10)

	Incumbent pairs		Role pairs	
Proportion continuous:	29%	(9)	30%	(3)
Proportion discontinuous:	71%	(22)	70%	(7)
Proportion perfectly mixed:	-----		0%	(0)
	100%	(31)	100%	(10)

greater physical destruction and social disruption, however, change of role allocation might become more pronounced.

3. ROLE PERFORMANCE

Recall that the focus of this dimension is the actual performance of roles by given individuals. Judgments have to be made in terms of the six types of performance represented in figure 4.1. As noted in table 4.3, of the nine participants there are four instances of formal role enactment, three instances of role prototyping, and two instances of working role enactment. Thus we judged seven of the nine enactments to be conventional role performances by either existing or new incumbents. Even assuming that all role performance involves improvising to some extent, we felt that these seven judgments were very clear-cut.

As existing incumbents, we judged the morgue director and

Table 4.3
Role Performance, Temporary Morgue

Postdisaster Role	Predisaster Role	Postdisaster Role Performance
Morgue director	Coroner/Funeral dir	Working role enactment
Clerical A	Marine recruiter	Role prototyping
Clerical B	Embalmer	Role prototyping
Clerical C	College student	Role prototyping
Minister A	Minister A	Formal role enactment
Minister B	Minister B	Formal role enactment
Pathologist A	Pathologist A	Formal role enactment
Pathologist B	Pathologist B	Formal role enactment
YMCA director	YMCA director	Working role enactment

Role-playing

Formal role enactment	45%	(4)
Working role enactment	22%	(2)
Radical role transformation	0%	(0)

Role-making

Role prototyping	33%	(3)
Role redefinition	0%	(0)
Radical role redefinition	0%	(0)
	100%	(9)

YMCA director to be improvising at the second level. With respect to the former, the demand on the coroner is clearly much greater than usual: a new facility has to be found, and new ways of meeting role expectations have to be improvised rapidly. That substantial improvisation is occurring seemed quite clear to us, but there was no compelling empirical case for concluding that a truly radical transformation of the morgue director role is occurring. With respect to the latter, the YMCA director's involvement is marginal, but critical. He provides access to the building and allows its use for a completely new purpose. But in so doing, he neither seeks nor receives formal authorization from his board of directors. Because he has redefined his facility, and gone outside of normal channels to do so, we judged his performance to be working role enactment.

The findings on the final dimension point to the importance of conventional arrangements even as a new and quite necessary social form is being created. With respect to role differentiation from the community and society to this emergent organization, then, the evidence of stability is very clear. But so also is the relative ease of modest role redifferentiation that is both functional and tenable at two (organized response, community) systemic levels.

Case Illustration II: Damage Control Crew

A large voluntary work center was organized in response to a tornado that left a mile-wide corridor of damage from one end of a city to the other. The center was chronicled in the archives and Kreps had earlier been able to use it as an example of an emergent organization. Unfortunately, the data on the center were not of sufficient quality to allow for an analysis of role dynamics. Fortuitously, however, one of twenty-five voluntary work crews who operated out of the center had been singled out for intensive study by one of its participants (Taylor, Zurcher, and Key 1970). The book that resulted provides precisely the kind of information our study demands. It also includes very rich details about the process of organizing and, in so doing, serves as a model of participant observation (Denzin 1989, 156–82). For summary purposes only, this emergent unit can be described briefly as a R-D-A-T form in Kreps's taxonomy:

The initiation of the damage control crew began with the mobilization of four volunteers—a heavy-equipment operator, a civil defense employee, a college student, and a social psychologist (one of the authors)—as well as some equipment provided by the volunteer center (Resources). The group would become as large as fourteen, but had ten core members during the three days of its existence. All except two (a clinical psychologist and a writer) were complete strangers prior to the disaster. Sent from the volunteer center, that umbrella organization provided legitimacy for the crew before its work began (Resources-Domain). But the conjoined actions that followed, perhaps even more so than the volunteer center, established the parameters of the group's existence (Resources-Domain-Activities). By the second day of its operation, the momentum of the crew's continuing activities led to an explicit division of labor, thus completing the origins of this small emergent organization (Resources-Domain-Activities-Tasks).

I. STATUS-ROLE NEXUS

The relevant postdisaster roles and predisaster statuses are described in the book as functions that evolved quickly in the damage control crew (Taylor, Zurcher, and Key 1970, 81). A preliminary comment is necessary about these postdisaster roles. The character of the group was tied to Monsterman and his truck. The truck and its power winch, nicknamed the Monster, enabled the crew far greater mobility and allowed it to tackle otherwise impossible jobs. Taylor, Zurcher, and Key (1970, 87) describe the evolution of the crew's ephemeral roles within the group as follows:

> The members gradually arrayed themselves in functional work roles to the best utilization of the machine. Consequently, toward the end of the work day, a rudimentary division of labor began to develop. When a job was nearing completion, Contactman would scout in advance of the truck, spot homes endangered by debris, and speak with the owners about the crew helping them. Monsterman drove the truck and operated the power winch. Climbers A and B scrambled on rooftops and up trees, setting the hook of the winch. Sawman A moved in with his power saw when rapid cutting was needed. Roper A, who had joined the crew late Friday afternoon, affixed guide or hauling ropes when necessary. If any member was not, at the moment, called upon to perform his specific work task, he would carry, clear, lift, or pull as the job demanded.

The relevant data are summarized in table 4.4. There are ten incumbents and seven postdisaster roles identified specifically in the book's account of what happened. It seemed to us that eight of the ten judgments were quite clear-cut. While certainly a tree surgeon or lumberman would have a consistent status-role nexus in performing most of the roles described, the range of occupations represented are generally far removed from what these people are doing. Only the judgments for Climber A (heavy equipment operator) and Sawman A (civil defense employee) seemed debatable to us.

Table 4.4
Status-Role Nexus, Damage Control Crew

Postdisaster Role	Predisaster Status	Consistent Nexus (Incumbent)	Consistent Nexus (Role)
1=Contactman	Social psychologist	no	no
2=Climber A	Heavy equipment operator	yes	mix
Climber B	College student	no	
3=Sawman A	Civil defense employee	no	no
Sawman B	Commodities inspector	no	
4=Monsterman	House painter	no	no
5=Roper A	Extension worker	no	no
Roper B	Clinical psychologist	no	
6=Rigger	Writer	no	no
7=Monster asst.	House painter	no	no

Number of postdisaster incumbents: N=10
Number of postdisaster roles: N= 7

	Incumbents		Roles	
Proportion consistent:	10%	(1)	0%	(0)
Proportion inconsistent:	90%	(9)	86%	(6)
Proportion evenly mixed:	-----		14%	(1)
	100%	(10)	100%	(7)

With respect to Climber A, while climbing trees, attaching winches, and doing whatever else is needed is not occupationally specified, there is no question that debris clearance is a routine expectation of heavy equipment operators. We therefore judged Climber A to be consistent. With respect to Sawman A, the incumbent has only recently been hired as a civil defense professional, and there is little information on his formal job. However, the general responsibility of civil defense workers is community coordination. We thought that so focused a role as running a power saw in a debris clearance operation is outside the routine expectations of civil defense professionals.

In contrast to the temporary morgue, these findings suggest that there is substantial inconsistency in the status-role nexus for this damage control crew. With respect to role allocation from the community and society to this organized disaster response, the evidence points primarily to reallocation and change. Note, however, that this particular crew was only one of twenty-five separate teams working out of the volunteer center, and we do not know whether its composition is representative of others. We do know from the archives and the book that the overall range of volunteers was far broader than professional tree surgeons and lumbermen.

Is the process functional? Just as with the temporary morgue, there is no question that this and the other damage control crews are providing a needed service in a timely fashion. Is the process tenable? One cannot possibly come away from a reading of Taylor, Zurcher, and Key's book and not conclude that this experience is a personally rewarding one for all those involved. Although these individuals are playing specialized roles within the group, they interact as equals, exhibit a strong sense of unity, and feel that they were helping victims of the disaster in a very personal way.

2. ROLE LINKAGES

The relevant data are found in table 4.5. In this case study there are seven roles, twenty-one possible role pairs, and forty-two incumbent pairs subsumed by them. Table 4.5 is a more simplified representation of role linkages than table 4.2 above (temporary morgue) because we assume that the reader now understands our procedure. So, for example, the role pair of Contactman (social psychologist) and Climber (heavy equipment operator and college student) subsumes two incumbent links, one that is discontinuous (social psychologist and heavy equipment operator) and the other that is continuous (social psychologist and college student), for a resulting perfect mix on this role pair. The process continues until judgments have been made on all possible role pairs and incumbent pairs.

We felt that all judgments were clear-cut on this case study. Accordingly, the pattern clearly is one of discontinuity except for links between the social psychologist (who also was a college professor) and college student, social psychologist and clinical psychologist, and two house painters. Similar to the temporary morgue, this case study points to substantial discontinuity among people who, with the exception of one incumbent pair (clinical psychologist and writer), did not know each other personally prior

Table 4.5
Role Linkages, Damage Control Crew

Postdisaster Role Pairs	Incumbent Pairs	Continuous Relationship Between Role Pairs
1=Contactman ——▸2=Climber A & B	(2)	mix
——▸3=Sawman A & B	(2)	no
——▸4=Monsterman	(1)	no
——▸5=Roper A & B	(2)	mix
——▸6=Rigger	(1)	no
——▸7=Monster asst.	(1)	no
2=Climber A & B ——▸3=Sawman A & B	(4)	no
——▸4=Monsterman	(2)	no
——▸5=Roper A & B	(4)	no
——▸6=Rigger	(2)	no
——▸7=Monster asst.	(2)	no
3=Sawman A & B ——▸4=Monsterman	(2)	no
——▸5=Roper A & B	(4)	no
——▸6=Rigger	(2)	no
——▸7=Monster asst.	(2)	no
4=Monsterman ——▸5=Roper A & B	(2)	no
——▸6=Rigger	(1)	no
——▸7=Monster asst.	(1)	yes
5=Roper A & B ——▸6=Rigger	(2)	no
——▸7=Monster asst.	(2)	no
6=Rigger ——▸7=Monster asst.	(1)	no
	(42)	(21)

	Incumbent Pairs		Role Pairs	
Proportion continuous:	7%	(3)	5%	(1)
Proportion discontinuous:	93%	(39)	86%	(18)
Proportion perfectly mixed:	------		9%	(2)
	100%	(42)	100%	(21)

to the emergency.[6] With respect to role complementarity from community and society to this emergent organization, the pattern is one of change rather than stability. More specifically, the role of volunteer brings people from widely varying employment backgrounds into direct contact, as they perform roles that are both functional and tenable.

3. ROLE PERFORMANCE

Once again, judgments have to be made with respect to the six types represented in figure 4.1 and the three levels of improvising represented by them. As noted in table 4.6, all ten participants are judged to be engaged in role redefinition (new incumbent, improvised performance). Our logic for this blanket judgment is as follows:

Table 4.6
Role Performance, Damage Control Crew

Postdisaster Role	Predisaster Role	Postdisaster Role Performance
Contactman	Social psychologist	Redefinition
Climber A	Heavy equipment operator	Redefinition
Climber B	College student	Redefinition
Sawman A	Civil defense employee	Redefinition
Sawman B	Commodities inspector	Redefinition
Monsterman	House painter	Redefinition
Roper A	Extension worker	Redefinition
Roper B	Clinical psychologist	Redefinition
Rigger	Writer	Redefinition
Monster asst.	House painter	Redefinition

Role-playing

Formal role enactment	0%	(0)
Working role enactment	0%	(0)
Radical role transformation	0%	(0)

Role-making

Role prototyping	0%	(0)
Role redefinition	100%	(10)
Radical role redefinition	0%	(0)
	100%	(10)

With respect to incumbency, the evidence suggests that none of the postdisaster roles is related to the broader status sets of the ten individuals. The ability to make contacts, operate certain equipment, or have physical dexterity does not define actual roles, and these skills have relevance far beyond the removal of fallen trees from houses. The role of Monsterman is perhaps the most questionable in this regard because he has a secondary status as a civil defense volunteer. In fact, Monsterman has been assigned the truck and told to "look around," whereupon he goes to the volunteer center and connects with the other early core members. But there is no evidence that he has any experience with what he is actually doing. Indeed it is Rigger (a writer) who is the chief tactical engineer for the crew. It is he who studies the problem and designs the strategy to tackle it.

With respect to level of improvising, the question is why the second level as opposed to the first or third? Prototyping seems an inappropriate judgment because these people are clearly defining and redefining what they are doing as they go along. In a very real sense, their individual improvisations are unique to the social structure they are creating. Rigger's boom-pulley technique is one example of an improvised effort that later becomes, in effect, institutionalized among the crew as Rigger's Law (Taylor, Zurcher, and Key 1970, 99). Proven successful on the second day, crew members soon become rather expert at this technique for lowering potentially dangerous debris to the ground. Radical role redefinition seems inappropriate, however, because a common sense approach to a known problem is being used throughout. Brief accounts of other teams, both volunteer and professional, indicate that performance differs only in terms of the limitations of the equipment and the experience of the crews (Taylor, Zurcher, and Key 1970).

With respect to the uniformity of our judgments, there is no evidence of any real differences among the ten people with respect to whether one of them is improvising more or less radically than the others. Although they are distinguished by their postdisaster roles, these roles only govern their activities part of the time. Otherwise, they are all engaged in the same tasks. Any rigging, roping, and sawing that occurs is the result of their coordinated team effort.

The findings on this dimension suggest that there is a good deal of role improvising going on that is responsive to incumbent levels of experience and interpretations of what is being done. With respect to role differentiation from the community and society to this emergent organization, the pattern is one of a nice mix of conventional practices and role redifferentiation that is unique to the people enacting new roles for themselves and the special circumstances in which their collective action takes place. Finally, strong arguments on the functionality and tenability of the role system can be sustained for this dimension as well.

In closing this section, one might argue that the above types of emergent units are not organizations at all, but rather a series of improvised arrangements that have little to do with the way real organizations work. As Kreps has responded in many different ways (especially Kreps 1989a, 186–96, 214–15, 229–30; 1991), this argument only makes (some) sense if the existence of organization is taken for granted. However, doing so is a serious mistake that has heretofore constrained a fruitful merger of collective behavior, organizational, and role perspectives. We believe that social structure should never be taken for granted at any level of scale or in any empirical setting, for to do so assumes away most of what is sociologically important to unravel.[7]

Summary Findings on Emergent Organizations

The original sample of fifty-two emergent organizations was identified initially by Kreps from analyses of 932 interviews and related documents on twelve natural disasters (one earthquake, four tornadoes, five floods, and two hurricanes). These fifty-two cases were then reanalyzed by Saunders and Kreps (1987) for purposes of modeling their life histories. The 107 archival interviews dealing specifically with these fifty-two cases and the book by Taylor, Zurcher, and Key (1970) form the data base upon which our refined conception and measurement of role was completed. This section summarizes briefly overall findings on twenty-nine of the fifty-two emergent organizations for which data were sufficient to implement our research design. The loss of well over 40 percent of the original sample speaks both to the incompleteness of the archives and the kinds of details that we were after. Weeding out good data from bad was a very lengthy but essential process.

Tables 4.7, 4.8, and 4.9 summarize the overall findings for the twenty-nine cases. The average proportion of roles and incumbents for status-role categories (role allocation) are arrayed in table 4.7. The average proportion of role pairs and incumbent pairs for role linkage categories (role complementarity) are arrayed in table 4.8. The average proportion of incumbents for the role performance categories (role differentiation) are arrayed in table 4.9. The latter table also breaks down the six types of role performance in terms of the three defined levels of improvising represented by them (uncertains are eliminated in computing these percentages). The substantial percentages uncertain in tables 4.7 and 4.8 speak very directly to missing data on occupations. The uncertain percentages in table 4.9 speak to this problem as well, and also to problems of identifying postdisaster roles for some participants in these emergent organizations.

The relative stability of role allocation is evidenced in table 4.7, with about two-thirds of the roles and incumbents showing consistency of the status-role nexus. The pattern for the temporary morgue, therefore, is fairly representative of the total sample, while the pattern for the damage control crew is a definite outlier. The findings for role complementarity, as summarized in table 4.8, pre-

Table 4.7
Summary Table
Status-Role Nexus for Twenty-nine Emergent Organized Responses

	Mean %	St.Dev.	Range	
Roles				
Consistent	.658	.301	.000	1.000
Inconsistent	.186	.243	.000	.857
Mixed	.008	.032	.000	.143
Uncertain	.148	.195	.000	.667
Incumbents				
Consistent	.673	.283	.100	1.000
Inconsistent	.161	.222	.000	.900
Uncertain	.166	.201	.000	.714

sent a different picture. Although one needs to be cautious given the substantial percentages uncertain, the highest percentages of role pairs and incumbent pairs are discontinuous. Here there is evidence of a much greater balance of stability and change. Recall that both the temporary morgue and the damage control crew exceeded to a substantial degree the overall sample percentages on this dimension.

Table 4.8
Summary Table
Role Linkages for Twenty-nine Emergent Organized Responses

	Mean %	St.Dev.	Range	
Role Pairs				
Continuous	.353	.376	.000	1.000
Discontinuous	.407	.375	.000	1.000
Mixed	.013	.037	.000	.167
Uncertain	.227	.305	.000	1.000
Incumbent Pairs				
Continuous	.329	.358	.000	1.000
Discontinuous	.436	.345	.000	1.000
Uncertain	.235	.305	.000	.951

Finally, table 4.9 points to an intermediate position with respect to stability and change of social structure. The stability of role differentiation is clearly evidenced, with formal role enactment and role prototyping representing over half of the cases; but so also is change of role differentiation, with over a third of the cases evidencing at least the second level of improvising (working role enactment and role redefinition). Neither the temporary morgue nor the damage control crew is particularly representative of the overall pattern. Perhaps most important, our earlier argument that roleplaying (social structure) and role-making (role invention) are two sides of the same coin receives strong empirical support.

Table 4.9
Summary Table
Role Performance for Twenty-nine Emergent Organized Responses

	Mean %	St.Dev.	Range	
Role-playing				
Formal role enactment	.353	.340	.000	1.000
Working role enactment	.188	.289	.000	.976
Radical transformation	.007	.028	.000	.143
Role-making				
Role prototyping	.167	.303	.000	1.000
Role redefinition	.162	.271	.000	1.000
Radical role redefinition	.006	.015	.000	.071
Uncertain	.122	.195	.000	.714
Level I Improvising	.588	.374	.000	1.000
Formal role enactment	.414	.362	.000	1.000
Role prototyping	.174	.305	.000	1.000
Level 2 Improvising	.390	.381	.000	1.000
Working role enactment	.202	.291	.000	.976
Role redefinition	.188	.292	.000	1.000
Level 3 Improvising	.024	.094	.000	.500
Radical transformation	.019	.093	.000	.500
Radical role redefinition	.005	.022	.000	.111

As noted earlier, the typical disasters studied originally by the Disaster Research Center had low ratios of impact to remaining local and certainly regional human and material resources. The general implication from tables 4.7 and 4.8 is that role reallocation is not a major requirement for such events, and that change of role complementarity is a natural and relatively easy accommodation to make. And as noted in table 4.9, when role redifferentiation is needed, it is as likely to involve existing as new incumbents. While we conclude that unique dimensions of role dynamics have been isolated in our research, it is interesting to ponder which of the three processes they represent is the most important. As Ralph Turner implies, perhaps relative importance is only determined situationally; and that, depending on the unique situation faced, changes in one process are substitutable for changes in another.

Once having documented patterns of role dynamics, the push toward trying to explain them became an exciting prospect. Analytically discrete, how does one dimension of role relate to another empirically? How does role enactment vary in terms of the form of organizing within which it occurs, or the kind of enacting organization, or the character of disaster impacts, or the type of impacted community? And last but not least, how do role dynamics vary in terms of the people actually performing roles? These are the kinds of questions we will address in chapters 6 and 7 of this book. But before even considering such questions, a major change in data production and level of analysis had to be made. That change is summarized in chapter 5.

Conclusion

The purpose of this chapter has been to summarize our refined conception and measurement of role dynamics. In completing the second phase of our research, we felt that we had isolated three important and unique dimensions of role, but we felt far less confident that we could apply them efficiently and effectively at the organizational level of analysis. The major problem we faced was incomplete data. How, indeed, could we maintain a focus on organizations, given the severe data problems we had encountered for the emergent units chronicled in the archives. Simply put, implementing our research design was very sensitive to size of an organization, and it was clear that many if not most of the remaining ones in the file (Types I, II, and III in the DRC typology) were larger. Missing data would quickly overwhelm us.

The solution to our problem was so obvious that it was amazing we had overlooked it for so long. If our conception of role was useful, it seemingly could be applied to any level of analysis. In fact, given the limitations of the archives, it was quite clear that we were working at the wrong level to begin with. While we had been treating interviewees as informants reporting on the units in which they were members, we could treat them more feasibly as respondents reporting only on themselves. To that end, we decided to change our unit of analysis to the individual for purposes of describing role dynamics, and then bring organizational variables in later as possible sources of explanation of individual role enactments (Barton 1969, especially chapter 5). We turn now to the third and final phase of our data production.

5

Role Dynamics at the Individual
Level of Analysis

This chapter summarizes the third and final phase of our conception and measurement of role. We originally had hoped to compare role dynamics in emergent as opposed to other organized responses, in part because Ralph Turner suggested it (see chapter 3), and also because we believed that patterns of structural stability and change might thereby be revealed. But at this point we were not at all interested in possible differences among the four types of organized responses (established, expanding, extending, and emergent) represented in the DRC typology. Instead, we wanted to see if or how patterns of organizing (from Kreps's taxonomy) and role enactment were related in new as opposed to already existing social entities.

It was becoming abundantly clear, however, that while the archives could provide descriptions that were sufficient for putting a structural code to work, they were far more limited for examining organizationally what we saw as three key dimensions of role. Incomplete data had been a major concern for emergent units, and, after several months of frustration, we concluded that it was an insurmountable problem for most of the remaining 371 organized responses in Kreps's data file. There was no choice but to revise our research design.

In effect, we were forced to change data production from the organizational to the individual level of analysis. But that decision proved to be reasonable on theoretical as well as practical grounds. First, we had learned a great deal about the subtleties of role by

This chapter is based on our collaborative research with Stephen Russell and Kristen Myers. Russell's study of role dynamics in emergent organizations is published in his master's thesis, "Role Enactment and Disaster Response: A Methodological Exploration" (1989). Myers's study of role dynamics in existing organizations is published in her master's thesis, "A Dialectical Analysis of Role Enactment During the Emergency Period of Natural Disasters" (1990).

trying to capture it organizationally, and we could envision easily how more highly structured field research could overcome the limitations of the archives for measuring the three dimensions we had isolated. Second, measuring role enactment at the individual level could both overcome some of the severe limitations of the archives, and it also could open the door to measuring other characteristics of role incumbents that might have explanatory value. It is important to note in this regard that the people described in the archives are, in virtually all cases, key participants in organized responses. That is why they were selected as informants in the first place. Third, working at the individual level of analysis would in no way preclude use of organizational variables for helping us later to unravel role dynamics of key participants (Barton 1969, 211–16). And so we made the switch.

Chapter 5 is divided into three sections. We initially specify and illustrate (with a detailed case description) the changes in our research design. We then summarize comparative findings on a sample of 257 participants (respondents now as opposed to informants) from a broad range of emergent as well as other types of organized responses in Kreps's data file. Interestingly enough, it was only at this rather late point in our research that we began to consider the possible value of the original DRC typology. By showing why and how that happened, the final section provides a necessary transition to the modeling of individual role dynamics that we report on in chapter 6.

Individual Role Enactments
Role Dynamics at the Individual Level of Analysis

As noted above, all interviewees played important roles in organized responses chronicled previously by Kreps. Focusing on these people now as individual participants, we applied the three dimensions of role largely the same way as before. However, a few refinements should be noted. The first refinement was quite important methodologically. Although we retained occupation as the standard referent for measuring the first and second dimensions, we noted also whenever another position in a status set pointed to either consistency of the status/role nexus or continuity of role linkages. This gave us a means of estimating the extent to which our measurement of the first and second dimensions was biased toward change rather than stability of structural arrangements.[1]

The second refinement involved being as precise as possible about

role linkages for each respondent. We no longer assumed that participant roles were linked to all other roles of respective organized responses for purposes of calibrating the second dimension. Instead,
we only made judgments about continuity or discontinuity of links
when there was evidence of direct contact between a respondent and
someone else. Moreover, that contact could be within or outside the
boundaries of the organized response. Any identified direct contacts
for the respondent were then broken down into four general categories: First, *intra-role organizational* links were ones with people
performing the same role as the respondent, and within the same organized response. Second, *inter-role organizational* links were ones
with people performing different roles than the respondent, but
within the same organized response. Third, *intra-role boundary
spanning* links were ones with people performing the same role as
the respondent, but not within the same organized response. Fourth,
inter-role boundary spanning links were ones with people performing different roles than the respondent, and not within the same
organized response. Regardless of whether links were intra- or inter-
role, we were most interested in summary percentages of continuous
and discontinuous links internal to the organized response, external
to the organized response, and overall.[2]

The third refinement, which is represented in figure 5.1, relates
to the improvisation component of role performance. While we
continued to believe that all three levels of improvising (see figure
4.1) should be measured at some point, we were not confident
about our own ability to distinguish reliably between the second
and third levels. Moreover, the number of instances of what we
thought might be radical role transformation or radical role redefinition were small in the previous phase. We concluded that for
purposes of later statistical analyses we would probably have to
collapse second- and third-level scores anyway. In effect, we felt
that the trade-off between reliability and validity was reasonable
at this point in our theory building.

Finally, we tried to document other variables that might be of
value later for purposes of modeling individual role dynamics.
Thus, we recorded the following information whenever it was available: the timing of the respondent's involvement in the organized
response; previous disaster or specific role experience of the respondent; the knowledge requirements (general, specific, technical) of the postdisaster role (Barton 1969); whether the respondent
was an instrumental leader, expressive leader, or both (Bales 1950);
evidence of conflict in the performance of a leadership role; and
finally, other personal characteristics of the respondent such as

Figure 5.1

Refined Measurement of Role Performance

IMPROVISATION

LEVEL 1

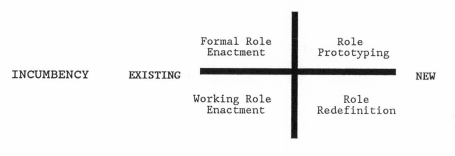

	Formal Role Enactment	Role Prototyping	
INCUMBENCY EXISTING			NEW
	Working Role Enactment	Role Redefinition	

LEVEL 2

1st Level of Improvising

Formal Role Enactment:
Existing incumbent, conventional performance

Role Prototyping:
New incumbent, conventional performance

2nd Level of Improvising

Working Role Enactment:
Existing incumbent, improvised performance

Role Redefinition:
New incumbent, improvised performance

gender, age, marital status, length of residence, and educational attainment. While we knew that missing data would be an endemic problem for most of the above factors, we were also thinking in terms of the kinds of data that could readily be collected in any subsequent field research.

Before proceeding with the case illustration, an additional methodological point is in order. The primary sources of data on individual role enactments are transcribed interviews with direct participants. In addition, other interviews were examined (typically three or four) that Kreps had identified earlier as providing relevant information on the organized responses of which these people were members. The latter interviews both confirmed what the participants did and provided supplemental information on their role links. Decisions about whether more than one participant in the same organized response would be a case in the sample depended on two considerations. The first one was data quality. Many cases were dropped because of inadequate information. The second one related to our broader purposive sampling plan (discussed below). We wanted to capture the full range of forms represented by Kreps's taxonomy and metric for both emergent and other organized disaster responses.

The following case description illustrates how we implemented the above refinements of our research design. Raw data on this particular case was extracted from six interviews. The case describes the actions of a structural engineer who becomes the leader of a disaster operations unit called "disaster control" following an earthquake. This emergent organized response was one of the first ones identified in the field by DRC researchers; and it was still being talked about when Kreps began working at the center four years later. In a very direct way, this case had served as a prototype for the original DRC typology.

Kreps later characterized this operations unit as a T-R-A-D form of organizing in his own taxonomy. As will be described below, the structural engineer plays an important role in an organizing process which begins with an elemental division of labor (T), followed by the rapid mobilization of resources (T-R) and performance of activities (T-R-A). The actual naming of the organization and the establishment of its domain (T-R-A-D) later completes the origins of this short-lived but very important social unit. The organization performs a critically needed coordination domain during the five days of its existence.

The Case Study

A state's largest city is impacted by an earthquake, the worst in the state's history. The superintendent of the city's building construction and maintenance department, a structural engineer and architect by training and experience (we will refer to him as SEA), becomes a key community leader in the immediate emergency period. Prior to the disaster, SEA is in charge of the maintenance of eighty-six buildings in the city and has three engineers, six mechanics, and one administrative assistant working directly under him. His primary job is to oversee the inspection and repair of these buildings. He also spends time reviewing architectural plans for new buildings, making corrections, and planning the division budget. SEA's unit is only one of several in the city's Department of Public Works.

The earthquake hits at approximately 5:30 P.M. on a Friday afternoon, a time when many people, including SEA, are on their way home from work. When the earthquake subsides, SEA again heads for his home and passes a friend with whom he had planned to have dinner. He learns from the friend that his home and his wife are safe, and immediately heads back toward town. He says that as a superintendent in the public works department, his services will be needed in response to the disaster.

SEA arrives at the Public Safety Building at about 5:45 P.M. and finds what he calls mass confusion. He goes to a desk and suggests that people be assembled into teams that might be useful for search and rescue or damage control. The teams are then formed and made up of volunteers, police and fire department personnel, city public works personnel, as well as national guardsmen. Within an hour of the earthquake, these teams are out in the impact area performing predesignated tasks. At about this time, a central desk in the building is being manned by members of the police department. People are asking questions that these policemen cannot answer. SEA goes to the central desk and starts answering questions, giving specific directions, and making specific decisions.

The organization works through the night and becomes identified as "disaster control" by Saturday afternoon. It is characterized frequently as the organization most involved in the disaster response. As national guard and army rescue teams become involved, they choose to receive their instructions from SEA and his organization. For the next five days SEA leads what is described as an effective response to the earthquake. In addition to forming search and rescue and damage assessment teams, the organization becomes involved in creating a filing system to catalogue all of their volunteers, commandeers fuel and other supplies, installs temporary city generators in public buildings, makes temporary toilets, opens shelters, provides security guards, and performs many other tasks. All of the disaster-related activities of "disaster control" are led by SEA in the name of the city, and without any official authority.

The legitimacy of this emergent organization continues to be evidenced by its role in coordinating the activities of the military, state and local government agencies, and private voluntary agencies. Moreover, several members of the city government, such as the city manager, city attorney, and members of the police department work out of "disaster control" for several days. It is also noteworthy that SEA, who has never previously attended city council meetings, is asked to be present at every emergency meeting following the earthquake. He plays a prominent role in these meetings, even though he has no place on the council and no real connection with it.

By late Tuesday the council decides formally that the city's emergency response should be handled by the various city agencies and departments that were intended to handle such problems. They decide also that "disaster control" should begin fading out of operation. By Wednesday afternoon "disaster control" is sending all requests for assistance to various city departments. The transition is difficult at first because local people have become use to its existence and coordination function.

The Three Dimensions of Role Enactment

With respect to status-role nexus (first dimension), we judge that SEA is inconsistent because neither expectations tied to his pre-disaster occupation nor his specific job title as building maintenance superintendent include being the leader of this emergent unit following the disaster. While certainly SEA is expected to be involved in some capacity because of possible damage to municipal buildings, the organization he heads performs a wide-ranging community coordination function that goes far beyond the mandate of his office. Had the mayor, city manager, or civil defense director played this leadership role, our judgment would have been different. But this case points to change rather than stability of role allocation. An individual not expected to enact a role, in effect, has risen to the occasion. The reallocation seems to be functional at both organizational and community levels. The reallocation seems to be tenable in the sense that it is personally gratifying for SEA. However, the archives indicate that there is some opposition to his assumption of a leadership role.

With respect to role linkages (second dimension), the worksheet presented in table 5.1 breaks down our judgments about SEA's predisaster status links by category of his postdisaster role links. All of the city employees listed in the table enact the same status roles pre- and postdisaster. Of those remaining on the list, the union business agent directs the secretarial staff of "disaster control," the bill collecting agent serves as its resources coordinator, the executive secretary (wife of the bill collecting agent) does clerical work, the local business owner (a former civil defense director) serves as local civil defense director, the army colonel provides security guards, the two national guardsmen do security work, the college professor serves as a search and rescue coordinator, and the person whose occupation is unknown is a member of a mountain rescue team.

Overall, SEA has a minimum of twenty-seven direct links with postdisaster role incumbents, and there are many more (e.g., several city councilmen) for whom we could not specify precisely the extent of direct contact. Some fifteen of the identified direct contacts are inter-role links within the organized response and twelve are boundary spanning inter-role links.[3] We judge eighteen of the twenty-seven inter-role links to be continuous (67 percent), five to be discontinuous (18 percent), and four to be uncertain (15 percent). The relatively high proportion of continuous links is clearly job related, with many links coming from the department of public works itself, and others to SEA's specific responsibility for maintaining municipal buildings.

Of the five discontinuous links, the status-role of secretary clearly is the most difficult to work with because it can be interpreted so broadly. In this instance, the person is an executive secretary for a federal aviation agency. Although all people in supervisory positions have regular contact with secretaries, we judged that routine contact between a local department of public works superintendent and an executive secretary for a federal aviation agency is highly unlikely. Of the four uncertain contacts, three result from the lack of information on employment (two national guardsmen and occupation unknown). Finally, the local business owner link is considered uncertain because we have no information on the type of business he was in. As part of his job, SEA would have regular contact with a number of venders. But in the absence of specific information, we thought it inappropriate to define regular contact with local business owners so inclusively.

While this case evidences a fruitful mixing of continuous and discontinuous role linkages, the general pattern is one of stability rather than change of role complementarity. Regardless of one's judgment (above) about role reallocation, therefore, there is no

Table 5.1
Predisaster Status Links by Category of Postdisaster
Role Links for Structural Engineer/Architect (SEA)

Predisaster Status Links	Link Continuous
WITHIN ORGANIZED RESPONSE	
Intra-role	
none	- - -
Inter-role	
union business agent	no
bill collecting agent	no
police captain	yes
police chief	yes
city attorney	yes
city planner	yes
public works building construction and maintenance foreman	yes
public works plumbing and heating foreman	yes
assistant to SEA (engineering side)	yes
public works maintenance person A*	yes
public works maintenance person B*	yes
public works maintenance person C*	yes
building inspector, public works	yes
chief of surveys, public works	yes
executive secretary	no
BOUNDARY SPANNING	
Intra-role	
none	- - -
Inter-role	
occupation unknown	unc
business owner	unc
mayor	yes
city manager	yes
administrative asst to city manager	yes
army colonel	no
national guard member A*	unc
national guard member B*	unc
public works street and sewer general foreman	yes
public works supervisor of design section, engineering division	yes
civil engineer, public works	yes
professor	no

Number of postdisaster incumbents   N=27
Number of postdisaster roles represented   N=24

Incumbent Links			
	Continuous	67%	(18)
	Discontinuous	18%	(5)
	Uncertain	15%	(4)
		100%	(27)

*Indicates that the incumbent played the same postdisaster role question that the stability of role complementarity facilitates greatly the actions of this emergent organization. While a series of new relationships are being improvised on the spot, they extend from established relationships that are longstanding. In this sense, the role dynamics are both functional for "disaster control" and quite tenable for its leader.

With respect to role performance (third dimension), we judged SEA to be engaged in role redefinition (role established, new incumbent, improvised performance). He states explicitly in the archives that being the leader of a community coordination unit like "disaster control" was a new role for him. As described, his role performance requires common sense and decisive action in the absence of authority. Therein lies the rationale for our characterization of his role performance. SEA orders specific actions (e.g., commandeering fuel and other supplies, controlling access to impacted areas) that even the city government itself may not have authority for at the time these actions are taken. Thus while SEA's role enactment may or may not entail radical role redefinition, there was no question in our minds that his level of improvising is far greater than role prototyping. From the standpoint of "disaster control," the role redifferentiation that occurs seems to be both efficient and effective (functionality). From SEA's own standpoint, there is no ambivalence about the fit between his capacities and dispositions on the one hand, and the requirements of the role he is performing on the other (tenability).

With respect to the other characteristics of role enactment we were interested in, the timing and duration of SEA's participation in "disaster control" can be pinned down precisely because he is involved throughout the five days of its existence. There is no evidence that SEA has any prior disaster or role experience. The knowledge required to perform his role exceeds what someone selected at random might possess. By that we mean that while the role calls for administrative as opposed to technical skills, anyone enacting it would have to know a great deal about the city and its daily routines (Barton 1969, 67–69). SEA's level of knowledge is very high along these lines. The evidence that SEA is an instrumental (task) leader is unequivocal. There is no evidence, however, that he is enacting an expressive leadership role. There is some evidence (but no specific details) on resistance by unnamed community leaders to SEA's heavy-handedness early on. Finally, we know little about SEA personally except his gender, marital status, and length of employment (three years) as superintendent of the city's building construction and maintenance department.

In conclusion, this case reveals once again the uniqueness of the three dimensions of role we have isolated in our research. In Ralph Turner's terms, the evidence for both role reallocation and role redifferentiation is quite compelling. But so also is the evidence for relative stability of role complementarity. In reconstructing this and many other cases from the archives, the difficulty of predicting one dimension of role enactment from knowledge of any other was becoming very apparent to us. Given our intense concern about isolating unique properties, we were quite encouraged by what such cases seemed to be saying about role dynamics. But an important measurement issue remained: namely to describe role enactment in its totality for any given individual. Before tackling that issue in the beginning of the next chapter, we will summarize what we learned about the three dimensions at the individual level of analysis, and then close by highlighting still another revision in our thinking about organizing and role dynamics.

Comparative Findings on Role Enactments in Emergent and Other Organized Responses

This section of the chapter has two parts: the first summarizes our purposive sampling plan and the resulting sample of 257 participants in emergent and other organized responses; and the second summarizes comparative findings on each of the three role dimensions for these participants. Note that for all participants selected for research, Kreps had previously constructed a data file on the organized response of which they were members.

Purposive Sampling Plan

Recall that Kreps (1985a) had created a data file on 423 organized disaster responses from 1,062 interviews in his original study. Some fifty-two of these organized responses were enacted by emergent units and the remaining 371 were enacted by already existing units of various types. In the first phase of our research (Bosworth and Kreps 1986), we analyzed thirty-nine organized responses (enacted by eighteen emergency-relevant bureaucracies, three other public bureaucracies, two private firms, one special interest group, one military unit, two radio-television stations, and eleven emergent units) whose structural forms seemed to balance the dynamics of formal organizing and collective behavior. The measure we used to represent this balancing is the social order–social action metric that was described in chapter 2 (see pages 44–46 and note 5 to chapter 2).[4]

In the second phase of our research, we analyzed only the fifty-two emergent units in Kreps's original data file, maintaining the organizational level of analyses as we tried to produce much more detailed data on three dimensions of role. That research was based primarily on examination of 107 interviews with people who served as informants on fifty-one of these emergent units; and secondarily on the book by Taylor, Zurcher, and Key (1970), which provided data on the one remaining case. Summarized in chapter 4, this research pointed both to the potential of our conception of role dynamics and the limitations of the archives for measuring them.

In the third phase of our research, we began with the above same 107 interviews and book to generate a new data file on respondents from emergent units. By now we knew these interviews very well and could locate the best possible information on individual participants. From these 107 interviews, we were able to complete role analyses of fifty-seven direct participants in twenty-nine emergent organized responses. Table 5.2 arrays these respondents in terms of structural forms and metric scores of the emergent units in which they participated. Notice the spread of cases by metric scores. Certainly the distribution deviates from statistical normality. However, all seven levels on the formal organizing-collective behavior metric include several cases or more. Given our central objective of comparing patterns of organizing and role dynamics, this distribution was a very satisfactory outcome.

Having accomplished the above, we then wanted to generate a parallel sample of respondents from other organized responses. But at this point we were not concerned at all about type of enacting units.[5] Instead, our objective was to generate a respondent sample from other organized responses that was reasonably comparable to the emergent sample along two lines: first, the forms of organizing in which individual role enactments occurred; and second, the types of events (earthquakes, tornados, floods, and hurricanes) in which individual role enactments occurred.

The importance of structural form and event differences had already been shown in our earlier work (Bosworth and Kreps 1986; Saunders and Kreps 1987). Please note in reviewing table 5.2 that, with the exception of the two extreme forms on the continuum (D-T-R-A and A-R-T-D), anywhere from three to six forms can receive the same metric score. While comparability by organizational form was an impossibility, comparability by metric score was a feasible objective. Obtaining relatively equal percentages of

Table 5.2
Respondents from Emergent and Other Organized Responses
by Structural Forms of Organized Responses

Organizational Forms	Logical Metric	Emergent Percentage	Freq.	Other Percentage	Freq.
D-T-R-A	(+3)	10.5%	6	22.5%	45
D-T-A-R		--	0	--	0
D-R-T-A	(+2)	12.3%	7	11.5%	23
T-D-R-A		--	0	--	0
	(subtotals)	(12.3%)		(11.5%)	
D-R-A-T		5.2%	3	15.5%	31
D-A-T-R		--	0	--	0
T-R-D-A	(+1)	3.5%	2	0.5%	1
T-D-A-R		--	0	--	0
R-D-T-A		28.0%	16	13.5%	27
	(subtotals)	(36.7%)		(29.5%)	
D-A-R-T		--	0	0.5%	1
T-R-A-D		7.0%	4	4.5%	9
T-A-D-R	(0)	--	0	--	0
R-D-A-T		7.0%	4	5.5%	11
R-T-D-A		1.8%	1	1.5%	3
A-D-T-R		--	0	2.5%	5
	(subtotals)	(15.8%)		(14.5%)	
T-A-R-D		--	0	--	0
R-A-D-T		1.8%	1	5.0%	10
R-T-A-D	(-1)	1.8%	1	0.5%	1
A-D-R-T		--	0	--	0
A-T-D-R		--	0	0.5%	1
	(subtotals)	(3.6%)		(6.0%)	
R-A-T-D		12.3%	7	4.5%	9
A-T-R-D	(-2)	--	0	3.5%	7
A-R-D-T		1.8%	1	5.5%	11
	(subtotals)	(14.1%)		(13.5%)	
A-R-T-D	(-3)	7.0%	4	2.5%	5
	(totals)	(100.0%)	(57)	(100.0%)	(200)

respondents by event type seemed much easier to achieve, given the large number of cases on each type in Kreps's file.

We set a target of two hundred cases from other organized responses, using data quality as the central criterion for data production. Of the remaining 371 cases in Kreps's data file, we selected fifty-six cases for which he thought archival data were of the highest quality. We gave no attention at this point to either metric scores or event types in selecting these cases. Then in order to expand the pool of cases from which reasonable comparability with the emergent file might be achieved, we randomly sampled thirty-four additional cases from the remaining 315 organized responses in

Kreps's file, using form type and event type as sampling criteria. This strategy yielded 420 interviews on ninety organized responses with which we hoped to complete data production on individual role dynamics.

Of these 420 interviews, respondent role analyses were possible for 172 participants in sixty-two organized responses. Still short of our objective of two hundred cases, and wanting to improve comparability with the emergent sample, an additional fifteen organized responses were purposively selected from the remaining 234 cases in Kreps's data file. This yielded the required twenty-eight additional participants in the respondent data file for other organized disaster responses. In the end, our analysis of 464 participants from 105 other organized responses produced adequate data on two hundred participants from seventy-seven of them.

Table 5.2 arrays these two hundred cases beside the fifty-seven participants from twenty-nine emergent organized responses. The percentages are reasonably close for all levels on the metric except the very top of the continuum (+3 or D-T-R-A), where participants from emergent units are underrepresented by over 10 percent. Overall, however, we were quite pleased with the comparability we had achieved on the metric derived logically from the formal taxonomy. Comparability was also quite satisfactory for type of event. For respondents from emergent as opposed to other organized responses, the distributions were as follows: 23 percent versus 26 percent for earthquakes; 19 percent versus 22 percent for tornados; 40 percent versus 39 percent for floods, and 18 percent versus 13 percent for hurricanes.

In summary, the final sample of 257 participants from 106 organized disaster responses (emergent and other) was created, first and foremost, to maximize the best transcribed archival material available for data production on individual role dynamics. While missing information remained an important concern, the archives could have served us worse, but probably no better for theory-building purposes. In maximizing data quality, we also achieved comparability in what we thought might be two important variables in any subsequent modeling of individual role dynamics. Pragmatically achieved, our sampling strategy was consistent with our theoretical needs (Glaser and Strauss 1967, 45–79).

Comparative Findings on the Three Dimensions of Role Enactment

Comparative findings on the first and second dimensions are summarized in table 5.3. With respect to status-role nexus (table

5.3A), the majority of participants in both emergent (51 percent) and other (79 percent) organized responses show consistency. Thus overall there is considerable evidence of stability of role allocation from pre- to postdisaster time periods.[6] At the same time, however, there is substantially greater inconsistency for respondents in emergent (49 percent) as opposed to other (21 percent) organized responses. The difference of 28 percentage points is statistically significant (Chi Square = 17.5, P<.0001), and it suggests that role reallocation is more likely for participants in new as opposed to already existing organizations.

Interestingly enough, if we compare findings on the status-role nexus at the individual versus the earlier aggregate levels of analysis for emergent organized responses (see table 4.7), we find somewhat stronger evidence for consistency at the aggregate level. Missing data aside, there may be a straightforward explanation for this difference. As respondents, these people are reporting only on themselves as key participants in organized responses. But earlier as informants, they were reporting on all participants in the same responses, many of whom were marginally involved. While stepping outside occupational expectations may not be required of participation in new social arrangements generally, it may very well be required of those who are key players. If this explanation is correct, then relative stability of role allocation will be evidenced overall for emergent organizations, and role reallocation will be more likely when the focus is only on key participants.

With respect to role linkages, table 5.3B arrays the total number of continuous and discontinuous links by the two categories of organized responses; and then table 5.3C arrays them by whether the links are within the organized response or boundary spanning. The number of missing cases (486) represent links for which data are inadequate on either postdisaster roles or predisaster occupations.[7] Notwithstanding our continuing problems with incomplete information, there is strong evidence of continuity of role linkages for respondents from both emergent (67 percent) and other (70 percent) organized responses; and there is no statistically significant difference between the two general types (table 5.3B). The pattern indicated is stability of role complementarity from pre- to postdisaster time periods.[8]

There is a quite notable difference, however, when continuous and discontinuous links are broken down with respect to their location (table 5.3C). Even though the majority of all links are within the organized response (1,476 or 72 percent), boundary spanning links are much more likely to be discontinuous than internal ones.

Table 5.3
First and Second Role Dimensions for Respondents
from Emergent and Other Organized Responses

5.3A
Status-Role Nexus by Type of Organized Response

	Emergent	Other
STATUS-ROLE NEXUS		
Consistent	51%	79%
Inconsistent	49%	21%
totals	100%	100%
	(55)	(185)

missing cases (uncertain) = 17
chi square = 17.5
p< .0001
phi = .27

5.3B
Discontinuity vs. Continuity of Role Linkages
by Type of Organized Response

	Emergent	Other
ROLE LINKAGES		
Continuous	67%	70%
Discontinuous	33%	30%
totals	100%	100%
	(736)	(1321)

missing cases = 486
chi square = 2.2
p< .20
phi = .03

5.3C
Type of Role Link

	Within Organized Responses	Boundary Spanning
ROLE LINKAGE		
Continuous	80%	40%
Discontinuous	20%	60%
	100%	100%
	(1476)	(581)

missing cases = 486
chi square = 298.1
P< .0000
phi = .38

The 40 percentage-point difference (60 percent versus 20 percent) is both large and statistically significant (Chi Square $=298.1$, $P<.0000$). These findings suggest that the closed system quality of organizing gives expression to stability of role complementarity. On the other hand, the open system quality of organizing, in this instance evidenced by boundary spanning links of key participants, gives expression to change of role complementarity.

The obvious follow-up question is whether there is any difference between respondents in emergent as opposed to other organized responses with respect to location of role linkages. The answer is no, with just under 30 percent of both categories having boundary spanning links. Regardless of category of organized response, therefore, the summary conclusion is quite clear: stability of role complementarity is largely an internal matter; change of role complementarity is largely an external matter. Individual role dynamics reflect the reality of organizations as boundary spanning social systems (Thompson 1967).

In comparing findings on role linkages at the individual versus the aggregate levels of analysis for emergent organized responses (see table 4.8), this time there is greater evidence for a balance of continuous (average of 33 percent) and discontinuous (average of 44 percent) incumbent links at the aggregate level. We first thought this difference was possibly a function of refinements in our research design. Recall that we analyzed only intra-organizational links in the second phase of data production. We also assumed that all postdisaster roles were linked. Our findings from the second phase suggested that while there is substantial consistency for status-role nexus (first dimension), the occupations represented in emergent organizations are diverse and often not linked predisaster. But in this third phase of data production all of the respondent's direct intraorganizational as well as boundary spanning links were documented to the extent possible. A fair comparison between individual and aggregate levels of analysis therefore required that we examine only intra-organizational links. In making that comparison, we still found greater evidence of a mix at the aggregate level.

Our interpretation of this intriguing difference is as follows: Participation generally in nascent organizations (the aggregate level) shows an internal balancing of continuous and discontinuous relationships that appears to be viable. The internal links of key participants, however, show greater evidence of continuity (individual level). This suggests that as key people are creating organization, they are turning to people they know (personally or categorically).

The people they know are more often than not linked to these key people occupationally. That being the case, what Ralph Turner calls functional and tenable role relationships exist already and are simply being applied to an unusual situation. But as implied above, the viability of any organization is not just an internal matter. Thus as key participants reach outside the boundaries of their nascent organizations—for communications, resources, or legitimacy— they must expand their routine social networks to do so.

The findings on role performance are summarized in table 5.4. The cases are arrayed at the top of the table (5.4A) by the four types of role performance represented in figure 5.1. The cases are then arrayed in the lower part of the table in terms of levels of improvising (5.4B) and types of role incumbency (5.4C) subsumed in figure 5.1. Note that all four types of role performance are evidenced for participants in both categories of organized responses, with role redefinition (44 percent) occurring most frequently for emergent cases and formal role enactment (51 percent) occurring most frequently for other cases. Role prototyping (9 percent and 9 percent) and working role enactment (30 percent and 28 percent) have almost identical percentages for emergent and other cases in the sample.

The evidence highlights beautifully the mutual relevance of role-making and role-playing, regardless of whether social structures are old or new. But it is also clear from table 5.4 that there are important differences between emergent and other organized responses with respect to both incumbency and level of improvising. With respect to incumbency, while only about 21 percent of the participants in other organized responses are new, about 53 percent of the participants in emergent ones are new (a difference of 32 percent, Chi Square = 22.0, P<.0000). With respect to level of improvising, while only 40 percent of the participants in other organized responses are at level 2, about 74 percent of participants in emergent ones are at level 2 (a difference of 34 percent, Chi Square = 20.2, P<.0000).

In comparing findings on role performance at the individual versus aggregate levels for emergent organized responses (see table 4.9), there is greater evidence for both new incumbency and improvising at the individual level. Similar to our explanation for the status-role nexus difference, these participants are more than just members. They are enacting key roles in demonstrably new organizations. It appears that the roles they enact require greater levels of innovativeness. The important conclusion can be stated as follows: While new organizations most certainly can be created without

Table 5.4
Third Role Dimension for Respondents from
Emergent and Other Organized Responses

5.4A

	Emergent	Other
Formal	17%	51%
Prototyping	9%	9%
Working	30%	28%
Redefinition	44%	12%
	100%	100%
	(57)	(200)

missing cases = 0
chi square = 35.1
p< .0000
Cramer's V = .37

5.4B

	Emergent	Other
IMPROVISATION		
Level 1		
Role-playing	26%	60%
Level 2	74%	40%
Role-making		
	100%	100%
	(57)	(200)

missing cases = 0
chi square = 20.2
p< .0000
phi = .28

5.4C

	Emergent	Other
ROLE INCUMBENCY		
Existing	47%	79%
Incumbent		
New	53%	21%
Incumbent		
	100%	100%
	(57)	(200)

missing cases = 0
chi square = 22.0
p< .0000
phi = .29

changes in incumbency and performance patterns, the circumstances in which these organizations emerge seem to require at least some redifferentiation.

In summary, participants in emergent organized responses are more likely to have an inconsistent status-role nexus than those in other ones. This pattern points to the relevance of role reallocation, and it appears to be greater for key participants in emergent organizations than for participation in general. Second, there are no noteworthy differences in role linkages for the two categories of participants, and a stable pattern of role complementarity is evident for the entire sample. However, the location of the linkages in both categories of organized responses is important, with external links showing much greater discontinuity than internal ones. Key participants in emergent organizations evidence more continuous relationships than do participants generally. Third, participants in emergent organized responses are more likely to be new incumbents and to improvise at a higher level than those in other organized responses. These patterns, which are stronger for key participants than for participants generally, point to the relevance of role redifferentiation as organizations come into being.

The above findings speak powerfully to the necessity of comparing role dynamics by category of organized response. But as we reviewed these findings, it became clear that the category of "other" organized responses was not very useful. Too many different types of enacting units were being represented in one catch-all category, and we felt compelled to break it down in some way. Our sampling plan had already ensured variation in terms of the formal organizing-collective behavior metric as well as type of disaster event. One other refinement was now needed, and it came almost as an afterthought. Simply put, we put back into use the original DRC typology that Kreps earlier thought was no longer of value. We close this chapter by describing briefly why and how this happened.

The Restoration of the DRC Typology

Recall from chapter 1 (see pages 22–25) that the DRC typology identifies four general classes of organized disaster responses. *Established* responses are enacted by existing units and much of what they do during a disaster is predetermined. Much of what *expanding* ones do is predetermined as well, but their structure changes from a small cadre of professionals to a much larger structure composed of officially designated volunteers. *Extending* ones are enacted by existing units, but much of what they do is unanticipated. Finally, the entire life history of *emergent* units is confined largely (in most cases exclusively) to the immediate emergency period.

After data production was completed, we came to see the DRC typology as a possible bridge between the process of organizing and role dynamics. The former was represented by the metric used in the first phase of our role analysis (see chapter 2). The latter was represented by what we hoped had become an increasingly precise conception and measurement of three core dimensions (status-role nexus, role linkages, role performance) and their respective underlying processes (role allocation, role complementarity, role differentiation). The realization of this bridging possibility did not emerge gradually. Instead, Kreps simply threw out the idea as we began modeling role dynamics. At this point we had little notion about how either Kreps's original 423 cases at the organizational level or our 257 cases at the individual level would distribute themselves in terms of the DRC typology. The typology had been ignored by Kreps for years, and most of the ten graduate students working on the project at one point or another were not even aware of its existence.

The distribution for the 423 case file turned out to be as follows: 65 percent established (N = 273), 9 percent expanding (N = 40), 14 percent extending (N = 58), and the remaining 12 percent emergent (N = 52). The distribution of the 257 case file turned out to be as follows: 49 percent established (N = 125), 24 percent expanding (N = 63), 5 percent extending (N = 12), and 22 percent emergent (N = 57). Established organized responses included those by police and fire departments, hospitals, departments of public works, military units, and the mass media. Expanding ones were enacted primarily by local Red Cross chapters, Salvation Army units, and local civil defense offices. Extending ones were enacted by special interest groups, other public bureaucracies, and private firms. Finally, emergent organized responses were composed of either unaffiliated individuals or previously existing social units.

The larger file had been constructed by Kreps as usable data allowed, and it is not a random sample. However, the distribution of 423 cases represents nicely the primary emphasis of early DRC field studies on emergency-relevant public bureaucracies and voluntary agencies. All of the remaining cases were documented by DRC field teams on a catch-as-catch-can basis. We then developed the smaller file from Kreps's larger one and, as described above, it is not a random sample either. Driven also by data availability, it is no less representative of the early DRC field studies.

Table 5.5
Formal Organizing—Collective Behavior Metric Scores
by DRC Typology of Organized Disaster Responses

	Mean	St.Dev.	Range	% of cases
DRC Typology				
Established	4.8	1.5	0-6	65%
Expanding	4.6	1.6	1-6	9%
Extending	4.0	4.4	1-6	14%
Emergent	3.3	1.6	0-6	12%
				100%
				(423)

Oneway analysis of variance
F = 17.4
p< .000

Perhaps the best way to communicate how the analytical potential of the DRC typology became apparent is summarized in tables 5.5 and 5.6. Using the 423 case file, table 5.5 provides the means, standard deviations, and ranges on Kreps's logical metric for each of the four types. Recall that the metric ranges from 0 to 6, with lower scores evidencing greater degrees of collective behavior (social action) and higher scores evidencing greater degrees of formal organizing (social order). Now observe the monotonic and statistically significant ($F = 17.4$, $P < .000$) increase in average metric scores, from a low of 3.3 for emergent organizations to a high of 4.8 for established organizations.

Next observe table 5.6, which cross-tabulates each of the three role dimensions for the 257 case file in terms of the same four DRC types. There are substantial and statistically significant differences on all three role dimensions. The patterns for participants in emergent organized responses have already been described. Being appropriately cautious about small numbers of cases, note the strong evidence of role reallocation (first dimension) and change of role complementarity (second dimension) for participants in extending organizations. Note also the balance of stability and change of role complementarity for participants in expanding organizations

Table 5.6
First, Second, and Third Role Dimensions by
DRC Typology of Organized Disaster Responses

Dimension 1: Status-Role Nexus

	Established	Expanding	Extending	Emergent
Consistent	87%	76%	--	51%
Inconsistent	13%	24%	100%	49%
	100%	100%	100%	100%
	(118)	(58)	(9)	(55)

missing cases = 17
chi square = 50.3
p< .0000
Cramer's V = .46

Dimension 2: Role Linkage

	Established	Expanding	Extending	Emergent
Continuous	81%	58%	32%	67%
Discontinuous	19%	42%	68%	33%
	100%	100%	100%	100%
	(787)	(460)	(74)	(736)

missing cases = 486
chi square = 125.3
p< .0000
Cramer's V = .25

Dimension 3: Role Performance

	Established	Expanding	Extending	Emergent
Formal/Prototyping	58%	65%	50%	26%
Working/Redefinition	42%	35%	50%	74%
	100%	100%	100%	100%
	(125)	(63)	(12)	(57)

missing cases = 0
chi square = 21.4
p< .0000
Cramer's V = .29

(second dimension). And perhaps most illuminating, note the substantial increases of role redifferentiation (third dimension) for respondents in extending and, in particular, emergent organizations that parallel somewhat the pattern evidenced for the formal organizing–collective behavior metric in table 5.5. It was very hard not to conclude from these tables that the DRC typology had major analytical potential for bridging analyses of organizing and role dynamics.

And so we became wedded to the idea that the DRC typology could be an important tool for purposes of modeling the 257-case file on role enactments. Precisely how it would be used remained to be determined. We saw four alternative modeling strategies. First, we could create a dummy variable that would include only participants from emergent organized responses. We had planned to do just that from the very beginning because we thought that this type would be most likely to evidence change of structural arrangements pre- to postdisaster. Second, we could create a dummy variable that would include only participants from established organized responses. We thought that this type was the most likely to evidence stability of structural arrangements pre- to postdisaster. Third, we could create a dummy variable that combined participants from emergent and extending organized responses. We thought that these two types were most likely to represent change of structural arrangements, and combining them would provide a better distribution of cases than the first alternative. Finally, we thought that expanding and extending organized responses represented an intermediate level of potential structural change vis-à-vis established (lowest potential) and emergent (highest potential) types. Grouping participants in this way would create a three-level ordinal measure.

There was a solid conceptual argument for each of the above alternatives, and each would also allow for independent variables with acceptable distributions. We therefore decided to experiment with them all in our subsequent model-building efforts. Our goal was to determine which one of them would yield the most powerful generalizations about role dynamics. We turn now to a reporting of those model-building efforts. As described in chapter 6, they serve as the final foundation for the formal theory of organizing and role dynamics that we construct in chapter 7.

6

Modeling Individual Role Dynamics

> There is an implication that associates "purely" descriptive re-
> search with empty-headedness; the label also implies that as a
> bare minimum every healthy researcher has at least an hypothe-
> sis to test, and preferably a whole model. This is nonsense.
> (Dubin 1978, 87)

The above passage implies that there are different ways of doing
science. One strategy is to seek adequate descriptions and explanations at the same time. The scientist starts with explanations of
social phenomena, tests their utility from one setting to the next,
refines them as needed, and determines their boundaries. Questions about why social phenomena are patterned in one way or
another are central. Another strategy is to seek precise descriptions of social phenomena before trying to explain them. The scientist starts with tentative definitions of social phenomena, refines
them as needed, and then crystallizes them after repeated observations. Questions about what social phenomena are and how they
are patterned precede attempts to explain the patterning that has
been observed (Kreps 1989b, 215–41; 1989c, 177–80).

We have chosen the second path, believing that the momentum of
improved conception and measurement of social phenomena leads
naturally, indeed inevitably, to more powerful explanations of them.
We agree with Dubin (1978, 87) that the more adequate the description, the more likely will the concepts derived from the description
be useful for the theory building that follows. In this instance, we
have tried to maximize the value of the archives for describing three
core properties of role. We have characterized our approach as a
variant of analytical induction to express the essential circularity of
conceiving and perceiving anything scientifically (Wallace 1971). In
this and the remaining chapter, we will construct a formal theory of
organization and role that tries to explain what we have observed.
Once constructed, we think the theory can best be tested through
primary data collection because many of the data problems we faced

could be overcome in the field. At the same time, the continuing value of the archives in this regard should not be underestimated.[1]

We trust that the momentum of description leading to explanation has been illustrated to some extent in the previous chapters. Once having isolated the patterns of role dimensions one, two, and three, the next obvious question is how are they related to each other. Logically, there are three potential empirical generalizations that specify the nature of their relationships (dimension one to two, one to three, and two to three).[2] The first section of this chapter summarizes what we have found in this regard and, in so doing, addresses the important issue of how to measure role enactment in its entirety for any given individual. We believe that developing a composite measure of role enactment is first and foremost a typological problem. Once constructed, the composite measure reveals an underlying continuum of structural change and stability that is logically consistent with the three dimensions of role that comprise it.

The next section of the chapter isolates possible correlates of role dynamics as we have now specified them for theory-building purposes. Recall from chapter 2 (see table 2.4) that we correlated a series of element, enacting unit, and event characteristics with our original measurement of role. Amended only slightly, these structural correlates now serve as contextual variables in our analysis of individual role enactments (Barton 1969, 211–16). We also measured a series of potentially important individual correlates of role enactments during the last phase of data production. The second section closes with a summary of how we operationalized them.

Using the above structural and individual correlates as independent variables, the last section of the chapter summarizes our exploratory modeling of the 257 individual role enactments. The findings for each dimension of role enactment will be discussed on their own terms and then compared with those on a composite measure. The latter will be used to summarize the overall patterns we have uncovered, patterns that obviously inform what we found during the first phase of this study (see chapter 2). The major continuity of results from first to most recent phases of our research provides a firm empirical foundation for the formal theory that concludes this book.

Empirical Relationships Among the Three Dimensions of Role

We begin with a summary of four separate measures of role enactment (one each for status-role nexus and role performance and two for role linkages) that are relevant to the statistical analyses which follows. In the process we will highlight empirical relationships among the three dimensions of role we have identified. Using three of the four separate measures, we then develop a typology from which a composite scoring of role enactment can be derived for all respondents in the sample.

Separate Measures of Role Enactment

For purposes of statistical analysis, we have treated status-role nexus (first dimension) as a dichotomous variable, with the respondent being scored as either inconsistent or consistent. The relevant percentages for the sample are 25 percent inconsistent (N = 65) 68 percent consistent (N = 175), and 7 percent uncertain (N = 17). The uncertain cases are those for which there is no information on the occupation of the respondent. These cases are excluded from all later statistical analyses.

We have treated role linkages (second dimension) in two different ways. First, we have computed the percentage of all links that are continuous. The higher the score, the greater the continuity of role linkages. With twenty-eight missing cases excluded from analysis, the mean percentage continuous is 66 percent (with a median of 75 percent and a standard deviation of 34 percent). The missing cases include those in which either no links were documented (ten cases) or there was missing occupational data for all of the respondent's role linkages (eighteen cases). While this continuous measure is very useful for statistical analysis as a measure of role linkages, it cannot readily be combined with the discrete measurement of the other two dimensions. For that purpose (discussed below), we reduced the second dimension to three levels: those respondents with less than 50 percent continuous relationships (26 percent, N = 60); those with a perfect mix (50 percent each) of continuous and discontinuous relationships (8 percent, N = 17); and those with more than 50 percent continuous relationships (66 percent, N = 152).

In conformity with the two levels of improvising (third dimension) highlighted in chapter 5, we have separated respondents engaged in formal role enactment and role prototyping (53 percent, N = 135) from those engaged in working role enactment and role redefinition (47 percent, N = 122). The percentages for each of the four types that we have reduced to a dichotomy are as follows: formal role enactment (44 percent, N = 112), role prototyping (9 percent, N = 23), working role enactment (28 percent, N = 73) and role redefinition (19 percent, N = 49). Recall that this gives us a measure of improvising during role performance that is equally relevant to existing as well as new incumbents (i.e., insensitive to incumbency).

Empirical relationships among the three dimensions of role are summarized in table 6.1. To simplify the table, only the second of the two possible measures for role linkages is included. It becomes immediately clear from the table that status-role nexus and role linkages (table 6.1A) evidence the strongest empirical relationship (Chi square = 54.2, P<.0000, r = .49). The correlation between status-role nexus and the interval (straight percentage) measure of role linkages is very similar (r = .54). These findings suggests that the stability of role allocation and role complementarity often work together as important sources of predictability during a disaster. In other words, who is going to do what is very clear, as is with whom it is going to be done.

There is only a slight positive relationship between status-role nexus and role performance (Chi Square = 2.6, P<.11, r = .10), and even less of a relationship between role linkages and role performance (Chi Square = 1.2, P<.55, r = .07). The correlation between the interval (straight percentage) measure of role linkages and role performance is about the same (r = .06). These findings suggest that processes related to stability or change of role allocation and role complementarity do not predicate how post-disaster roles are actually performed (i.e., stability or change of role differentiation). We must therefore look elsewhere for more important correlates of the presence or absence of improvisation.

It is very important to recognize in this regard that role allocation and role complementarity tie more directly to postdisaster role incumbency rather than its performance. In our sample the correlation between status-role nexus and the incumbency component (new versus existing) of the third dimension (r = .70) is quite substantial because many respondents have predisaster statuses and postdisaster roles that are one and the same. Similarly, the modest correlation between role linkages and the incumbency component of role performance (r = .25) is a statistical artifact of the correlation between status-role nexus and role linkages (table 6.1A) noted above. However, our measurement of improvising is completely insensitive to incumbency, as it must be if we are to have a pure measure of role performance.

Composite Measure of Role Enactment

Regardless of the extent to which the three dimensions of role are correlated, we think it is important to capture individual role enactments in their entirety. The low to moderate relationships

Table 6.1
Relationships Among Three Dimensions of Role

6.1A Status-role Nexus and Role Linkages

		Status-Role Nexus	
		Inconsistent	Consistent
Role	Discontinuous	60%	13%
Linkages	Mixed	9%	7%
	Continuous	31%	80%
		100%	100%
		(64)	(165)

missing cases = 28
chi square = 54.2
p< .0000
Pearson r (phi) = .49

6.1B Status-role Nexus and Role Performance

		Status-Role Nexus	
		Inconsistent	Consistent
Role	Working/Redefinition	57%	45%
Performance	Formal/Prototyping	43%	55%
		100%	100%
		(65)	(175)

missing cases = 17
chi square = 2.6
p< .11
Pearson r (phi) = .10

6.1C Role Linkages and Role Performance

		Role Linkage		
		Discontinuous	Mixed	Continuous
Role	Working/Redefinition	55%	47%	47%
Performance	Formal/Prototyping	45%	53%	53%
		100%	100%	100%
		(60)	(17)	(152)

missing cases = 28
chi square = 1.2
p< .55
Pearson r (Cramer's V) = .07

among the three dimensions depicted in table 6.1 suggest that there are many different ways people adapt to the changing conditions of disaster. But how many? Using the same set of variable categories found in table 6.1, the twelve-fold property space depicted at the top of table 6.2 arrays all logically possible combinations of the three dimensions. Thus cell A represents an inconsistent status-role nexus, discontinuous role linkages, and the highest level of improvising (working role enactment or role redefinition). And so on. The numbers in parentheses are the actual frequencies for the twelve types in our sample. Note that there are multiple empirical examples for all of them. The disproportionate stability as opposed to change of social structure that is evidenced speaks directly to the kinds of disasters typically studied by the Disaster Research Center—i.e., largely low-impact disasters in an economically advanced society. Notwithstanding that important contextual factor, the amount of variation evidenced in this property space provides an adequate foundation for constructing a composite measure of role enactment.

Once having specified the twelve types of role enactments, it is then possible to derive logically a composite score for each respondent in the sample. The strategy for accomplishing that is depicted in the middle of table 6.2. We believe that the twelve-fold property space reveals an underlying continuum of change and stability of social structure. One extreme on the continuum is represented by cell A (inconsistent status-role nexus, discontinuous role linkages, working role enactment/role redefinition). Here all three dimensions of role evidence change of social structure. The other extreme on the continuum is represented by cell L (consistent status-role nexus, continuous role linkages, formal role enactment/role prototyping). Here all three dimensions of role evidence stability of social structure. The other five gradations represent symmetrical distances from each extreme to the midpoint of the continuum where there is a perfect balance between change and stability of social structure. The balance is represented by cell E (consistent status-role nexus, mixed role linkages, working role enactment/role redefinition) and cell H (inconsistent status-role nexus, mixed role linkages, formal role enactment/role prototyping).

With seven levels, it then becomes a matter of assigning higher or lower scores that maintain the logical integrity of the continuum. In this case, we construct a 0–6 ordinal measure, with lower scores reflecting greater change and higher scores reflecting greater stability. The bottom of table 6.2 arrays these scores, the twelve types

Table 6.2
Composite Measurement of Role Enactments

		STATUS-ROLE NEXUS					
		Inconsistent			Consistent		
ROLE LINKAGES		Discon	Mixed	Contin	Discon	Mixed	Contin
ROLE PERFORMANCE	Working/ Redefinition	A (22)	B (4)	C (11)	D (11)	E (4)	F (60)
	Formal/ Prototyping	G (16)	H (2)	I (9)	J (11)	K (7)	L (72)

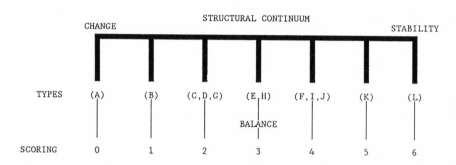

STRUCTURAL CONTINUUM

CHANGE   STABILITY

| TYPES | (A) | (B) | (C,D,G) | (E,H) | (F,I,J) | (K) | (L) |

BALANCE

| SCORING | 0 | 1 | 2 | 3 | 4 | 5 | 6 |

SAMPLE DISTRIBUTION

CHANGE

		Percent	
0	INCONSISTENT, DISCONTINUOUS, WORKING/REDEFINITION	10%	(22)
1	INCONSISTENT, MIXED, WORKING/REDEFINITION	2%	(4)
2	INCONSISTENT, CONTINUOUS, WORKING/REDEFINITION CONSISTENT, DISCONTINUOUS, WORKING/REDEFINITION INCONSISTENT, DISCONTINUOUS, FORMAL/PROTOTYPING	16%	(38)
3	CONSISTENT, MIXED, WORKING/REDEFINITION INCONSISTENT, MIXED, FORMAL/PROTOTYPING	3%	(6)
4	CONSISTENT, CONTINUOUS, WORKING/REDEFINITION INCONSISTENT, CONTINUOUS, FORMAL/PROTOTYPING CONSISTENT, DISCONTINUOUS, FORMAL/PROTOTYPING	35%	(80)
5	CONSISTENT, MIXED, FORMAL/PROTOTYPING	3%	(7)
6	CONSISTENT, CONTINUOUS, FORMAL/PROTOTYPING	31%	(72)

STABILITY

MISSING = 28   TOTALS   100%   (229)

of enactments subsumed by them, and their respective distributions in our sample of respondents. The mean score for the sample is 3.9, with a median of 4, and a standard deviation of 1.9.[3]

The result of the above exercise is a fourth specification of role enactment as the dependent variable. If a composite measure is a good one, it is not likely to provide much new information as a dependent variable when correlated with the same independent variables as are its component parts. However, it becomes a very efficient way of expressing role enactment as an independent variable. We will illustrate the latter use in the final chapter for purposes of examining what Ralph Turner refers to (see chapter 3) as the functionality and tenability of role dynamics.

The conceptual as well as empirical foundation for each of the four measures of role enactment has hopefully been affirmed above and in the preceding chapters. Successful or not, we have pushed analytical description as far as the archives and our capacities have allowed. The next step in theory building is to summarize structural and individual correlates of the role enactments we have observed. There are sixteen of the former and eight of the latter. The discussion of those correlates speaks again to the continuity as well as expansion of data production during the course of our research. The discussion speaks also to the boundaries of our theorizing about organization and role (Dubin 1978, 126).

Structural and Individual Correlates of Role Dynamics

With a few modifications, the structural correlates are the same as those used in the first phase of our research (see table 2.4 and related discussion on pages 55–58). The revised set of structural element, enacting unit, and disaster event characteristics, and their distributions for the sample of 257 respondents, are summarized in table 6.3. As specified in chapter 2, these variables now represent broader social and physical contexts in which individual role enactments take place. As such, they serve as potential explanations of role dynamics.

The modifications of these structural correlates are as follows: First, the initial appearing element (R or A versus D or T) of organizing was used earlier because all cases in the sample of thirty-nine organizational enactments had the same (midpoint) metric score. As noted in chapter 5 (see table 5.2 and related discussion on pages 125–27), the full range of scores subsumed by Kreps's formal organizing (social order)–collective behavior (social action)

Table 6.3
Structural Correlates of Role Enactment

Correlate Type	Measurement
ELEMENT CHARACTERISTIC	
Metric score	0 (N=9); 1 (N=35); 2 (N=14); 3 (N=38); 4 (N=80); 5 (N=30); 6 (N=51) Mean=3.71 st.dev.=1.73 range=0-6
Domain problem	Absent=0 (N=155); present=1 (N=102)
Task problem	Absent=0 (N=108); present=1 (N=149)
Resource problem	Absent=0 (N=130); present=1 (N=127)
Activities problem	Absent=0 (N=69); present=1 (N=188)
ENACTING UNIT CHARACTERISTIC	
DRC typology	Established/expanding=0 (N=188); extending/emergent=1 (N=69)
Size of unit	Number of participants: 9 or fewer=1 (N=38); 10-20=2 (N=48); 21-50=3 (N=57); over 50=4 (N=114)
Preparedness	No formal preparedness=1 (N=129); formal preparedness=2 (N=128)
Complexity of response	4 or fewer tasks=1 (N=101); more than 4 tasks=2 (N=156)
Social network relevance	Links: local, state, or national=0 (N=176); self-contained at initiation=1 (N=81)
Number of network links	None=0 (N=81); 1-3=1 (N=107); more than 3=2 (N=69)
Time network established	Established prior to event=0 (N=176); specific to event=1 (N=81)
Community type	Metropolitan: no=0 (N=106); yes=1 (N=151)
Disaster experience	No disaster experience, few threats=1 (N=49); no disaster experience, several threats=2 (N=142); one or more disasters=3 (N=66)
EVENT CHARACTERISTIC	
Length of forewarning	Earthquakes=1 (N=65); tornadoes=2 (N=55); floods=3 (N=101); hurricanes=4 (N=36)
Magnitude-scope of impact	Severity: low=0 (N=91); high=1 (N=166)

metric are represented in the sample (mean = 3.71, standard deviation = 1.73, range = 0–6). Second, the timing of the first appearing element has been dropped from analysis because of its very high multicolinearity (r = .88) with the timing of the respondent's involvement in the responses (discussed below).

Third, domain, tasks, resources, or activities problems are documented as present if they occurred at any point during the history of the response. The more precise fine tuning of the earlier study could not be accomplished here. Fourth, recall from chapter 5 (see pages 133–37) that we decided to experiment with four alternative expressions of the DRC typology. Although the patterns of relationships with role enactments are quite similar across these four alternatives, the third option consistently evidences the most powerful effects. Thus type of enacting unit is now measured as a dichotomous variable with respondents in extending and emergent organized responses being separated from those in established or expanding ones.[4] This use of the DRC typology maximizes the potential for examining structural change at both organizational and individual levels of analysis. Finally, the measure of concern for victims has been dropped from analysis because of missing data on too many cases in the sample.

The eight individual correlates arrayed in table 6.4 all are new variables measured in the last phase of data production. With respect to timing of initiation, in proposing the DRC typology Dynes (1970, 163–73) argued that established and expanding organizations tend to be involved earlier in an emergency because they are expected to be. It follows that respondents in extending and emergent organizations tend to become involved somewhat later, as needed. The correlation between the DRC typology measure and timing of the respondent's involvement (r = .24) is consistent with Dynes's prediction. If the potential for structural change is greatest in extending and emergent organized responses, and if key participants in them tend to become involved somewhat later during an emergency, it is possible that timing of involvement and degree of change evidenced in role enactment are related.

The measure of individual disaster experience parallels the structural measure of community disaster experience. In this case respondents were coded as "yes" on experience if they were ever involved in a disaster as either a victim or provider of emergency services. The measure of broad postdisaster role repertoire distinguishes respondents who enacted only our referent postdisaster role from those who enacted one or more other roles as well. We thought that multidimensional involvement during the emergency

Table 6.4
Individual Correlates of Role Enactment

Correlate Type	Measurement
RESPONDENT CHARACTERISTIC	
Time of initiation in organized response	Hrs from impact: 0-2=1 (N=87); 3-24=2 (N=127); 25-72=3 (N=25); more than 72 hrs=4 (N=18)
Disaster experience	No=0 (N=161); yes=1 (N=96)
Broad postdisaster role repertoire	No=0 (N=143); yes=1 (N=114)
Instrumental leader	No=0 (N=70); yes, in sub-unit of organized response=1 (N=101); yes, in overall organized response=2 (N=86)
Experience in disaster role	No=0 (N=92); yes=1 (N=165)
Knowledge required for role performance	General=1 (N=28); specific=2 (N=187); technical=3 (N=42)
Boundary spanning respondent links	Proportion of total respondent links external to organized response Mean=.296 st.dev.=.302
Complexity of role enactment	Total number of roles represented by all of the respondent's links (internal and external to organized response) to other role incumbents Mean=5.914 st.dev.=5.017 range=0-24

period might be related to role dynamics and, if so, we wanted to discover whether structural stability or change was being evidenced in the process.

The measure of instrumental leadership is a three level ordinal variable—with those who were not leaders at the low end, those enacting a subunit leadership role at the middle level, and those enacting an overall leadership role at the high end. The fact that 73 percent of the respondents played some kind of leadership role is not surprising given the fact that DRC field researchers were always looking for key participants. Leadership has been an important dimension of role research at least since Bales's (1950) classic study, and we had hoped to isolate both instrumental and expressive leadership roles in data production. Information was completely lacking on expressive leadership, however, and this was also the case with respect to evidence for conflict in the performance of leadership roles.[5]

With respect to the measure of experience in the postdisaster role, respondents were coded "yes" if they had ever enacted the specific postdisaster role we had identified. This would certainly be the case for those respondents whose predisaster occupation and postdisaster roles were one and the same. Our speculation here was very straightforward, i.e., that role experience and structural stability evidenced by role enactment would be positively related. The measure of knowledge requirements is a three-level ordinal score. At the low end are postdisaster roles about which knowledge is widespread in the public at large (e.g., much clerical activity or manual labor). At the middle level are postdisaster roles that call for more specific training and/or experience (e.g., government administration or shelter management). At the high end are roles that require specific technical skills (e.g., inspection of physical structures and infrastructures or providing medical care). Just as with previous role experience, we suspected that the greater the knowledge requirements of the role, the greater the structural stability—in this case because of a more selective range of people who can enact a role.

The measure of boundary spanning links is an outgrowth of the findings reported in chapter 5 (see pages 128–30). Recall that boundary spanning links are much more likely to be discontinuous than internal ones. This suggests that the open system quality of organizing impels change of role complementarity. We therefore decided to include the proportion of the respondent's total incumbent links that were boundary spanning as a separate independent variable. Our hypothesis in this regard was quite explicit: the greater the proportion of an individual's links that are boundary spanning, the greater the evidence of structural change during role enactment.

The final individual correlate, complexity of role performance, derives from the exchange with Ralph Turner highlighted in chapter 3 (see pages 81–83 in particular). As noted in table 6.3, the number of tasks is a structural correlate that represents the overall complexity of the division of labor in an organized response (complexity of response). We had hoped to develop an analytically comparable measure of role complexity such as the total number of roles performed in an organized response. But because the organizational level of analysis was precluded by insufficient data, we had to come up with an alternative measure of complexity of role enactment at the individual level.

The question can be posed in the following way: Improvised or not, to what extent is the respondent's role performance part of a broader postdisaster role system during its enactment? To answer this question, the total number of roles (internal or boundary spanning) represented by all of the respondent's linkages to other incumbents can be aggregated. It logically follows that the greater the number of roles represented, the more complex the role system of which the respondent's postdisaster role is a part.[6] The correlation of this measure with complexity of response at the organizational level is in the expected direction ($r = .22$). Given our findings from phase one (see page 61), we suspected that both measures of complexity would be associated with structural change during role enactment.

In summary, the above structural and individual correlates serve as independent variables in the exploratory modeling which follows. The generally crude ordinal distinctions that are captured represent what we believe the transcribed archives can maximally yield. The four-fold specification of the dependent variable, when combined with the twenty-four independent variables that have been identified, represent also our attempt to converge organizational, collective behavior, and role theories in trying to unravel the drama of social structure and disaster (Kreps 1978).

Patterns Among Role Dynamics and Their Correlates

All four measures of role enactment are coded so that higher scores represent greater stability of social structure. Thus status-role nexus (dimension 1) is a dummy variable, with inconsistency coded as 0 and consistency coded 1. The interval (percentage) measure of role linkages (dimension 2) is scored so that the higher the score the greater the proportion of linkages that are continuous. Role performance (third dimension) is a dummy variable, with working role enactment/role redefinition coded as 0 and formal role enactment/role prototyping coded as 1. Finally, the composite measure is a seven-level ordinal scale that ranges from 0 (structural change) to 6 (structural stability).

Our findings are summarized in tables 6.5 and 6.6 and Appendix B. Consistent with the procedure followed in chapter 2, the tables do three things. First, they array all bivariate correlations that are statistically significant at the .10 level (two-tailed test) for each of the four specifications of individual role enactments.[7] Positive signs reveal a strain toward structural stability. Negative signs indicate a strain toward structural change. All but one (length of forewarning) of the structural or individual correlates show statistically significant correlations with role enactments one or more times. The tables then present partial standardized regression coefficients for a second subset of correlates that meet a .10 inclusion criterion for adding variables to equations. The vast majority (85 percent) of the statistically significant Beta's meet the more stringent .05 inclusion criterion or better, however. Finally, the variance explained by the subset of statistically significant partials is included for each specification of role dynamics. All four stepwise regression equations are statistically significant (P<.0000).[8] Finally, Appendix B provides a correlation matrix for all twenty-eight independent and dependent variables we have analyzed.

In the summary of findings that follows we will reference tables 6.5 and 6.6 and also Appendix B when it is relevant to a point we want to make. We will discuss initially each of the three dimensions of role dynamics in some detail, and then follow with comments on the composite measure so that the reader can easily compare findings here with those from the first phase of our research (chapter 2). The considerable continuity we can report suggests that even though our original measurement of role was less precise than it is now, we were on the right track from the very beginning.

Status-Role Nexus (Role Allocation)

The first thing to note in table 6.5 is the range of both structural and individual measures that show significant correlations with the respondent's status-role nexus. Stability of role allocation is associated with respondent role experience ($r = .52$, Beta $= .40$), size of organized responses ($r = .27$, Beta $= .19$), respondent disaster experience ($r = .20$, Beta $= .12$), knowledge requirements of the respondent's role ($r = .27$), responses that are self-contained at initiation rather than boundary spanning (social network relevance, $r = .18$), and formal organizing (as opposed to collective behavior) in the enactment of organization ($r = .16$). Change of role allocation is associated with the DRC typology measure ($r = -.40$, Beta $= -.29$), respondent boundary spanning links ($r = -.12$, Beta $= -.11$), social networks that are established during rather than before the disaster (time network established $r = -.20$), delayed involvement in the emergency by the respondent (time of initiation $r = -.13$), domain problems ($r = -.12$), task problems ($r = -.11$), and greater magnitude and scope of disaster impact ($r = -.11$).[9]

The most powerful among these variables are respondent role experience and the DRC typology measure. The relationship of role experience to stability of role allocation is not surprising, given the

Table 6.5
Correlation and Regression Analysis:
Status-Role Nexus (role allocation) and Role Linkages (role complementarity)

Correlate	Status-Role Nexus (consistency)		Role Linkages (continuity)	
	r	b	r	b
ELEMENT CHARACTERISTIC				
Metric score	.16		.11	
Domain problem	-.12			
Task problem	-.11			
Resource problem				
Activities problem			.12	
ENACTING UNIT CHARACTERISTIC				
DRC typology	-.40	-.29****	-.25	-.19***
Size of unit	.27	.19****	.19	.11*
Preparedness				
Complexity of response				
Social network relevance	.18		.19	
Number of network links			-.11	
Time network established	-.20			
Community type				
Community disaster experience				
EVENT CHARACTERISTIC				
Length of forewarning	--------------		--------------	
Magnitude-scope of impact	-.11			
RESPONDENT CHARACTERISTIC				
Time of respondent initiation in organized response	-.13		-.21	-.10*
Respondent disaster experience	.20	.12**		
Broad postdisaster role repertoire				
Instrumental leader			.13	.18***
Experience in disaster role	.52	.40****	.25	.17***
Knowledge required	.27		.21	
Boundary spanning respondent links	-.12	-.11**	-.32	-.31****
Complexity of role enactment			-.12	
Constant	.33		.61	
R² (stepwise)	.43		.26	
N=	(240)		(229)	

* P< .10   ** P< .05   *** P< .01   **** P< .001

substantial number of respondents whose predisaster occupations and postdisaster roles are one and the same. The relationship of the DRC typology with change of role allocation, however, shows how critical is the kind of organized response within which postdisaster roles are enacted. In this case, stability of role enactment is associated with established and expanding organized responses, and change of role enactment is associated with extending and emergent ones.[10]

We learn more about stability and change of role allocation by examining the pattern of correlations between role experience and the DRC typology measure, respectively, and other independent variables in the equation. Note from Appendix B that respondent role experience is positively correlated with respondent disaster experience (r = .22), formal organizing (metric r = .16), and responses that are self-contained at initiation rather than boundary spanning (social network relevance r = .10); and that it is negatively correlated with the DRC typology measure (r = − .24).[11]

On the other hand, the DRC typology is negatively correlated not only with respondent role experience, but also with size of organized responses (r = − .10), responses that are self-contained at initiation (social network relevance r = − .30), knowledge requirements of the postdisaster role (r = − .18), and formal organizing (metric r = − .12). It is positively correlated with time of respondent initiation (r = .24) and the time the social network of the organized response is established (r = .36). Such relationships suggest that different kinds of social structuring occur in extending and emergent as opposed to established and expanding organized responses.[12]

Finally, recall that status-role nexus and role linkages (discussed below) are themselves positively correlated (r = .54). Thus while these two dimensions are treated only as dependent variables, if the second dimension is added to the equation for status-role nexus, it becomes the most powerful predictor, and the total variance accounted for in the equation increases by 26 percent (to $R^2 = .54$).[13] Thus any inference about stability and change of role allocation must specify continuous role linkages as a component of stability and discontinuous linkages as a component of change.

The inferred scenario for stability of role allocation is as follows: Consistency of the status-role nexus is more likely where there is continuity of role linkages; during events that are less harmful and socially disruptive (with respect to problems of organizing); where there is evidence of formal organizing in larger and self-contained units that are expected to be involved during the immediate emergency period (established and expanding organized responses in the DRC typology); where key participants become involved sooner and have experience with both disasters generally and the postdisaster roles they enact; and where knowledge requirements attached to these roles are higher.

The inferred scenario for change of role allocation is as follows:

inconsistency of the status-role nexus is more likely where there is discontinuity of role linkages; during events that are more harmful and socially disruptive (with respect to problems of organizing); where there is evidence of collective behavior in smaller but more boundary spanning units that are not expected to become involved during the emergency period (extending and emergent organized responses in the DRC typology); where key participants become involved later and do not have experience with either disasters generally or the postdisaster roles they enact; and where knowledge requirements attached to these roles are lower.

While one must always be cautious about making too much of small to moderate relationships, a substantial amount of variance (43 percent or 54 percent, depending on whether the second dimension is included) in the status-role nexus has been accounted for by the equation. More specifically, the two scenarios inferred above are consistent with assumptions of linearity and additivity in regression models, the actual correlations reported in table 6.5, and the low to modest covariances among independent variables reported in Appendix B. The empirical patterns we have reported point to potentially powerful explanations and predictions about processes of role allocation and reallocation during the emergency periods of disasters (Dubin 1978, 18–32).

Role Linkages (Role Complementarity)

Note for the role linkages equation from table 6.5 the range of structural and individual measures that show significant correlations with the dependent variable. Stability of role complementarity is associated with respondent role experience (r = .25, Beta = .17), respondent instrumental leadership (r = .13, Beta = .18), size of the organized response (r = .19, Beta = .11), responses that are self-contained at initiation rather than boundary spanning (social network relevance, r = .19). knowledge requirements of the role (r = .21), activities problems (r = .12), and formal organizing (as opposed to collective behavior) in the enactment of organization (r = .11). Change of role complementarity is associated with respondent boundary spanning links (r = − .32, Beta = − .31), the DRC typology measure (r = − .25, Beta = − .19), time of respondent initiation (r = − .21, Beta = − .10), complexity of respondent role enactment (r = − .12), and the number of network links (r = − .11).[14]

Similar to the above scenarios for status-role nexus, any inference about stability and change of role complementarity should specify a consistent status-role nexus as a component of stability and an inconsistent status-role nexus as a component of change. Thus if we add status-role nexus to the equation for role linkages, it becomes the most powerful predictor in the equation, and the variance accounted for increases by 50 percent (to $R^2 = .39$).[15] While a smaller amount of variance overall is captured for the second dimension of role enactment (26 or 39 percent depending on whether the first dimension is included), the empirical patterns evidenced, in no small way, parallel those for status-role nexus.

What is perhaps most interesting about the equation for role linkages is that some eight correlates (role experience, DRC typology measure, size of organized response, respondent boundary spanning links, time of respondent initiation, knowledge requirements of role, social network relevance, and metric score) operate in the same direction here as they do for status-role nexus; and among these eight correlates, role experience, the DRC typology measure, size of organized response, and respondent boundary spanning links have statistically significant Beta's for both equations. We conclude that the above scenarios for role allocation can, with slight modifications, be generalized to role complementarity. These modifications are described below.

First, physical harm and social disruption (as represented by magnitude-scope of impact and problems of organizing) are less important for distinguishing between stability and change on this dimension. The correlations between the DRC typology and problems of organizing suggest that established and expanding organized responses are somewhat more likely to have activities problems ($r = -.19$) and somewhat less likely to have domain problems ($r = .19$) than extending and emergent ones.[16] Second, while respondent role experience is important in both equations, direct disaster experience shows no relationship with role linkages. The two independent variables themselves, however, are positively related ($r = .22$).

Third, the time social networks of organized responses are established is a component of change for status-role nexus, while the number of social network links is a component of change for role linkages. But consistent with the above scenarios, the two variables themselves are positively related ($r = .27$) and both are positively related with the DRC typology measure ($r = .36$ for time network established and $r = .23$ for number of network links). Fourth, while complexity of role enactment is a modest source of structural change on this dimension, its major influence is on role performance (see table 6.6). As we will discuss there, it is part of a nexus of variables that point to a notable pattern of relationships among measures of physical harm and social disruption, and cultural and structural capacities to deal with them.

Finally, instrumental leadership newly appears as a correlate of role complementarity. Its positive sign here means that when a postdisaster role has a leadership component, there is continuity in the incumbent's linkages with other role incumbents. This correlation is important because the majority of participants in the sample (73 percent) enact an instrumental leadership role at the subunit level or higher (see table 6.4). When they do so, it is clear that they are well connected with existing social networks.

The only slightly altered scenarios for stability and change of role complementarity are as follows: Continuity of role linkages is more likely where there is consistency of the status-role nexus; where there is evidence of formal organizing in larger and more self-contained units that are expected to be involved during the immediate emergency period (established and expanding types); where key participants become involved sooner and have experience with postdisaster roles they enact; where knowledge requirements of these roles are higher; where these roles include a leadership component; and where the role enactment is less complex.

Discontinuity of role linkages is more likely where there is inconsistency of the status-role nexus; where there is evidence of collective behavior in smaller but more boundary spanning units that are not expected to be involved during the emergency period (extending and emergent types); where key participants become involved later and do not have experience with the postdisaster roles they enact; where knowledge requirements of these roles are lower; where these roles do not include a leadership component; and where the role enactment is more complex.

Role Performance (Role Differentiation)

The third dimension of role enactment, which as noted above shows only slight correlations with the other two, evidences the largest number of statistically significant correlations (seventeen) and Beta coefficients (nine). The total variance accounted for by the equation in table 6.6 ($R^2 = .32$) stands in an intermediate position with respect to status-role nexus and role linkages. As might be expected, the equation for role performance is not improved by adding either or both of these other role dimensions to it. Notwithstanding that important point, however, the patterning of significant correlations and regression coefficients shows important similarities as well as differences when compared with those for the earlier equations.

Table 6.6
Correlation and Regression Analysis:
Role Performance (role differentiation) and Composite Measure

Correlate	Role Performance		Composite	
	r	b	r	b
ELEMENT CHARACTERISTIC				
Metric score				
Domain problem	-.26	-.12**	-.23	-.14***
Task problem	-.11			
Resource problem	-.14			
Activities problem				
ENACTING UNIT CHARACTERISTIC				
DRC typology	-.27	-.13**	-.45	-.31****
Size of unit			.23	.12**
Preparedness	.12	.15**	.11	
Complexity of response	-.27	-.17***		
Social network relevance	.14		.25	
Number of network links	-.15		-.16	
Time network established			-.19	
Community type	.12		.12	
Community disaster experience	-.26	-.18***	-.12	-.11**
EVENT CHARACTERISTIC				
Length of forewarning	--------------		--------------	
Magnitude-scope of impact	-.28	-.10*	-.18	
RESPONDENT CHARACTERISTIC				
Time of respondent initiation in organized response	-.11		-.21	
Respondent disaster experience	-.10		.11	
Broad postdisaster role repertoire	.16		.12	
Instrumental leader	-.26	-.19****		
Experience in disaster role	.22	.17***	.48	.37****
Knowledge required			.15	
Boundary spanning respondent links			-.19	-.17***
Complexity of role enactment	-.26	-.10*	-.15	
Constant		1.23		3.84
R^2 (stepwise)		.32		.42
N=		(257)		(229)

* P< .10   ** P< .05   *** P< .01   **** P< .001

Stability of role differentiation is associated with respondent role experience (r = .22, Beta = .17), disaster preparedness of the organized response (r = .12, Beta = .15), the respondent having a broader postdisaster role repertoire (r = .16), responses that are self-contained at initiation rather than boundary spanning (social network relevance r = .14), and responses occurring in metropolitan as opposed to nonmetropolitan communities (community type r = .12). Change of role differentiation is associated with respondent instrumental leadership (r = − .26, Beta = − .19), community disaster experience (r = − .26, Beta = − .18) as well as respondent disaster experience (r = − .10), the DRC typology measure (r = − .27, Beta = − .13), complexity of the division of labor as it relates to both the organized response (complexity of response r = − .27, Beta = − .17) and the participant's role performance (complexity of role enactment r = − .26, Beta = − .10), magnitude and scope of impact (r = − .28, Beta = − .10) as well as three of four problems of organizing (domain problems r = − .26, Beta = − .12; task problems r = − .11; resources problems r = − .14), time of respondent initiation (r = − .11), and number of network links (r = − .15).

Some eleven of the above seventeen correlates have appeared in one or both of the previous equations. Perhaps most notable, the DRC typology measure and role experience are the only two correlates that have statistically significant Beta's for all three equations, attesting to their centrality for theory building purposes. The directions of the effects for the seventeen correlates are the same except for instrumental leadership and respondent disaster experience. Here leadership is part and parcel of working role enactment or role redefinition. This finding is quite in keeping with requirements for adaptiveness during an emergency.

Respondent disaster experience earlier showed a positive relationship with status-role nexus, suggesting that where occupation predicates role allocation, a disaster experience factor goes along with it. But this says nothing about whether experience has anything to do with improvisation. It appears from the equation in table 6.6 that both respondent and community disaster experience are cultural resources that promote individual adaptations. Note also that the two experience variables are correlated themselves (r = .23), which is important because experienced communities represented in the sample tend to suffer from events that have greater physical impact and social disruption. The correlation between community disaster experience and magnitude-scope of impact is noteworthy (r = .40), and so are the correlations of these two variables with various problems of organizing.[17]

Four variables (metric score, size of organized response, knowledge required, and respondent boundary spanning links) that were correlates of status-role nexus and role linkages no longer operate. However, the DRC typology measure is significant across the board, and three of the omitted variables (size $r = -.10$, metric score $r = -.12$, and knowledge required $r = -.18$) are correlated with the DRC measure in a manner that is quite consistent with earlier scenarios for role allocation and role linkages. Moreover, the positive correlations of respondent boundary spanning links with three change factors in this equation (time of respondent initiation $r = .14$, magnitude-scope of impact $r = .12$, and instrumental leadership $r = .10$) is consistent with its characterization as a factor of change for role allocation and role complementarity.

There are six correlates for this equation that have not appeared before: disaster preparedness of the organized response, role enactments in metropolitan as opposed to nonmetropolitan communities, and role enactment as part of a broader postdisaster role repertoire are associated with stability of role differentiation (lower levels of improvising); and resource problems, complexity of the organized response, and community disaster experience are associated with change of role differentiation (higher levels of improvising).

With respect to stability factors, preparedness is a cultural resource similar to respondent and community disaster experience.[18] However, the effects of these three variables on role performance are quite different. Disaster plans are manifest cultural advantages for organized responses. They contribute to clarity of role enactments as extensions from established practices. Key participant and community disaster experience are latent cultural advantages. They contribute to flexibility of role enactments as adjustments to postdisaster demands. The greater stability of role differentiation in metropolitan areas results from the fact that, when disasters occur, the ratios of damages to remaining human and material resources is generally lower, and social routines are less severely disrupted. Finally, role enactment as part of a broader postdisaster role repertoire is negatively correlated with the DRC typology measure ($r = -.17$), suggesting that it happens more often in established and expanding organized responses. But regardless of whether one or more roles are performed in these two types, much of what goes on is expected. The role performance pattern that results points to stability.

With respect to change factors, resources problems, complexity of organized response, and community disaster experience are both positively related to each other,[19] and parts of a broader network of variables that associate the destructive and disruptive effects of disasters with cultural and structural capacities to deal with them (Haas and Drabek 1970). The destructive and disruptive effects of disasters are represented by the already reported set of correlations among magnitude-scope of impact and the four problems of organizing (see notes 9 and 17). With the sole exception of activities problems in the role linkage equation, all of these variables are associated with structural change. As noted earlier, respondent and community disaster experience are latent cultural capacities for change. Recall also that we identify the number of tasks performed and the number of roles represented by the respondent's linkages as parallel measures of structural complexity. As structural capacities, these two variables are correlated with each other ($r = .22$), the two measures of disaster experience, and also the various measures of physical disruption and social disruption.[20]

This consistent pattern of relationships among variables that reflect the destructive and disruptive effects of disaster, cultural capacities, and structural capacities reinforces quite consistently the regression equation for role performance. When we consider change factors along with those pointing to structural stability, in effect, we are able to see how the forces of social action and social order actually work during an emergency (Alexander 1982). Such findings are, indeed, gratifying because they render more precise the disaster research legacy on individual and social response to crisis events (Fritz 1961; Barton 1969; Dynes 1970; Quarantelli and Dynes 1977; Kreps 1984; Drabek 1986).

The scenarios for stability and change of role differentiation need to be amended somewhat, but they still parallel the others on many key factors. Lower levels of improvising are more likely to occur where events are less harmful and socially disruptive (with respect to problems of organizing); where the organizing occurs in self-contained units that are expected to be involved during the immediate emergency period (established and expanding types); where key participants are involved sooner and have experience with postdisaster roles they enact; where the disaster roles performed do not include a leadership component, but are part of broader role repertoires; where complexity of the division of labor is lower at the organizational and key participant levels; where formal preparedness is evidenced at the organizational level, but disaster experience is not evidenced at either the individual or community level; and where the impacted community is metropolitan.

Higher levels of improvising are more likely to occur where events are more harmful and socially disruptive (with respect to problems of organizing); where the organizing occurs in boundary spanning units that are not expected to be involved during the immediate emergency period (extending and emergent types); where key participants are involved later and are not experienced in the postdisaster roles they enact; where the disaster roles performed include a leadership component, but are not part of broader role repertoires; where complexity of the division of labor is higher at the organizational and key participant levels; where disaster experience is evidenced at the individual and community levels, but formal preparedness is not evidenced at the organizational level; and where the impacted community is nonmetropolitan.

Composite Measure of Role Enactment

Our discussion of the correlation and regression analysis for the composite measure (see table 6.6) can be brief because there is relatively little new information to report other than a solid amount of variance explained ($R^2 = .42$). Recall that all independent variables except length of forewarning evidence correlations with one or more of the above three dimensions of role. By simply knowing the direction of their relationships with status-role nexus, role linkages, and role performance, one can predict with great certainty whether they will be stability or change factors on the composite measure. This point is communicated in table 6.7 as part of an overall summary of our findings.

The table cross-classifies the four specifications of role and twenty-four structural and individual correlates. Each independent variable is characterized as a stability or change factor for each specification of role enactment, depending on its zero-order correlation from the regression tables or (when not statistically significant) from Appendix B. The asterisks indicate variables that have statistically significant Beta coefficients in one or more of the four regression equations. Note that for all but one independent variable (instrumental leadership) the direction of the correlation on the composite measure can be predicted correctly from the pattern of correlations on the three dimensions of role that compose it.

The certainty achieved is, in no small way, a statistical artifact of index construction. The components must be correlated with the composite ($r = .75, r = .70$, and $r = .61$) because it is constructed from them, and the independent variables associated with each component (particularly those with higher correlations) are likely also to show at least some association with the composite. More important for theory-building purposes, however, is very high consistency in the direction of empirical relationships summarized in the table.

The table also communicates the centrality of two key independent variables: the DRC typology measure (a structural correlate) and respondent role experience (an individual correlate). The former is a major factor of change for all specifications of role enact-

Table 6.7
Predicting Stability (S) and Change (C) Factors
for the Composite Measure of Role Enactment

Independent Variables	Specifications of Role Enactment			
	Allocation	Complementarity	Performance	Composite
ELEMENT CHARACTERISTIC				
Metric score	stability	stability	(c)	(s)
Domain problem	change	(c)	change*	change*
Task problem	change	(s)	change	(c)
Resource problem	(c)	(s)	change	(c)
Activities problem	(s)	stability	(c)	(s)
ENACTING UNIT CHARACTERISTIC				
DRC typology	change*	change*	change*	change*
Size of unit	stability*	stability*	(s)	stability*
Preparedness	(s)	(c)	stability*	stability
Complexity of response	(s)	(c)	change*	(c)
Social network relevance	stability	stability	stability	stability
Number of network links	(c)	change	change	change
Time network established	change	(c)	(c)	change
Community type	(s)	(s)	stability	stability
Community disaster experience	(s)	(c)	change*	change*
EVENT CHARACTERISTIC				
Length of forewarning	(s)	(s)	(c)	(s)
Magnitude-scope of impact	change	(c)	change*	change
RESPONDENT CHARACTERISTIC				
Time of respondent initiation in organized response	change	change*	change	change
Respondent disaster experience	stability*	(s)	change	stability
Broad postdisaster role repertoire	(s)	(s)	stability	stability
Instrumental leader	(s)	stability*	change*	(c)
Experience in post-disaster role	stability*	stability*	stability*	stability*
Knowledge required	stability	stability	(c)	stability
Boundary spanning respondent links	change*	change*	(c)	change*
Complexity of role enactment	(c)	change	change*	change

* Indicates statistically significant Beta coefficient
() Indicates direction of correlation in Appendix B

ment, and the latter is a major factor of stability for all specifications as well. And as noted above, the two variables are inversely related to each other ($r = -.24$). Not only are they important in their own right, but their respective patterns of associations with other independent variables has made the preceding scenarios that much easier to construct.

These scenarios themselves point to the closed system dynamics of social structuring in established and expanding units and the open system dynamics of social structuring in extending and emergent ones.[21] They also highlight the mutual relevance of disaster event, cultural, and structural forces for unraveling what goes on during the emergency period. Using table 6.7 as our guide, we infer overall scenarios for role enactment in its totality as a means of highlighting the continuity of findings from this chapter with those found (in chapter 2) during the first phase of our research.

Stability of role enactment is more likely to occur during events that are less harmful and socially disruptive (with respect to problems of organizing); where there is evidence of formal organizing in larger and self-contained units that are expected to be involved during the immediate emergency period (established and expanding types); where key participants become involved sooner and have experience with both disasters and the postdisaster roles they enact; where the disaster roles performed do not include a leadership component, but do require greater knowledge, and are parts of broader role repertoires; where complexity of the division of labor is lower at both the organizational and key participant levels; where formal preparedness is evidenced at the organizational level, but disaster experience is not evidenced at the community level; and where the community is metropolitan.

Change of role enactment is more likely to occur during events that are more harmful and socially disruptive (with respect to problems of organizing); where there is evidence of collective behavior in smaller and boundary spanning units that are not expected to be involved during the immediate emergency period (extending and emergent types); where key participants become involved later and do not have experience with either disasters or the postdisaster roles they enact; where the disaster roles performed include a leadership component, but do not require greater knowledge, and are not parts of broader role repertoires; where complexity of the division of labor is higher at the organizational and key participant levels; where disaster experience is evidenced at the community level, but formal preparedness is not evidenced at the organizational level; and where the community is nonmetropolitan.

If you review the findings from the first phase of our work (see chapter 2), you will see how remarkably consistent they are.[22] Thus despite the fact that Ralph Turner and we were not quite sure about what we were after during the first phase; despite the fact that we made major revisions in our conception and measurement of all three dimensions of role and, in particular, role linkages and role performance dimensions; and despite the fact our unit of analysis and sampling plan were completely different; the findings from the latest phase of our work are both consistent with and extend considerably those from the first phase. We, of course, hoped that we were on the right track several years ago. We are convinced now that we are on the right track. The final chapter will formalize what we are learning about organization and role.

7

A Theory of Disaster, Organization, and Role

The "need" for theory lies in the human behavior of wanting to impose order on unordered experiences. . . . It goes without saying that the same set of experiences may be ordered, or theorized about in very different ways.

(Dubin 1978, 6)

We have attempted to order our observations of social response to disaster in two different ways: initially as a process of organizing with reference to a structural code; and then as a process of role enactment in terms of three core dimensions. But in conceiving and measuring organizing and role enactment as discrete processes, our theoretical vision has always been that they are mutually related. Thus for theory-building purposes, we believe they can be independent or dependent with respect to each other.

We have observed social structure at two different levels of analysis—the organizational and the individual. The organizational level was used earlier in our research program to describe the commonality of formal organizing and collective behavior. We then attempted to describe role enactment at the same level of analysis. This proved to be impossible given the limits of the archives. Thus we switched to the individual level in specifying role allocation (status-role nexus), role complementarity (role linkages), role differentiation (role performance), and a composite measure as dependent variables. The previously constructed formal organizing–collective behavior metric now serves, along with many other correlates, as an explanatory variable in our efforts to unravel individual role enactments.

We hope that the details of the exploratory modeling were communicated thoroughly in chapter 6 because they provide the empirical foundations for what is to follow. The theory can now be specified succinctly because, to a large extent, it simply formalizes the empirical generalizations we have already documented. The substantive foundations of the theory are obviously multifaceted. As we tried to show in several previous chapters, however, Ralph Turner's influence on our thinking has been singularly important. The very practical problem remains of what procedural steps should be taken to actually construct a formal theory. We have found Robert Dubin's (1978) programmatic treatment of the problem to be a valuable intellectual tool.[1]

Dubin identifies five components of any theory that we will use to organize our presentation in this chapter. We have amended them slightly to make more explicit the empirical side of theory building. Our characterization of these components should orient the reader to the sociological subject matter at hand (Dubin 1978, 7–8):[2]

> A sociological theory of disaster, organization, and role starts with *(1) concepts* which can be used to describe social structure during the emergency period of disaster. The theory then specifies the manner in which these concepts relate to each other, or their *(2) laws of interaction* (empirical generalizations). Because most sociological theories capture limited portions of social reality, the empirical limits or *(3) boundaries* of the theory must be defined within which the theory is expected to hold. Because social structure is complex, all sociological theories must identify the structural conditions or *(4) system states* within which concepts are presumed to interact in different ways. Once concepts, laws of interaction, boundaries, and system states have been specified, the theorist is then able to derive truth statements or *(5) predictions* which represent logical and empirical conclusions about the theory in operation.

The heart of any theory is its concepts, laws of interaction, and boundaries. If they are well-stated, then system states (additional boundary conditions) and predictions (truth claims of a fully specified theory) can be communicated in a straightforward manner.[3] While the above statement gives explicit expression to key parts of any theory, we think it is equally important to begin with a very clear understanding of its overall structure. Figure 7.1 communicates that structure for the theory being proposed in this chapter.

Note initially in figure 7.1 that role enactment and organizing are inclusive (summative) constructs, which specify what is to be explained.[4] The arrows going to and from these two endogenous constructs indicate that they are reciprocally related. However, only the arrow pointing from organizing to role enactment is solid, indicating that this is the causal direction we have focused on in

Figure 7.1

A Theory of Disaster, Organization, and Role

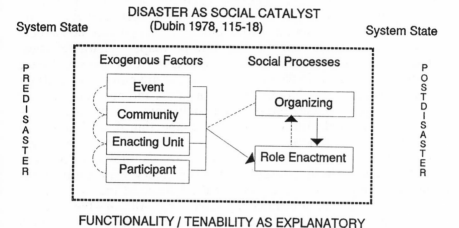

FUNCTIONALITY / TENABILITY AS EXPLANATORY
PRINCIPLES (R. Turner 1980, 128-30)

EVENT CHARACTERISTICS
Length of forewarning
Physical harm (magnitude-scope)
Social disruption (domain, tasks,
    resources, activities problems)
*Duration of impact

COMMUNITY CHARACTERISTICS
Type (metropolitan/nonmetropolitan)
Disaster experience
*Demographic, economic, and
    political indicators

ENACTING UNIT CHARACTERISTICS
DRC typology measure
Disaster preparedness
Size
*Other structural indicators

PARTICIPANT CHARACTERISTICS
Role experience
Disaster experience
Leadership
    instrumental
    expressive
*Other status characteristics
    ascribed
    achieved
*Orientations (perceptions, values, attitudes, beliefs)

ORGANIZING
Structural form (metric score)
Timing
*Duration
Complexity of organizing
Knowledge required (aggregated)
Social networking (number of
    network links)

ROLE ENACTMENT
Structural form
    Role allocation (status-role nexus)
    Role complementarity (role linkages)
    Role differentiation (role performance)
    Overall stability/change (composite
        measure)
Timing
*Duration
Complexity of role enactment
Knowledge required
Social networking (boundary spanning
    links)

*represents new variables which can be used to expand boundaries of the theory the exploratory modeling summarized in the previous chapter. While our level of analysis remains the individual participant, we believe that with more complete aggregate data on role enactments, the theory can be tested at the organizational level as well.[5]

The figure also identifies four blocks of exogenous constructs (event, community, enacting unit, and participant characteristics) that are causally related to role enactment (solid arrow). As we showed many times in the last chapter, there are numerous relationships among the five blocks (four exogenous and one endogenous) of contextual variables that we think help unravel empirically how roles are enacted. The dashed lines connecting these blocks are apropos of this point, but in the interest of parsimony (i.e., reducing the number of possible laws of interaction), such relationships will not be specified in the presentation of the theory. Both endogenous and exogenous blocks are listed at the bottom of the figure along with the variables subsumed by each one. All variables except those with asterisks have been measured in some fashion through spadework with the archives.

Notice how the rectangular block both bounds the theory and expresses its permeability. We will highlight that permeability in our later discussion of boundaries. Two system states of the broader impacted community are indicated on the left and right hand margins. They serve as further boundary conditions. As illustrated many times in the previous chapters, our theory speaks directly to the transition from one system state (predisaster) to another (postdisaster). Our continuing use of disaster as social catalyst (from Dubin) is specified at the top of the rectangle. The possible utility of functionality and tenability (from Ralph Turner) as explanatory principles is specified at the bottom of the rectangle.

The theory will be presented as a linear recursive system. This is consistent with the correlation and regression analysis employed in the previous chapter, the sequential time order implied by relationships between the four blocks of exogenous variables and role enactment, and the causal assymetry we have imposed on all relationships between organizing and role enactment. Obvious problems of imperfect measurement and potential problems of nonadditivity and nonlinearity aside, the result is the most logically coherent, realistic, and parsimonious theory we can muster at this point.

Concepts

We begin with brief discussions of disaster as social catalyst and the two explanatory principles of role enactment (functionality and tenability) proposed by Ralph Turner. This is followed by respective discussions of organizing and role enactment as analytically parallel blocks of endogenous variables. The section closes with a discussion of the four blocks of exogenous variables. In discussing what is a large number of variables, we will provide formal definitions only when they are necessary to the exposition, or to introduce concepts that we have not measured in our prior work.

Disaster as Social Catalyst

Similar to their use in chemistry, Dubin (1978, 115) characterizes social catalysts as empirical concepts whose presence (some non-zero value) in a social system is necessary for two or more other concepts to relate in specific ways. Such relationships can then be expressed as laws of interaction based on the presence of the catalyst. Interestingly enough, one of Dubin's primary examples of social catalysts is disaster. It is therefore appropriate that some formal definition of disaster be provided.

In a summary article for the *Annual Review of Sociology,* Kreps (1984) revised only modestly Fritz's (1961) earlier definition of disaster because it continues to serve the field well. Kreps amended it slightly again in a special issue on taxonomy for the *International Journal of Mass Emergencies and Disasters* (Kreps 1989b, 219) to distinguish defining characteristics from antecedents or consequences. Thus disasters are defined as

> nonroutine events in which societies or their larger subsystems (e.g. regions, communities) are socially disrupted *and* physically harmed. The key defining characteristics of such events are (1) length of forewarning, (2) magnitude of impact, (3) scope of impact, and (4) duration of impact.

Thus disasters (natural, ecological, technological, economic, civil, military, or whatever other type might be of interest) have life histories, which can be designated in time and space. The phrase "nonroutine events" is used to distinguish disasters as unusual and dramatic happenings from the reservoir of everyday problems and concerns of humankind. The conjunctive *and* is emphasized to distinguish disasters from emergencies. The designation "societies or their larger subsystems" means that social disruption and physical harm, however they may be measured, must be observable at relatively high levels of aggregation.

As social catalyst, the above definition of disaster does two very important things. First, it subsumes the four variables in the block of event characteristics represented in figure 7.1. We have measured, albeit crudely, three of the four defining properties of disaster during our research. Length of forewarning is the time lag between threat cues and first onset of disaster impacts. Magnitude and scope of impact subsume a variety of measures of physical harm. Social disruption is multifaceted as well, but we have focused on problems of organizing (as they relate to Kreps's structural code) in our work thus far. Duration of impact is a very elusive temporal variable that has not been addressed in our research or disaster research generally.[6]

Second, using the disaster as a social catalyst places very important boundaries on the theory being proposed. All disasters have life histories. Thus their pre-, trans-, and postimpact time phases can (and arguably should) be given commensurate attention. By implication, disasters can (and arguably should) be treated as social constructions. This means that their defining properties can just as easily be considered as dependent variables for theoretical purposes. The theory being proposed is therefore bounded by the immediate emergency period for a very narrow range of events, and the properties of these events are seen as determinants rather than consequences of social structure. Such boundary specifications are very important because issues of disaster prevention and mitigation are both interesting to disaster researchers and major public policy concerns.

Functionality and Tenability as Explanatory Principles

As noted in chapter 3, Ralph Turner invokes the above principles to answer questions about why there is stability or change of role allocation, role complementarity, and role differentiation. For our purposes, we think the functionality principle is best considered as a systemic property. The focus is on how well the organized response is working. An efficient organized response is one that minimizes the human effort needed to mobilize resources and perform tasks. An effective organized response is one that fulfills its reason for being. We think the tenability principle is best considered as an individual property. The focus is on the extent to which involvement in the organized response is personally rewarding to a participant. For Turner, tenability can be determined in at least two ways: first, the extent to which the most desirable postdisaster roles go to the most powerful participants or categories of participants; and second, the extent to which there is a fit between individual dispositions (attitudes, preferences, skills, and aptitudes) and the requirements of roles that are enacted. In either case, patterns of cooperation and conflict with respect to the extrinsic and intrinsic rewards of role enactmant become central.

Turner's conceptions of functionality and tenability are easy to grasp and very interesting. We do not consider them to be unmeasured explanatory principles, however, because they can just as easily be treated as antecedents or consequences of role processes. Efforts should therefore be made to measure functionality and tenability directly. We will illustrate how this might be done later in the chapter. Treating Turner's explanatory principles in this way expands the boundaries of the theory in directions that we think can make it more powerful and complete.

Social Structuring: Organizing and Role Enactment

Our conception and measurement of Kreps's structural code and three core dimensions of role have already been discussed in great detail. The formal organizing–collective behavior metric (metric score) and the four specifications of role enactment are measures that describe social process. They are represented in figure 7.1 as parallel measures of structural form because we suspect that explanations of organizational and role dynamics ultimately will turn out to be substitutable. With that hypothetical possibility in mind, it is very important to have as many other parallel measures of social structuring as possible.

Five additional sets of analytically parallel variables are listed in figure 7.1. Measuring the two temporal variables (timing and duration) requires using the onset of disaster impacts as a reference point for determining both when organizing or individual involvement begins, and then how long each continues. Unfortunately, Kreps overlooked these key temporal variables in constructing the original data file on 423 organized responses. However, timing of organizing was measured in the first phase of our role study (see chapter 2), and both timing and duration of organizing were examined in a study of emergent organized responses by Saunders and Kreps (1987). While individual measures of timing and duration were introduced in the latest phase of our research as well, sufficient data could only be produced for the former.

The idea of parallel measures of structural complexity was introduced in the previous chapter. Complexity at the organizational level was measured as the total number of tasks performed (complexity of response). Complexity at the individual level was measured as the total number of roles represented by all of respondent's links with other role incumbents (complexity of role enactment).[7] While knowledge required for the enactment of roles may be seen as a related (technological) component of complexity, for the time being it should remain a separate concept. Because knowledge required has only been measured at the individual level of analysis, any subsequent organizational comparisons will require an aggregated measure.

Social networking at the organizational level was measured as the total number of social units linked to the organized response during the emergency period (number of network links). Social networking at the individual level was measured as the proportion of the respondent's links that are boundary spanning (boundary spanning links). In pursuit of simplicity, we have dropped from consideration other networking variables at the organizational level of analysis (social network relevance and time network established). The pattern of covariances among social networking variables for the respondent and earlier organizational samples suggests that little is lost theoretically by doing so.[8]

Exogenous Variables (Event, Community, Enacting Unit, and Participant Characteristics)

The event characteristics listed in figure 7.1 have already been discussed in relation to disaster as a social catalyst. Obviously we have only scratched the surface for the community block with our metropolitan/nommetropolitan distinction and measure of community disaster experience. Demographic, economic, and political indicators are listed as potential new variables whose measurement can specify a great deal more about the social structure of the impacted community. Many such measures are readily available through public access data, and they can be produced at low cost.

The block of enacting unit variables includes three measures we have used already, with the DRC typology proving to be a powerful variable at both organizational and individual levels of analysis. We list other structural indicators whose measurement can specify further details about the enacting unit. At both organizational and community levels, however, we suggest that size is perhaps the most powerful generator of structural form (Kreps 1989a, 197–207).

The last block, labeled participant characteristics, includes two variables we have measured before, with role experience proving to be consistently powerful at the individual level of analysis for the four specifications of role enactment. We list status characteristics (ascribed and achieved) and orientations (perceptions, attitudes, values, and beliefs) to focus attention on a wide range of variables that may be quite important for explaining role enactments, quite simply, because they tell us much more about role incumbents as individuals. Two examples will illustrate what we have in mind.

First, once occupations have been identified for responding individuals, they can immediately be given prestige scores using the standard National Opinion Research Center (NORC) rating system. One might hypothesize, for example, that occupational prestige and knowledge requirements of postdisaster roles are positively related because of the substantial education and training components of jobs having higher prestige. One might argue also that people having higher occupational prestige will be more likely to exercise leadership roles in an organized response because they are experienced in doing so. Along the same line, one might hypothesize that the greater the difference in prestige scores for an incumbent pair, the more likely will there be a power differential operating in the relationship.

Second, it is important to learn more about why people become involved during the emergency period, and how they feel about it later (Zurcher 1989). This becomes particularly interesting when such involvement is not expected (i.e., it has not been institutionalized prior to the disaster). It is conventional wisdom among disaster researchers that altruism is an important and powerful motive for sustaining prosocial action during certain types of crises (Fritz 1961; Barton 1969). If that is the case, then expressions of altruistic motivations for involvement and expressions of intrinsic satisfaction when that involvement has ended should be related.

At this point we have no clear hypotheses about how orientations or status characteristics relate to the three dimensions of role enactment. However, focused attention on the measurement of these and other variables would make it easy to find out. Such measurement would also have important implications for empirically grounding Turner's explanatory principles. With respect to tenability (and the individual), for example, we can measure participant perceptions of the personal rewards of role enactment, the relevance of role conflict, and the exercise of power vis-à-vis other role incumbents. With respect to tenability (and the social system), we can determine the degree of fit between human capacities and organizational requirements by documenting more thoroughly the status characteristics of participants.

Learning more about role incumbents as individuals is important for still another reason. As noted in chapter 3 (see page 85), one of the major limitations of our work is that we have had little to say about role enactment and the self concept (Turner 1976, 1978, 1980). We continue to believe that greater knowledge about the Meadian self will lead to more powerful explanations of disaster, organization, and role. By expanding the boundaries of the theory to include a broader range of participant characteristics, we can begin to show how and why this is so.

Laws of Interaction

A general determination of the number of possible laws in any theory can be derived by the formula for combinations of N things taken two at a time $[N(N-1)/2]$.[9] In chapter 6, for example, with twenty-eight variables there were 378 correlations (empirical generalizations) that might be of theoretical interest. However, we have simplified matters considerably by specifying only the three core dimensions of role enactment as our focus dependent variables. As such, laws of interaction are needed to connect stability and change of role allocation (status-role nexus), role complementarity (role linkages), and role differentiation (role performance) with other characteristics of role enactment, organizing as a contextual process, and the four blocks of exogenous variables.

Table 7.1 specifies some fifty-eight laws of interaction that are important theoretically at this point in our theory building. Three general types are highlighted. The first type are laws for which no empirical examination has been undertaken. The statements are speculations on our part, but illustrate how the theory can be expanded by adding explanatory concepts. The major sources of new explanatory concepts are illustrated in the community (demographic, economic, and political indicators), enacting unit (other structural indicators), and participant (status characteristics and orientations) blocks of variables. The second (significant bivariate correlations) and third (significant multiple regression coefficients) types of laws represent weaker to stronger empirical generalizations from our archival studies. The laws themselves are arranged in terms of the blocks of variables to which they refer.

All laws of interaction are determinant (Dubin 1978, 109–112) because direction of covariation (positive or negative) is made explicit. All laws are assymetric (Mullins 1974, 4–5) and, with the exception of the relationship between role allocation and role complementarity, the three dimensions of role enactment are never identified as independent variables. This certainly does not mean that they cannot be. As noted earlier, we think that organizing and role enactment will ultimately be evidenced as parallel processes that are reciprocally related.[10] Finally, with the possible exception of leadership (instrumental or expressive), the laws of interaction connecting role enactment with the exogenous variables are sequential (Dubin 1978, 101–4) because time can readily be used to order the relationships.

Table 7.1 communicates formally the laws we identify as important theoretically. There are several points we wish to make about them. First, note the many parallels stipulated between the effects of organizing and other role enactment variables on one or more of the three basic dimensions (e.g., I.3 and II.3, I.4 and II.4, I.5 and II.5 and so on). The comparable empirical patterns for complexity, social networking, and timing dimensions that we have uncovered give us considerable confidence that many laws of interaction about organizing and role enactment are substitutable. When sufficient organizational-level data on these parallel processes become available, the result may be a much more parsimonious expression of the theory.

Second, duration of role enactment and duration of organized response currently are unmeasured variables so the laws related to them are hypothetical. We reason that duration factors and role allocation are positively related (I.11 and II.11) and, in this instance, role allocation might better serve as an independent variable. In other words, sustained participation is a more likely consequence when there is consistency of the status-role nexus because it is part and parcel of expected involvement. On the other hand, we suspect that the potential for discontinuous role linkages (I.12 and II.12) and improvised performance (I.13 and II.13) will increase with longer duration of participation because of the fluid nature of demands during the emergency period.

Third, it is important to recall that variables representing physical harm and social disruption are themselves positively related. Thus the preponderance of inverse relationships between impact variables and role enactment (III.1 to III.11) point to the obvious theoretical importance of disaster as an agent of social change. Currently unmeasured, we speculate that duration of impact will operate in the same way as other measures of impact. Finally, although it did not show any significant relationships in the present study, length of forewarning is included (III.12 to III.14) because it was related with role-making during the first phase of our research. Physical harm and social disruption are change factors because they create unique demands. Forewarning is a change factor because it provides time to adapt existing social arrangements to unique demands.

Fourth, community level variables are important theoretically

Table 7.1
Laws of Interaction for a Theory of
Disaster, Organization, and Role

I. ROLE ENACTMENT ON ITS OWN TERMS

1. Role allocation and role complementarity are positively related.[c]
2. Complexity of role enactment and role complementarity are inversely related.[b]
3. Complexity of role enactment and role differentiation are inversely related.[c]
4. Knowledge required for role enactment and role allocation are positively related.[b]
5. Knowledge required for role enactment and role complementarity are positively related.[b]
6. Social networking of role enactment and role allocation are inversely related.[c]
7. Social networking of role enactment and role complementarity are inversely related.[c]
8. Timing of role enactment and role allocation are inversely related.[b]
9. Timing of role enactment and role complementarity are inversely related.[c]
10. Timing of role enactment and role differentiation are inversely related.[c]
11. Duration of role enactment and role allocation are positively related.[a]
12. Duration of role enactment and role complementarity are inversely related.[a]
13. Duration of role enactment and role performance are inversely related.[a]

II. ORGANIZING AND ROLE ENACTMENT

1. Formal organizing-collective behavior metric and role allocation are positively related.[b]
2. Formal organizing-collective behavior metric and role complementarity are positively related.[b]
3. Complexity of organizing and role differentiation are inversely related.[c]
4. Knowledge required for enactment of organized response and role allocation are positively related.[a]
5. Knowledge required for enactment of organized response and role complementarity are positively related.[a]
6. Knowledge required for enactment of organized response and role differentiation are positively related.[a]
7. Social networking of organized response and role allocation are inversely related.[b]
8. Social networking of organized response and role complementarity are inversely related.[b]
9. Social networking of organized response and role differentiation are inversely related.[b]
10. Timing of response initiation and role complementarity are inversely related.[b]
11. Duration of organized response and role allocation are positively related.[a]
12. Duration of organized response and role complementarity are inversely related.[a]
13. Duration of organized response and role differentiation are inversely related.[a]

Table 7.1
Laws of Interaction for a Theory of
Disaster, Organization, and Role (cont.)

III. EVENT CHARACTERISTICS AND ROLE ENACTMENT

1. Magnitude-scope of impact and role allocation are inversely related.[b]
2. Magnitude-scope of impact and role differentiation are inversely related.[c]
3. Domain problems and role allocation are inversely related.[b]
4. Domain problems and role differentiation are inversely related.[c]
5. Task problems and role allocation are inversely related.[b]
6. Task problems and role differentiation are inversely related.[b]
7. Resource problems and role differentiation are inversely related.[b]
8. Activities problems and role complementarity are positively related.[b]
9. Duration of impact and role allocation are inversely related.[a]
10. Duration of impact and role complementarity are inversely related.[a]
11. Duration of impact and role differentiation are inversely related.[a]
12. Length of forewarning and role allocation are inversely related.[b]
13. Length of forewarning and role complementarity are inversely related.[b]
14. Length of forewarning and role differentiation are inversely related.[b]

IV. COMMUNITY CHARACTERISTICS AND ROLE ENACTMENT

1. Community type and role differentiation are positively related.[b]
2. Disaster experience and role differentiation are inversely related.[c]

V. ENACTING UNIT CHARACTERISTICS AND ROLE ENACTMENT

1. DRC typology measure and role allocation are inversely related.[c]
2. DRC typology measure and role complementarity are inversely related.[c]
3. DRC typology measure and role differentiation are inversely related.[c]
4. Disaster preparedness and role differentiation are positively related.[c]
5. Unit size and role allocation are positively related.[c]
6. Unit size and role complementarity are positively related.[c]

VI. PARTICIPANT CHARACTERISTICS AND ROLE ENACTMENT

1. Role experience and role allocation are positively related.[c]
2. Role experience and role complementarity are positively related.[c]
3. Role experience and role differentiation are positively related.[c]
4. Disaster experience and role allocation are positively related.[c]
5. Disaster experience and role differentiation are inversely related.[b]
6. Instrumental leadership and role complementarity are positively related.[c]
7. Instrumental leadership and role differentiation are inversely related.[c]
8. Expressive leadership and role allocation are positively related.[a]
9. Expressive leadership and role complementarity are positively related.[a]
10. Expressive leadership and role differentiation are inversely related.[a]

---

[a] indicates no empirical examination undertaken
[b] indicates statistically significant bivariate correlation
[c] indicates statistically significant multiple regression coefficient

because they represent what Kreps (1984, 323–24) refers to as the absorptive capacities of social systems. Our most interesting finding in this regard is that community disaster experience is an important cultural resource for responding flexibly to the demands of disaster (IV.1). But the crude measure of community type (IV.2) needs to be replaced by indicators that provide a more precise demographic, economic, and political profile. That profile should reflect the cultural and structural capacities of the impacted community. While there certainly are limits to the absorptive capacities of social systems, we know precious little about them.

Fifth, it is important to emphasize again that the DRC typology is a consistently powerful variable (V.1 to V.3). Established and expanding responses are very different from extending and emergent ones with respect to both how roles are enacted and how organizing occurs. Preparedness is a source of clarity in role performance (V.4), but as findings from the first phase of our research suggest, it may have dual value as a source of flexibility. The consistent pattern for enacting unit size is stability of role enactment (V.5 and V.6). We think this is a function of the greater (i.e., bureaucratic) need for predictability that comes with increasing size. And while this variable can readily serve as a general referent for a variety of organizational characteristics, efforts to measure such characteristics may have theoretical payoffs.

Sixth, role experience has proven to be a powerful individual correlate of role enactment, and the consistent direction of its relationships (VI.1 to VI.3) points unambiguously to structural stability. However, disaster experience (VI.4 and VI.5) and the two dimensions of leadership (VI.6 to VI.10) operate in different ways, depending on which dimension of role enactment is being considered (allocation or complementarity versus differentiation). The reason for this difference is subtle but important.

Recall from chapters 5 and 6 that where postdisaster role incumbency is existing as opposed to new, such incumbency is occupationally based to a very substantial degree. Our findings suggest that disaster experience and instrumental leadership are part and parcel of many occupations that are at once expected to be involved (consistent status-role nexus) and linked to each other (continuous role linkages) during the emergency period. But such patterns do not allow us to predict how postdisaster roles will actually be performed. Disaster experience and instrumental leadership are positively correlated with improvised performance. We think that once measured, expressive leadership will evidence a similar pattern.

Finally, we think that measurement of other status characteristics and orientations of participants has great potential for putting Ralph Turner's functionality and tenability principles to work. We have proffered no laws of interaction in this regard because we have little idea as to how they might relate to the three dimensions of role. We suspect, however, that functionality and tenability are better treated as dependent rather than independent variables. We will illustrate this strategy in the next section as it relates to expanding the boundaries of the theory.

Boundaries

Dubin's treatment of boundaries (1978, 125–43) is important; not because it makes their determination a simple matter, but because it forces theorists to be sensitive to the limitations of their explanations and predictions. Attention always begins and ends with concepts because a theory's explanations and predictions must be constructed from them. A theory is bounded when the limiting values of its concepts are known. Its boundaries are closed when all concepts are specified logically and empirically. Its boundaries are opened when the specification of existing concepts is being changed, or when new concepts are necessary to make explanations more powerful and predictions more precise.

While boundary specification is both a logical and an empirical matter, we will focus largely on the empirical side for two basic reasons. First, we have found the logical tools Dubin provides to be of limited value when they are divorced from the empirical side of our work.[11] Second, the empirical consideration of dependent and independent variables raises a number of boundary conditions that are quite specific. In effect, our discussion of boundaries extends from the conception and measurement problems we have grappled with throughout the various phases of this research program. In what follows, therefore, we will take another brief look at the concepts represented in figure 7.1 and table 7.1 with limiting values in mind, and then illustrate how the boundaries of the theory can be expanded.

Closed Boundaries and the Limiting Values of Existing Concepts

Boundary specification becomes an elaborate exercise with over thirty variables because each one of them raises both logical and empirical issues. Accordingly, we have identified what for us, at least, are only the most obvious and compelling boundary conditions of the theory. These conditions derive from our conception and measurement of the six blocks of variables summarized earlier. We have tried to formalize them with the set of explicit statements found in table 7.2. The statements are arrayed in terms of the block of variables to which they refer.

Several comments are in order. First, it must be remembered that the theory only addresses role dynamics at the individual level of analysis (I.1). Expansion to the organizational level remains critically important, but the data production required to aggregate individual role enactments is a major undertaking (witness chapter 4). The larger the enacting unit studied, the more difficult do data production problems become. Some sort of participant sampling plan that is proportional to unit size is essential. Given the difficulties of doing fieldwork during the emergency period, more intensive studies of fewer organizations seems to be the appropriate strategy for primary data collection.

Second, it is important to emphasize that role enactments can occur in a wide variety of structural contexts, only some of which evidence organization (I.2). The theory is therefore bounded in this respect. Kreps's structural code identifies some forty nonorganizational forms of association within which role enactment takes place. By breaking organizing down into stages, we addressed many of these nonorganizational forms in the first phase of our research. It would be very interesting to compare role enactment in successful versus unsuccessful attempts to organize.

Third, the standardization achieved by using occupation to calibrate stability/change of role allocation and role complementarity may have a theoretical cost (I.3 and I.4). Stability may be underrepresented because other parts of participant status sets are excluded from analysis. In our research, however, we were able to estimate the biasing effects of standardization. They appeared to be slight for role allocation and modest for role complementarity. We continue to believe that standardization by occupation is the right strategy.

In the kinds of disasters we have studied, there is substantial evidence of structural stability because the impact ratios are low. In these circumstances, standardization by occupation provides a useful way of identifying change in the face of stability. In more severe disasters, however, standardization by occupation provides a useful way of identifying stability in the face of change. For the same reason, more severe disasters would undoubtedly provide greater opportunity to calibrate role differentiation in terms of all three levels of improvising (I.5 and pages 92–95).

Fourth, complexity of role enactment is an inferior measure to the one we were after. The preferred measure (I.6) requires aggregate-level data on the number of roles performed in the organized response. Along the same line, it is important to note that we did not capture the full range of values that are theoretically important for variables such as complexity of organizing (II.1), magnitude-scope of impact (III.2), length of forewarning (III.3), community type (IV.1), and unit size (V.2). Thus all laws of interaction involving these variables are limited to the lower ends of their respective distributions.

Fifth, variables such as social networking (I.7 and II.2), disaster experience (IV.2, IV.3, and VI.2), disaster preparedness (V.1), and role experience (VI.1) are limited to presence rather than degree (intensity, duration) during or prior to the emergency. Obviously expanded measurement for these and other variables would be valuable theoretically.[12] Sometimes important improvements are relatively easy to accomplish, such as timing of organizing problems (III.4) and instrumental leadership (VI.3). For example, had we simply determined whether instrumental leadership was established during or prior to a disaster, it would have been much easier to compare its relationships with role linkages (positive) and role performance (negative).

Finally we think the last boundary condition is the most important one. At this point the theory is limited empirically to the emergency periods of a small set of natural disasters in the United States (II.3 and III.1). We have made some progress in unraveling role enactment and organizing in these social contexts. We strongly suspect, however, that the theory can be applied to the emergency periods of any disaster (natural or otherwise), in any society, and during any historical period. We also believe that the theory has relevance for all time phases (predisaster, emergency period, long-term recovery) of disasters.[13] These are bold claims, certainly, but they derive from the fact the basic constructs we work with are not confined to the empirical materials we are using.

Expanding the Boundaries of the Theory

As noted earlier, one can open the boundaries of a theory by changing the specification of existing concepts or by adding new ones. Our discussion of table 7.2 relates to the former strategy, but we think the latter is equally important. We close our discussion of boundaries by illustrating empirically how this can be done. In this regard, we suggest that a theoretically critical expansion of the

Table 7.2
Boundary Conditions for a Theory of
Disaster, Organization, and Role

I. ROLE ENACTMENT ON ITS OWN TERMS

1. The level of analysis is the individual. Role enactments are not aggregated for purposes of organizational comparisons.
2. Individual role enactments only occur in organized as opposed to other structural contexts.
3. Consistency/inconsistency of status-role nexus (role allocation) is based strictly on pre-disaster occupation of participants. Other parts of status sets are excluded from consideration.
4. Continuity/discontinuity of role linkages (role complementarity) is based strictly on pre-disaster occupations of role pairs and incumbent pairs. Other parts of status sets are excluded from consideration.
5. Role performance (role differentiation) does not include the highest level of improvising (only two of three original levels captured).
6. Complexity of role enactment is based only on the total number of roles represented by all of the participant's relationships with other individuals within or external to the organized response of which the participant is a part. The preferred contextual measure is the total number of roles enacted in the organized response.
7. Social networking of role enactment is based on the number of boundary spanning linkages, but not their intensity.

II. ORGANIZING AND ROLE ENACTMENT

1. Complexity of organizing does not capture higher levels of complexity.
2. Social networking of organized response is based on the number of boundary spanning links but not their intensity.
3. Organizing and role enactment only occurs during the immediate emergency period of disaster events.

III. EVENT CHARACTERISTICS AND ROLE ENACTMENT

1. The theory applies only to disaster events that are earthquakes, tornadoes, floods, or hurricanes.
2. Magnitude-scope of impact does not capture higher levels of physical harm.
3. Length of forewarning does not capture longer degrees of forewarning.
4. Measures of organizing problems (domain, tasks, resources, or activities related) do not specify when they occur during the life history of organizing, and if or when they are resolved.

IV. COMMUNITY CHARACTERISTICS AND ROLE ENACTMENT

1. Community type does not capture higher levels of population size in metropolitan areas
2. Disaster experience is limited to the previous ten years.
3. Disaster experience is based on the presence but not intensity of experience

Table 7.2
Boundary Conditions for a Theory of
Disaster, Organization, and Role (cont.)

V.   ENACTING UNIT CHARACTERISTICS AND ROLE ENACTMENT

1.   Disaster preparedness is based on the existence of written plans or formal training, but not their content or intensity of use prior to or during the disaster.
2.   Unit size does not capture higher levels of organizational size.

VI.   PARTICIPANT CHARACTERISTICS

1.   Role experience is based on presence but not duration of experience.
2.   Disaster experience is based on presence but not intensity of experience.
3.   Instrumental leadership is based on presence but not timing of incumbency.

theory is the measurement of functionality and tenability as consequences of organizing and role enactment.

Recall that Ralph Turner's functionality principle is best considered at the systemic level of analysis. It has two components: efficiency as that relates to the effort expended during the course of organizing; and effectiveness as that relates to fulfilling the organized response's reason for being. While we have no measure of efficiency, we do have at least a crude measure of the effectiveness component. It is one that Kreps referred to earlier as reason for suspension (Saunders and Kreps 1987).

The central question being addressed is how and why does organization go out of existence (Faia 1986). Kreps measured suspension of organization in his original data production by identifying a successful end state: *need met, organization ended.* Measurement involves using a dummy variable to distinguish this reason for suspension from other ones (e.g., the loss of resources or absorption by another entity).[14] The relevant distributions for the 423 (organizational) file are as follows: reached the successful end state (coded 1, N = 300, 71 percent); and did not (coded 0, N = 123, 29 percent). The relevant distributions for the 257 (participant) file are as follows: reached the successful end state (coded 1, N = 161, 63 percent); and did not (coded 0, N = 96, 37 percent).

We thought it would be interesting to see if patterns of organizing, role enactment, and functionality are related. In an earlier study of emergent organized responses (Saunders and Kreps 1987), we found that the probability of reaching the successful end state was increased by the dynamics of formal organizing (as opposed to collective behavior), as described by Kreps's metric. Recall from table 7.1 and chapter 6 that formal organizing is also a stability factor with respect to role enactment. We therefore concluded that scenarios of stable (as opposed to changing) role enactment would predict reaching the successful end state as well.

To test this prediction, we ran separate statistical models on the participant and organizational data files. For each file we regressed reason for suspension with as many common variables as possible. The role composite measure was used for the participant file to express role dynamics more efficiently as an independent variable. The obvious difference in the two data files is that there are no aggregated data on role enactment variables for the organizational file. Our findings are reported in tables 7.3 (participant file) and 7.4 (organizational file).

The prediction is confirmed.[15] The overlap of significant Beta coefficients is notable, with the formal organizing–collective behavior metric being the most powerful predictor in both equations. Much more important, however, is that all significant correlations and Beta coefficients in both equations are consistent with (1) a scenario that equates formal organizing and stable role enactment with reaching the successful end state and (2) a scenario that equates collective behavior and changing role enactment with not reaching the successful end state. Such scenarios dovetail beautifully with those developed earlier for stability and change of role enactment. The key question becomes: can we conclude from these findings that the dynamics of collective behavior and changing role enactment are less effective (dysfunctional) than those related to formal organizing and stable role enactment?

As Saunders and Kreps (1987) argued, it depends very much on whether the social system referenced is the organized response or the impacted community. From the standpoint of the organized response, death is death. The dynamics of formal organizing and stable role enactment work to prevent that from happening prematurely during the emergency period. But from the standpoint of the impacted community, survival of a particular organized response is not an imperative. Systemic adaptiveness at this level is represented by often rapid changes in the mix of responding groups and organizations. The dynamics of collective behavior and changing role enactment are likely to be at work when that happens. Thus while suspension in process may be dysfunctional at one level (in this case the organized response), it may point to systemic looseness that is highly functional at a broader level (in this case the impacted community).[16]

A much better test of the functionality principle will be possible when aggregate data on role enactment are available for a relatively

Table 7.3
Correlation and Regression Analysis:
Suspension of Organization (participant sample)

Correlate	Suspension of Organization	
	r	b
ELEMENT CHARACTERISTIC		
Metric score	.29	.23****
Domain problem	-.23	-.16***
Task problem	-.23	-.11*
Resource problem		
Activities problem	-.20	
ENACTING UNIT CHARACTERISTIC		
DRC Typology	-.19	
Size of unit	.13	.11*
Preparedness		
Complexity of response		
Social network relevance	.14	
Number of network links		
Time network established	-.31	-.18***
Community type		
Community disaster experience	-.19	-.18***
EVENT CHARACTERISTIC		
Length of forewarning		
Magnitude-scope of impact	-.17	
RESPONDENT CHARACTERISTIC		
Time of respondent initiation in organized response		
Respondent disaster experience	.13	
Broad postdisaster role repertoire		
Instrumental leader		
Experience in disaster role	.30	.18***
Knowledge required	.16	
Boundary spanning respondent links		
Complexity of role enactment	-.15	
Role composite	.27	
Constant	.60	
R^2 (stepwise)	.30	
N = 257		

* P < .10   ** P < .05   *** P < .01   **** P < .001

large sample of organized responses. Still, the findings reported in tables 7.3 and 7.4 are highly suggestive. They also show how the boundaries of the theory can be expanded in very productive ways.. While we have no way of providing even preliminary tests for either the efficiency component of functionality or the tenability principle, we think Turner's explanatory principles can and should be measured directly during subsequent (primary) data production. As noted earlier, we are particularly interested in relationships between status characteristics and orientations on the one hand, and the power and fit of postdisaster roles on the other.

In closing this section, we believe that the boundaries of this

Table 7.4
Correlation and Regression Analysis:
Suspension of Organization (organized response sample)

Correlate	Suspension of Organization	
	r	b
ELEMENT CHARACTERISTIC		
Metric score	.37	.31****
Domain problem	-.17	
Task problem	-.12	
Resource problem		
Activities problem		
ENACTING UNIT CHARACTERISTIC		
DRC Typlogy	-.25	-.13***
Size of unit		
Preparedness	.09	
Complexity of response		
Social network relevance	.09	
Number of network links		
Time network established	-.19	
Community type	.14	.20****
Community disaster experience	N/A	
EVENT CHARACTERISTIC		
Length of forewarning		
Magnitude-scope of impact	-.20	-.19****
RESPONDENT CHARACTERISTIC		
Time of respondent initiation in organized response	N/A	
Respondent disaster experience	N/A	
Broad postdisaster role repertoire	N/A	
Instrumental leader	N/A	
Experience in disaster role	N/A	
Knowledge required	N/A	
Boundary spanning respondent links	N/A	
Complexity of role enactment	N/A	
Role composite	N/A	
Constant		.36
R^2 (stepwise)		.21
N = 423		

* P < .10   ** P < .05   *** P < .01   **** P < .001

theory can be defined either narrowly or broadly. As Dubin aptly notes (1978, 19–32, 134–35), the greater the number of boundary conditions, the narrower the scope of the theory, regardless of the power of its explanations or the precision of its predictions. Obviously with the twenty-two boundary conditions formalized in table 7.2 (which is only a minimum), the empirical boundaries of this theory are rather restrictive. But please note how quickly and usefully the boundaries can be opened along the lines we have suggested. This is because we are dealing with basic sociological concepts that have wide applicability. The domain of any theory based on them is potentially broad indeed.

System States

As implied earlier (see note 3), our discussion of the last two components of the theory will be brief: system states because they are best thought of as boundary conditions; and predictions because they necessarily derive from laws of interaction.

Dubin argues (1978, 143–46) that one must always refer to the system as a whole in addressing its various conditions. The relevant empirical questions are as follows:[17] first, what is the system; second, what are its various states; third, what are the key components of the system; and fourth, how do these components operate in one system state as opposed to another? We stated earlier that the theory speaks directly to stability/change of role enactment from predisaster to postdisaster time phases. The broadest system referenced is the disaster impacted community. The relevant system states are the community's predisaster as opposed to postdisaster structural arrangements. The relevant components of the community are basic sociological concepts that specify these structural arrangements (status-roles, organizations, and social networks) and the people who enact them. How these components operate differently in predisaster and postdisaster time periods is what the theory is trying to describe and explain.

Predisaster states of the system are represented by values on most of the community, enacting unit, and participant exogenous variables.[18] Event exogenous variables serve as specifications of disaster as a social catalyst. The presence of the catalyst is the point of transition from pre- to postdisaster time periods. The transition from steady state to emergency conditions of the community is represented as patterns of stability/change of role enactment. These patterns are explained by laws of interaction that relate role enactment to forms of organizing and the exogenous variables. The more powerful the laws, the more precise should be the predictions of structural stability and change.

Characterized in this way, system states are best described as further boundary conditions of the theory. There are only two system conditions, one catalyst, and one transition being addressed here. The situation is therefore much simpler than it could be. For example, no attempt is being made to capture the transition from emergency to recovery time periods. Although many postdisaster roles and organized responses are ephemeral, neither is there any attempt to capture the return to normalcy in the community. Finally, no attempt is being made to capture cycles of stability and change in the community across two or more disasters. Although all of these matters are very interesting, they most certainly fall outside the boundaries of the current theory.

One reason core concepts are so important is that their variability means that something very interesting is happening to the system as a whole. In this case, role enactment (especially its three basic dimensions) and organizing (especially the formal organizing–collective behavior metric) serve as state coordinates (Dubin 1978, 151–52) because their values describe the transition from predisaster to postdisaster system states. Moreover, the laws of interaction (empirical generalizations) that connect core concepts with the most powerful independent variables, in this case the DRC typology (an organizational measure) and role experience (an individual measure), are strategic because they order the theory's explanations and predictions about what is happening or will happen to the system as a whole (Dubin 1978, 168–69).

Predictions

As noted earlier, predictions are logical and empirical conclusions from a theory when it is fully specified in terms of concepts, laws of interaction, boundaries, and system states (Dubin 1978, 160–74).[19] The key thing to keep in mind is the essential asymmetry between laws of interaction and propositions. Laws of interaction direct our attention to social process. In this theory, they help us to explain how and why role enactment occurs during the emergency period of disaster. Predictions direct our attention to social outcomes. In this theory, they help us to determine under what circumstances stable as opposed to changing forms of role enactment will occur. We think it follows both logically and empirically that as our descriptions and explanations become more powerful, the predictions that can be derived from them will necessarily become more precise.[20]

The distinction between explanation and prediction is represented very nicely in chapters 3–7. Conceptualization and measurement problems are addressed initially as we attempt to describe patterns of role enactment. What is to be explained becomes more explicit, and a quite natural transition from description to explanation unfolds. The reason for this transition is clear: questions of how and why role enactment occurs become obvious and compelling. We then invent/discover laws of interaction (empirical generalizations) that provide possible answers to these questions through comparative examination of cases. In a very direct way, the correlation analysis formalizes laws of interaction, and the multiple regression analysis identifies those laws that are potentially the most powerful (e.g., the DRC typology and role experience). These analyses, and inspection of covariances among independent variables, allow us to construct summary scenarios of how and why role dynamics work. Within the boundaries specified above, the scenarios we reported in chapter 6 (see pages 153–54, 156, 160–161) represent the predictions (truth claims) of the theory.

The previously reported scenarios could be expanded to include predictions about functionality (reason for suspension) as an outcome of organizing and role dynamics. Reaching the successful end state would have to extend from scenarios predicting stability of role enactment, and not reaching the successful end state would have to extend from scenarios predicting change of role enactment. The scenarios are precisely stated; they derive logically from the laws of interaction; and they derive empirically from the correlation and regression analysis. Having said that, there is still the question of the empirical accuracy of these scenarios.

The predictions are moderately precise, first because there is much residual variance in the respective dependent variables and, second, because the theory is bounded in many important ways. Some important laws of interactions have been empirically grounded, however, and a number of others that may be important have been identified. As a result, much more can be said than that things just happen during the emergency period of disaster. There is a patterning to what occurs, one that can be described, explained, and predicted through reliance on basic sociological concepts. The better our measurement of these concepts, the better will our predictions become.

Conclusion

We close this chapter and book by providing a simple graphic representation of the expanded theory. We hope, of course, that it is worthy of more systematic testing than we have been able to complete. As noted in figure 7.2, the exogenous blocks of constructs remain the same as before. They subsume both the variables we have measured and the several new ones we have suggested in this chapter. Organization and role enactment are reciprocally related social processes. Given the availability of aggregated data on role enactment, these processes can be examined through use of nonrecursive modeling techniques.

Figure 7.2

An Expanded Theory of Disaster, Organization, and Role

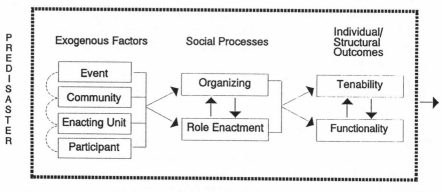

POSTDISASTER

We see similar possibilities for examining Ralph Turner's functionality and tenability principles. Accordingly, they are identified as reciprocally related individual and structural outcomes of organizing and role dynamics. We hope our crude measure of the effectiveness dimension of functionality has illustrated the direction we have in mind. Finally, the arrow extending from the theory is apropos of the point that a single disaster event is but a small part in the life of the impacted social system. Patterns of systemic stability and change over time may reveal trends that, at this point, we can only imagine.

Appendix C is a data protocol that can be used to develop a research design for further testing of the theory. The protocol is arranged in terms of the blocks of variables represented in figure 7.2. While continuing work with the archives is feasible (and much cheaper) for purposes of testing the theory, the most complete tests require primary data collection. To that end, we think the best data production strategy for field research should include strategic sampling of each type in the DRC typology. Where the organized responses are larger, some sort of sampling of participants will be needed to produce the necessary aggregated data. It will also be important to study a much broader range of events than natural disasters.

Testing cannot take place overnight. It will require a coordinated effort and sustained funding over a much longer period of time than is usually the case with social science research. But on the more positive side, it must be remembered that no particular study has to test the entire theory in order to be of value.[21] We can envision studies that focus only on relationships among participant characteristics, role enactment, and tenability; or studies that focus only on demographic characteristics, organizing, and functionality; and so on. Thus the theory can be broken down in any number of different ways. But because its laws of interaction are interrelated, all partial tests have important implications for the entire theory.

The DRC typology will continue to be a very efficient and effective analytical tool, regardless of whether subsequent studies are at the individual or organizational level of analysis. The typology is efficient because it is easy to measure and provides for mutually exclusive and exhaustive classes. It is effective because once having identified what type of organized repsonse is relevant, we can predict with some confidence the structural form of its organizing and role enactment. Intended or not, therefore, the DRC typology specifies nicely a micro-macro link between the individual and social structure.

When all is said and done, crisis events (of whatever type) are intriguing and obviously important social phenomena. Because social structure cannot be taken for granted in such situations, its origin, transformation, and demise can often be observed quite vividly. Certainly social structure is no less interesting or important in everyday affairs; but it is more likely to be taken for granted in these contexts; and its processes are more subtle as a result. By using basic sociological constructs to observe the transition of social structure from more routine to crisis circumstances, we are able to learn more about each of these systemic conditions. A convincing case can then be made that disaster research is a theoretically important specialty and an eminently practical one as well.

Means, Standard Deviations, and Correlations of Model Variables (Chapter 2)

	V1	V2	V3	V4	V5	V6	V7	V8	V9	V10	V11	V12	V13	V14	V15	V16	V17	V18	V19	V20	V21
V1	1.00	.72	.41	.65	-.07	.13	-.29	-.01	.11	.10	-.03	.27	-.28	-.13	.35	-.37	-.40	.25	-.22	-.18	-.03
V2		1.00	.49	.40	-.02	.19	-.28	.03	.07	.18	-.04	.18	-.22	-.32	.23	-.16	-.49	.00	-.10	.06	.00
V3			1.00	.26	-.38	.03	-.27	.04	-.33	.11	.39	-.22	-.16	-.05	.17	-.04	-.16	.22	.20	-.23	.11
V4				1.00	-.25	.20	-.31	.13	.19	.22	-.11	.14	-.26	.03	.54	-.48	-.36	.19	-.47	-.29	-.04
V5					1.00	.05	.09	-.23	-.13	-.32	-.05	-.07	.08	.03	-.22	.17	.15	-.30	-.08	.30	-.23
V6						1.00	.12	-.05	.11	-.08	.27	.03	.04	.05	.09	-.20	-.14	-.08	.10	.04	
V7							1.00	.27	.02	.02	-.28	.14	.27	-.10	-.31	.32	.12	-.02	.05	.12	.21
V8								1.00	.35	.31	-.25	.22	.04	.06	-.07	.01	.11	.02	-.01	-.09	-.05
V9									1.00	.22	-.31	.46	-.03	-.01	.04	.01	-.19	-.03	-.09	.15	.01
V10										1.00	.08	.37	.00	.12	.32	-.28	-.32	.40	-.03	-.10	-.04
V11											1.00	-.06	.10	.24	.34	-.21	-.09	.21	.42	-.17	-.06
V12												1.00	.11	.06	.25	-.27	-.36	.24	-.07	.23	-.07
V13													1.00	.05	.06	.04	.16	.11	.20	.18	.34
V14														1.00	.24	-.22	.08	.28	.16	-.09	.15
V15															1.00	-.86	-.65	.32	-.06	-.12	.01
V16																1.00	.48	-.37	.11	.11	.15
V17																	1.00	-.19	.06	-.18	.16
V18																		1.00	.15	-.34	.07
V19																			1.00	.25	.31
V20																				1.00	-.02
V21																					1.00
Mn	2.13	2.50	2.50	.55	2.24	1.71	1.76	1.45	2.18	.47	2.58	1.37	1.50	.61	.34	.82	.45	.63	2.13	2.55	.68
StD	.84	.60	.50	.50	1.05	.84	.88	.69	.90	.50	1.08	.49	.51	.50	.48	.69	.50	.49	.66	1.03	.47

VARIABLE NAME
V1 = ROLE CONTINUUM STAGE 1
V2 = ROLE CONTINUUM STAGE 2
V3 = ROLE CONTINUUM STAGE 3
V4 = FIRST APPEARING ELEMENT
V5 = TIMING OF FIRST ELEMENT
V6 = DOMAIN PROBLEM
V7 = TASK PROBLEM

VARIABLE NAME
V8 = RESOURCE PROBLEM
V9 = ACTIVITIES PROBLEM
V10 = TYPE OF ENACTING UNIT
V11 = SIZE OF UNIT
V12 = PREPAREDNESS
V13 = COMPLEXITY OF RESPONSE
V14 = CONCERN FOR VICTIMS

VARIABLE NAME
V15 = SOCIAL NETWORK RELEVANCE
V16 = NUMBER OF NETWORK LINKS
V17 = TIME NETWORK ESTABLISHED
V18 = COMMUNITY TYPE
V19 = DISASTER EXPERIENCE
V20 = LENGTH OF FOREWARNING
V21 = MAGNITUDE-SCOPE OF IMPACT

Means, Standard Deviations, and Correlations of Model Variables (Chapter 6)

	V1	V2	V3	V4	V5	V6	V7	V8	V9	V10	V11	V12	V13	V14	V15	V16	V17	V18	V19	V20	V21	V22	V23	V24	V25	V26	V27	V28
V1	1.00	.54	.10	.75	.16	-.12	-.11	-.01	.06	-.40	.27	.07	.06	.18	-.10	-.20	.03	.03	.08	-.11	-.13	.20	.02	.06	.52	.27	-.12	-.0
V2		1.00	.06	.70	.11	-.05	.02	.05	.12	-.25	.19	-.00	-.00	.19	-.11	-.08	-.06	-.03	.09	-.05	-.21	.07	.07	.13	.25	.21	-.32	-.
V3			1.00	.61	-.06	.26	-.11	-.14	-.05	-.27	.04	-.12	-.27	.14	-.15	-.09	.12	-.26	-.01	-.28	-.11	-.10	.16	-.26	.22	-.08	-.03	-.
V4				1.00	.09	-.23	-.08	-.02	.05	-.45	.23	.11	-.08	.25	-.16	-.19	.12	-.12	.06	-.18	-.21	.11	.12	-.05	.48	.15	-.19	-.
V5					1.00	-.04	-.01	-.07	-.02	-.12	.02	.07	.07	.27	-.02	.11	-.33	.09	.18	-.14	.05	.12	.22	.20	.16	.31	.02	.
V6						1.00	.32	.09	.19	.19	.04	-.09	.12	-.11	.23	-.04	-.13	.11	-.12	.25	.05	-.13	-.16	.09	-.05	.09	.04	-.08	.
V7							1.00	.46	.27	.04	-.20	.06	.11	-.08	.13	.09	.28	.16	-.14	.33	.07	-.04	-.14	-.04	-.06	.10	-.06	.
V8								1.00	.34	-.07	-.18	.12	.19	-.03	.02	.19	-.01	.41	.05	.14	-.11	-.04	.02	.05	.04	.05	.
V9									1.00	-.19	-.08	.04	.14	.13	-.15	-.06	.15	.18	-.16	.32	-.22	-.02	-.04	.00	.04	.01	-.02	.
V10										1.00	-.10	-.36	.02	-.30	.23	.36	-.17	-.07	.04	.04	.24	.02	-.17	.11	-.24	-.18	.02	.
V11											1.00	-.11	.09	.11	.07	-.14	.03	-.00	.11	-.29	-.12	-.06	.01	.03	.10	.16	-.03	-.
V12												1.00	.12	-.16	.15	-.11	.17	.17	.07	.12	.07	.18	.02	-.05	.01	-.13	.07	.
V13													1.00	-.07	.24	.03	-.04	.37	-.05	.20	.15	.23	-.32	.02	.06	.15	.06	.
V14														1.00	-.85	-.46	.26	-.12	-.33	-.25	-.35	-.02	-.02	-.09	.10	.09	-.21	-.
V15															1.00	.27	-.25	.15	.28	.17	.36	.09	-.01	.13	-.01	-.02	.13	.
V16																1.00	-.03	-.02	.03	.24	.06	-.11	.05	-.02	-.26	-.22	.07	-.0
V17																	1.00	.19	-.46	-.02	-.03	-.06	.08	.03	-.01	.1
V18																		1.00	.07	.40	.05	.23	-.14	.05	.03	.10	.1
V19																			1.00	-.15	.40	.16	.22	.04	.01	-.05	-.00	.2
V20																				1.00	.01	.05	-.14	.09	-.08	-.09	.12	.2
V21																					1.00	.08	-.04	.03	-.06	-.02	.14	.0
V22																						1.00	.02	.09	.22	.10	.05	.1
V23																							1.00	-.02	-.05	-.14	-.10	-.1
V24																								1.00	-.03	.03	.10	-.2
V25																									1.00	.27	-.01	-.0
V26																										1.00	-.06	.0
V27																											1.00	.1
V28																												1.0
Mn	.73	.66	.53	3.86	3.71	.40	.58	.49	.73	.27	2.96	.50	1.61	.68	.95	.32	.59	2.07	2.42	.65	1.90	.37	.44	1.06	.64	2.05	.30	5.9
StD	.45	.34	.50	1.92	1.73	.49	.49	.50	.44	.44	1.11	.50	.49	.47	.76	.47	.49	.67	1.02	.48	.84	.48	.50	.78	.48	.52	.30	5.0

VARIABLE NAME
V1 = DIMENSION 1
V2 = DIMENSION 2
V3 = DIMENSION 3
V4 = COMPOSITE OF CRITERIA
V5 = METRIC SCORE
V6 = DOMAIN PROBLEM
V7 = TASK PROBLEM
V8 = RESOURCE PROBLEM
V9 = ACTIVITIES PROBLEM

VARIABLE NAME
V10 = DRC TYPOLOGY
V11 = SIZE OF UNIT
V12 = PREPAREDNESS
V13 = COMPLEXITY OF RESPONSE
V14 = SOCIAL NETWORK RELEVANCE
V15 = NUMBER OF NETWORK LINKS
V16 = TIME NETWORK ESTABLISHED
V17 = COMMUNITY TYPE
V18 = COMMUNITY DISASTER EXPERIENCE

VARIABLE NAME
V19 = LENGTH OF FOREWARNING
V20 = MAGNITUDE-SCOPE OF IMPACT
V21 = TIME OF RESPONDENT INITIATION IN ORGANIZED RESPONSE
V22 = RESPONDENT DISASTER EXPERIENCE
V23 = BROAD POST-ROLE REPERTOIRE
V24 = INSTRUMENTAL LEADER
V25 = EXPERIENCE IN DISASTER ROLE
V26 = KNOWLEDGE REQUIRED
V27 = BOUNDARY SPANNING RESPONDENT LINKS
V28 = COMPLEXITY OF ROLE ENACTMENT

192

Appendix C: Data Protocol for the Theory

The data protocol provides guidance and easy reference for those wanting to develop research designs that can test the theory. Our recommendations are outlined in terms of the blocks of variables from figure 7.2 to which they refer. As noted in earlier discussions, we believe the theory can be tested at either the individual or organizational level of analysis. However, the latter requires aggregating data for the theoretical blocks termed *participant characteristics, role enactment,* and *tenability.* For larger enacting units, aggregation will undoubtedly be based on samples of participants. The aggregation requirement is referenced by the asterisks placed next to these three blocks of variables. Finally, the theory can be broken down in any number of ways for testing purposes. This is an important consideration, given data production requirements and costs related to them.

Event Characteristics

Type of Event: Any event (e.g., natural, technological, ecological, medical, political, military) with an emergency period that can be specified socially, temporally, and geographically.

Forewarning: Time lag between explicit threat cues and onset of physical harm and social disruption.

Physical Harm: Variety of possible measures of physical effects (e.g., impact ratios of deaths, injuries, illnesses, and damages to the natural or built environment) and the spatial parameters of these effects.

Social Disruption: Problems of organizing and more direct measures of suspension or breakdown of normal routines.

Duration: Time lag from onset of physical harm and social disruption until point at which disaster event has ended.

Community Characteristics

Type: Metropolitan/nonmetropolitan, length of existence, and country of origin (developed, newly industrialized, less developed).

193

Disaster Experience:	Number of threats and actual disaster events that have occurred during a specified historical period (including measures of physical harm and social disruption related to these events). Document any evidence of disaster subcultures.
Profile Measures:	Population size, growth rate and age distribution, employment by sector, per capita retail and wholesale trade, percent unemployed, median income, median education, percent racial, minority, and religious groups, housing stock, form of government, per capita government expenditures, and other measures.

Enacting Unit Characteristics

DRC Typology:	Established, expanding, extending, and emergent (Dynes 1970 is a valuable conceptual resource).
Preparedness:	Evidence of written disaster plans and/or formal training, regular updating, field tests, or use in actual emergencies (Drabek and Hoetmer 1991 is a valuable conceptual resource).
Size:	Number of identifiable members (full-time, part-time, and volunteer) for established, expanding, and extending types in the DRC typology. Number of participating individuals and social units for emergent type in the DRC typology.
Other Indicators:	Various structural measures (e.g., bureaucratization, specialization, formalization, and hierarchy of control) that can be derived from organizational theory (March and Simon 1958, Thompson 1967, and Hall 1982 are valuable conceptual resources).

Participant Characteristics*

Role Experience:	Prior experience performing the postdisaster role (include measurement of the frequency or, if occupationally based, the duration of that experience).
Disaster Experience:	If victim, measure frequency and seriousness of victimization. If responder, measure frequency and extensiveness of involvement. If victim and

responder, determine how these roles were related.

Leadership: Document instrumental and expressive leadership roles, noting any negotiation or conflict in their performance. Determine if leadership roles were established prior to or during the disaster (Bales 1950 is a valuable conceptual resource).

Status
Characteristics: Document occupational prestige (in terms of NORC prestige ratings) education, professional training, status as formal volunteer, income, age, gender, race and ethnicity, family status, and religion.

Orientations: Document motivation for involvement in disaster response, with attention to such factors as personal victimization, knowledge of or personal relationships with victims (social or physical proximity), occupational or avocational motivations, community involvement (social integration), and altruistic values (Barton 1969 is a valuable conceptual resource).

Organizing

Structural Form: Qualitative description of content using Kreps's structural code. Quantitative expression of form using Kreps's metric.

Timing: Before or after impact, measure the time lag between initiation of organizing and occurrence of the disaster event.

Duration: Measure total time of organizing during the emergency period from point of initiation until activities are suspended.

Complexity: Describe each task that is collectively represented in the division of labor. Quantify the total number of tasks performed.

Knowledge
Required: Aggregated measurement of role enactment property (see below).

Social Networking: Measure the total number of links with other social units responding at local, regional, and national levels. Calibrate the frequency and duration of each contact. Determine if each contact was established prior to or during the emergency. Quantify the centrality of the organization in its broader social network

(Drabek et al. 1981 is a valuable conceptual and methodological resource).

Role Enactment*

Structural Form: For each participant measure role allocation (status-role nexus), role complementarity (role linkages), role differentiation (being sensitive to all three levels of role performance), and composite measure in terms of the operationalization proposed in this monograph. Ask participants to give their own assessments of stability/change on the three core dimensions of role.

Timing: Before or after impact, measure the time lag between initiation of participation and occurrence of disaster event.

Duration: Measure the total time of participation during the emergency period from point of initiation until participation is suspended.

Complexity: At individual level, measure the total number of roles represented by the participant's links with other role incumbents. At organizational level, measure the total number of roles performed by all participants in the organized response.

Knowledge Required: Three measurement levels for each role performance: postdisaster role about which knowledge is widespread (general knowledge required); postdisaster role that calls for some training or experience (specific knowledge required); postdisaster role that calls for highly technical skills (technical knowledge required).

Social Networking: Determine the proportion of participant links with other role incumbents that are boundary spanning. Calibrate the frequency and duration of each boundary spanning link. Quantify the centrality of the participant in his or her broader social network.

Functionality

Effectiveness: Measure dichotomously: Does the organized response (of which participants are members) fulfill its reason for being (i.e., reach the successful end state)?

Efficiency:

Measure the time lag between when organizing begins and the enacting unit becomes fully operational during the emergency period. Document any evidence of inadequate communications, wasted resources, or unnecessary duplication of activities.

Tenability*

Personal Rewards:

Measure the extent to which instrumental and expressive leadership roles are enacted by people with higher prestige scores on NORC rating system. Measure perceptions of personal rewards of role enactment, the relevance of role conflict, and the exercise of power among role incumbents. Barton (1969), R. Turner (1980), Taylor, Zurcher, and Key (1970), and Zurcher (1989) are valuable conceptual resources.

Role/Person Fit:

Measure the extent to which role requirements (general, specific, technical) are coterminous with the capacities represented by the status characteristics of role incumbents. Measure participant perceptions of the fit between role requirements and their individual capacities and dispositions (R. Turner 1976 and 1978 are valuable conceptual resources).

Notes

Chapter 1. Disaster Archives, a Research Program, and Sociological Theory

1. In studying social networks both the DRC archives and data provided by Thomas Drabek from his earlier research on search and rescue responses were analyzed (Drabek et al. 1981). Drabek's data were potentially useful because he and his colleagues attempted to describe emergency social networks on their own terms, using blockmodeling techniques (White, Boorman, and Breiger 1976). While this is an important exercise, we were interested in exploring Drabek's case materials to compare relationships among network members (dyads) as forms of association. From 1,122 possible dyads, there were sufficient data on 130 of them to describe the content of each relationship from informant accounts of what happened, and then to characterize the form of each relationship in terms of our structural code. Findings from this study are reported in Kreps and Bosworth (1987) and Kreps (1991).

2. The dialectic of social action and social order has been a central metatheoretical theme of our research program (Alexander 1982). That theme was highlighted in the *American Sociological Review* article that follows, most pointedly as a more abstract expression of the formal organizing–collective behavior continuum discussed above. While we will not dwell on that theme in this monograph, we continue to believe that scientists engaged in substantive theory should never overlook broader epistemological issues that underly the subject matter of their research programs.

3. Our original measurement of the third dimension (as reported in the next chapter) was nowhere close to this ideal. While the measurement should have been based on the actual performance of postdisaster roles, we were more concerned about incumbency. In that regard, we equated greater creativity with new incumbency (unique role performance) and less creativity with already established incumbency (role boundary expansion). As Ralph Turner points out in chapter 3, this does not have to be the case at all.

Chapter 2. Structure as Process: Organization and Role

1. Locating instances of organization in disaster is tied critically to the identification of domains (Kreps 1985a). Whether before or after impact, many domains (e.g., providing victims basic needs, damage control) are not predesignated, and quite often there are multiple but independent enactments of the same ones. Thus, boundary specification is a continuing methodological concern because discrete instances of organization are linked to broader networks of social units, some of which are doing the same thing. In this

sense, domain is akin to the ecological concept of niche. The latter points to issues of power and legitimacy of single units, or the population of organizations of which they are members. The focus here is on origins of member unit. We do not address the problem of determining population boundaries. Moreover, the theory proposed is developmental rather than evolutionary (Carroll 1984).

2. The conventional factorial approach for expressing possible combinations of elements must be amended to include permutations. As is shown below, the difference between four-element forms like A-R-T-D and D-T-R-A is analytically central. This is equally true for one-, two-, and three-element forms that formally represent organization in a state of becoming. There is also one remaining possibility—no elements present. By the logic of the theory proposed here, this condition represents the absence of structure.

3. The theory and findings reported here are based on reanalyses of data collected by the Disaster Research Center (formerly of the Ohio State University and now the University of Delaware). Disasters are not easy to research (Drabek 1970; Kreps 1981). The center's earliest studies—largely unstructured and descriptive—focused on the emergency period of selected natural disasters in the United States. The resulting several thousand interviews and documents are located in the center's well-maintained archives. Studies done between 1963 and 1974 are particularly relevant for our purposes because data were reported on a wide range of activities in an effort to document what happened during the emergency period. The major strength of the original research was the attempt to document sequences of events in time and space. The resulting archives provide an essential foundation for studying organization and role as interrelated processes. The major weakness of the archives is that one never knows where or even if useful data can be found. Considerable digging is therefore required. Our methodology, which is reported in detail elsewhere (Kreps 1985b), involves comparative case studies of organizing as we are able to reconstruct them from spadework with the archives. From 1,062 transcribed interviews with informant participants and hundreds of related documents (meeting minutes, after-action reports, communications logs, news accounts, tape-recorded direct observations), a data file of 423 instances of organization from fifteen natural disasters has been constructed thus far. The findings on role dynamics reported in this chapter have been developed from further data production on a subsample of thirty-nine cases from the original data file.

4. The DRC studies focused on the functioning of local agencies that had obvious responsibilities in disasters (e.g., police and fire departments, hospitals, departments of public works, voluntary agencies). The result is that about 60 percent of the 423 cases in the reconstructed data file were enacted by such units. Reported on below is a subsample of thirty-eight cases from the total sample. About 47 percent of those cases (18) were enacted by the above types of units. For purposes of the analyses reported in this paper, those units normally expected to be involved in emergencies are distinguished from all others. The remaining cases in the subsample include three nonemergency public bureaucracies, two private firms, one special interest group, one military unit, two radio-television stations, and eleven emergent organizations.

5. The key requirement for constructing the metric is to capture all of the transitivities between D-T-R-A or social order and A-R-T-D or social action. This is done in the following way: At the social order end of the continuum, D

precedes T, R, and A (3 points); T precedes R and A (2 points); and R precedes A (1 point). Given one point for each conforming transitivity (3 + 2 + 1), D-T-R-A receives a score of 6, while at the social action end of the continuum, A-R-T-D receives a score of 0. Beginning at the social action end would simply reverse the scores, but not change the distribution in any way. By subtracting a constant 3 from each derived level of social order or social action, the resulting metric is +3 to −3 with a 0 midpoint. This was done to highlight where balance or tension between social action and social order is greatest.

6. A major methodological problem here is determining when there is a mix of role-making and role-playing. The archives do not generally provide clear documentation of what all participants are doing at each stage of organizing. The more people involved, the greater the methodological problem. The result is imprecision in determining proportions of role-making and role-playing. In effect, we made judgments of a mix whenever the dominance of role-making or role-playing was not absolute as depicted in the archives. Given primary data collection designed with this approach in mind, greater precision about proportions of role-making and role-playing would be possible. But whether it is role or organization, attribute thresholds of presence are analytically critical. Debates about these thresholds are therefore essential.

7. The continuum can also be represented as a polytomous variable that subsumes three dimensions: role-making; mixed role-playing and role-making; and role-playing. For purposes of the illustrative modeling reported in the next section, we replicated everything presented there with different cut points to make sure that findings were not artifactual. Given the negative skewness in the data, we tried throughout to create statistically manipulable marginal splits that retained meaningful substantive distinctions (see Bosworth and Kreps 1984).

8. For example, any questioning of the appropriateness of an enacting unit's involvement in the event was recorded as a domain-related problem. Confusion or conflict about how things were being done was recorded as a task problem. Depletion of resources related to the response (e.g., damaged equipment or losses of personnel) was recorded as a resources-related problem. Finally, disruption of activities (e.g., blocked access, overloaded communications, secondary impacts) was recorded as an activities problem.

Chapter 4. Role Dynamics and Emergent Organizations: Conception and Measurement

1. Any time there is an even number of roles or incumbents in the organized response, the possibility exists of a perfect mix (50 percent) of consistent and inconsistent role allocation. We would duly note that result whenever it occurred.

2. Here again, any time there is an even number of either inter-role or incumbent pairs, the possibility exists for a perfect mix of continuous and discontinuous role linkages. Interestingly enough, this possibility became an important nuance in our later modeling of role enactment (see chapter 6).

3. We agree with Hilbert's (1981, 213–14) position that human beings routinely invoke ideas of role-playing (acceptance of structural constraints) or role-making (rejection of structural constraints) to clarify for themselves and

others what they are doing. His important implication is that neither human beings nor the people who study them require literal conceptions of social structure and role invention to describe how roles are enacted. Dubin's (1978, 66–88) reference to summative terms is relevant also in this regard. Role-playing and role-making are summative terms because they represent an entire complex thing, i.e., role dynamics. But it is the properties of such things that must be captured conceptually and empirically.

4. It should be noted that both incumbent and role proportions are needed. This is because the latter may underrepresent the overall extent of consistency or inconsistency of the status-role nexus, depending on how simple majorities of incumbents are judged for each postdisaster role.

5. Similar to the measurement of status role nexus, there is potential imprecision in the role pair proportions. For each role pair, a simple majority of incumbent pairs judged to be continuous or discontinuous yields an associated judgment for that role pair regardless of the actual number of incumbent pairs. A great deal of continuity or discontinuity can therefore be hidden by using only the role pair proportions.

6. The clinical psychologist and writer had interacted previously as psychoanalyst and patient. But because people from virtually any occupation can become patients, it seemed inappropriate to us to define the clinician's status-role linkages that broadly. For subsequent data production, however, we decided to document linkages through secondary statuses of one or both members of incumbent pairs.

7. Supposedly the two most important distinguishing qualities of organizations are their size and longevity. But if size is going to be used seriously as a core defining property, then most of what are now called organizations (e.g., relatively small firms and public agencies) will have to be eliminated from consideration. Longevity is not a particularly useful core property either because most organizations go out of existence in a relatively short period of time (Starbuck 1983). Important for sure, size and longevity are more appropriately observed developmentally in life history studies of organizing (Bosworth and Kreps 1986; Saunders and Kreps 1987; Kreps 1989a, 166–86).

Chapter 5. Role Dynamics at the Individual Level of Analysis

1. Just as we had done in the second phase of data production, if a respondent was performing more than one postdisaster role, we singled out one of them as being the most central for purposes of measuring the three dimensions of role.

2. Our focus was only on the total number of *incumbent* links for each respondent as opposed to the total number of postdisaster *role* links represented by them. We would later use the total number of role links to represent (as an independent variable) the complexity of the respondent's role enactment.

3. As best as we could determine, a total of twenty-four postdisaster roles are represented by SEA's twenty-seven incumbent links. Only the three public works maintenance people and two national guardsmen, respectively, seem to be playing similar postdisaster roles when they are in direct contact with SEA. The relatively high role differentiation being evidenced for SEA might be expected for someone enacting a leadership role.

4. Recall that the higher the score, the greater the evidence of formal organizing

(and social order); and the lower the score, the greater the evidence of collective behavior (and social action).

5. In Kreps's (1985b) original data file, enacting unit types included emergency relevant public bureaucracies (50.8 percent), other public bureaucracies (5.2 percent), emergency relevant voluntary agencies (9.5 percent), special-interest groups (6.4 percent), private firms (2.1 percent), military units (8.7 percent), mass media (5 percent), and emergent units (12.3 percent).

6. The percentages consistent increase very little for participants in either emergent or other organized responses when statuses other than occupation are identified as relevant to the postdisaster role. Thus within the limits of information provided by the archives, our measurement of status-role nexus is not biased toward change rather than stability of role allocation.

7. The average number of links for respondents from emergent and other organized responses, respectively, is 14.5 and 8.5. But this difference is at least partly explained by the greater problems with missing data on participants from other organized responses. While about 64 percent of the cases are from other organized responses, about 78 percent of the cases for which there are missing data come from that category. It is also possible that key participants in emergent organizations require broader networks of direct interaction as they enact postdisaster roles.

8. The percentages continuous increase by 8 and 9 points for participants in emergent and other organized responses when statuses in addition to occupation (e.g., friend, relative, volunteer) are identified as relevant to the role linkage. This means that we have underrepresented somewhat the degree of continuity of role linkages by using only occupation as our referent in table 5.3B.

Chapter 6. Modeling Individual Role Dynamics

1. Subsequent model testing is certainly feasible with the DRC archives because there are several thousand tape-recorded interviews that have not been transcribed. While the same data problems that we faced would remain, the number of potential role enactments about which useful data could be extracted is enormous and continually growing.

2. Dubin (1978, 89–123) refers to laws of interaction in order to communicate possible links among theoretical concepts. While we prefer his terminology, it is not a part of standard parlance in sociology. In this and the remaining chapter, therefore, we will exploit Dubin's work as an analytical rather than linguistic tool. With that in mind, in determining how many laws of interaction are possible among concepts, Dubin suggests that both their number and their character as attributes or variables must be taken into account. Even though attributes are now treated routinely in sociology as if they were variables, Dubin's general point remains well-taken.

3. In subsequent regression analyses we ran this composite measure as is. But then to ensure that findings were not an artifact of its distribution, we ran the same equation after reducing the composite measure to only three levels: 0–2 (28 percent of the sample); 3–4 (38 percent of the sample); and 5–6 (34 percent of the sample). The major findings for the two equations are the same.

4. While the earlier measure of enacting unit type was not constructed with the DRC typology in mind, it overlaps considerably with the more recent one. In order to make the two operational definitions equivalent, one military unit

and two radio stations from the earlier study would have to be recoded as established organized responses (see chapter 2, note 4).

5. The lack of information on expressive leadership and conflict is primarily the result of the design of the original research. These simply were not topics of interest in the field.

6. The correlation between the number of roles and the total number of respondent links subsumed by them is $r = .44$. While the correlation is in the expected direction, its moderate magnitude suggests that the complexity of role enactment is more than a simple function of the sheer number of people linked to key participants.

7. This means that a bivariate correlation of .11 or higher is statistically significant for the first dimension ($N = 240$), second dimension ($N = 229$), and composite measure ($N = 229$); and a correlation of .10 or higher is statistically significant for the third dimension ($N = 257$). Two variables, metric score in the second equation ($r = .105$) and respondent disaster experience in the fourth equation ($r = .107$) are included because we rounded all correlations to two places. Their respective significance levels ($P < .113$ and $P < .107$) are slightly above our specified criterion. Just as in the first phase of our work, we have tried to balance the discovery of insights with concern about Type I error.

8. A few other comments on the multivariate techniques are in order. First, we later ran the four regression equations with all significant correlates listed in tables 6.5. and 6.6 included to assess the stability of the significant Beta coefficients from the earlier stepwise equations. That stability was very high, suggesting that we had identified important subsets of variables for the four specifications of role enactment. Second, because the measures of status-role nexus and role performance are dichotomous dependent variables, we replicated the findings for these two dimensions through discriminant analysis. Using variables with significant Beta's for grouping purposes, the discriminant analysis yields a correct classification of 83 percent of the cases for status-role nexus categories and 77 percent for role performance categories. Finally, an analysis of residuals for the role linkages and composite measures of role enactment showed no major abnormalities that we could detect.

9. There is also an interesting set of correlations between magnitude-scope of impact and problems related to the elements of organizing (domain problems $r = .25$, task problems $r = .33$, resources problems $r = .41$, and activities problems $r = .32$) that argues for defining disaster in terms of physical impact and social disruption (Fritz 1961, Kreps 1989b). It is also clear from Appendix B that this disaster event characteristic is correlated with a fair number of other independent variables as well. Thus the fact that the only significant partial Beta for magnitude-scope of impact is on the third dimension (role performance) understates its analytical importance for explaining individual role dynamics. The other measure of disaster events (length of forewarning) shows no significant relationship with any specification of role enactment. This deviates from the performance of this variable during the first phase of our research, where it was related to role-making at the third stage of organizing.

10. Recall from chapter 5 that the DRC typology and Kreps's structural metric are inversely related ($r = -.32$ for Kreps's original sample of 423 organized responses). This means that established and expanding organized responses tend to evidence greater degrees of formal organizing, while extending and emergent ones tend to evidence greater degrees of collective behavior.

11. Note also that respondent disaster experience and knowledge requirements of

the role, respectively, are positively correlated with formal organizing (metric score r's = .12 and .31). Such findings are consistent with the scenario of stable role allocation that we are about to propose.

12. Consistent with Dynes's (1970, 163–73) prediction, for example, the positive correlation of the DRC typology with time of initiation suggests that respondents in extending and emergent organized responses tend to become involved later during the emergency period. Its positive correlation with time the network is established suggests that social networks of extending and emergent organized responses tend to be improvised during the emergency rather than established prior to the disaster.

13. With the exception of respondent boundary spanning links, the coefficients for the other key independent variables (role experience, type of enacting unit, size of organized response, and respondent disaster experience) remain statistically significant when the measure of role linkages is added to the equation for status-role nexus. It must be remembered also that role linkages and respondent boundary spanning linkages are themselves correlated $(r = -.32)$. Thus some of their covariance with status-role nexus is common rather than unique.

14. Please note that because social network relevance and number of network links are highly multicolinear $(r = -.85)$, we ran them separately as well as together in this and the remaining two equations. In no case did a statistically significant Beta emerge for either of these independent variables.

15. Boundary spanning incumbent links, instrumental leadership, and time of respondent initiation continue to have statistically significant Beta's when status-role nexus is added to the equation, while role experience, DRC typology measure, and size of organized response drop out. It must be remembered, however, that status-role nexus is correlated with all of these variables $(r = .52$ for role experience, $r = -.40$ for DRC typology measure, and $r = .27$ with size of organized response). Thus some of its covariance with role linkages is common with these three remaining independent variables.

16. The fact that activities problems show a modest positive correlation with continuous role linkages does not tell us very much, except perhaps that they are more likely to be handled through normal channels. Perhaps more interesting is the negative correlation between the DRC typology measure and activities problems $(r = -.19)$, and its positive correlation with domain problems $(r = .19)$. These correlations suggest that participants in established and expanding organized responses are more likely to report operational (activities) problems, while those in extending and emergent ones are more likely to report legitimacy (domain) problems. What is involved here is a potentially critical difference between expected and unexpected involvement during the emergency period of crisis situations (Saunders and Kreps 1987). While domain problems tend to be resolved quickly during the emergency periods of natural disasters, such resolution may not be so easy for other types of crises (Barton 1969; Perrow 1984; Drabek 1989; Kreps 1989b).

17. As noted in the appendix, the correlations between magnitude-scope of impact and the four problems of organizing are as follows: domain problems $(r = .25)$, task problems $(r = .33)$, resources problems $(r = .41)$, and activities problems $(r = .32)$. The correlations between community disaster experience and the four problems of organizing are as follows: domain problems $(r = .11)$, task problems $(r = .16)$, resources problems $(r = .19)$, and activities problems $(r = .18)$.

18. Their commonality as cultural resources is reflected by the positive correlation between preparedness and both respondent disaster experience (r = .18) and community disaster experience (r = .31).

19. The correlations are as follows: resources problems and complexity of organized response (r = .19); resources problems and community disaster experience (r = .19); and complexity of organized response and community disaster experience (r = .37).

20. The correlations for complexity of organized response are as follows: respondent disaster experience (r = .23); community disaster experience (r = .37); magnitude-scope of impact (r = .20); domain problems (r = .12); task problems (r = .11); resources problems (r = .19); and activities problems (r = .14). The correlations for complexity of role enactment are as follows: respondent disaster experience (r = .13); community disaster experience (r = .14); magnitude-scope of impact (r = .25); domain problems (r = .15); task problems (r = .33); resources problems (r = .29); and activities problems (r = .15).

21. An interesting nuance in this regard is that size of the organized response is an important component of stability of role enactment (and closed system dynamics), while complexity of the organized response is an important component of change (and open system dynamics). The two variables themselves evidence only a slight correlation (r = .09) for this sample of respondents. But this is not surprising because the measurement of size is ordinal (an upper limit of fifty or more eliminates considerable variance) and the measurement of complexity is quite crude.

22. The most important exceptions are as follows: First, our initial measure of enacting unit type, which was not measured with the DRC typology in mind, showed no statistically significant relationships with role enactment. However, the earlier and more recent measures for this variable overlap considerably, and the direction of their respective relationships with role enactment are consistent. Second, while length of forewarning was evidenced as a resource for role-making in the first phase of our research, it shows no statistically significant correlations with role enactment now. Third, while magnitude-scope of impact did not evidence relationships with role enactment during the first phase, it clearly does so now. We suspect that both event variables are change factors: length of forewarning because it provides time for adaptation; and magnitude-scope of impact because it necessitates adaptation.

Chapter 7. A Theory of Disaster, Organization, and Role

1. There is an important procedural side to Ralph Turner's (1980) theorizing about role as well, but it necessarily is far less complete than that provided by Dubin. Please note also that theory builders like Dubin (1978), Blalock (1969) and Mullins (1971; 1974), in particular, do not intend that their ideas should serve as rigid prescriptions or proscriptions. Instead, they offer practical guidelines that working scientists should find enabling rather than constraining.

2. While very sensitive to the necessary relationship between theorizing and doing research, for both analytical and stylistic purposes Dubin treats separately the logical (mental) and empirical (observational) sides of theory build-

ing. Feeling no need to do so, we do not refer to his final two components of a theory (empirical indicators and hypotheses). Nor do we treat the determination of laws of interaction and propositions (predictions) only as logical matters.

3. Most of the following discussion focuses on concepts, laws of interaction, and boundaries; first because system states are best considered as boundary conditions; and second, because predictions derive from laws of interaction. As Dubin notes (1978, 170–72), one can begin a theory with predictions (he uses the term propositions), but one must then make the inductive leap backward to identify the laws of interaction that produce them. We work in the opposite direction, and the whole process has evolved developmentally from the empirical side of our work.

4. In Dubin's (1978, 66) terminology, summative concepts stand for entire complex things. While they have value as communication devices, it is their properties that are important for theory-building purposes. Dubin's characterization of summative concepts is similar to Blalock's (1969, 29) reference to theoretical blocks of variables. In our case, the six blocks of variables represented in figure 7.1 are nominally labeled in summative terms.

5. If or when aggregate data on role enactments are produced in sufficient numbers for all four types of organized responses in the DRC typology, then more complicated models that address reciprocal causation could become very powerful tools. For the time being, our data base and level of analysis calls for one-way causation: with the four exogenous blocks and organizing serving as explanatory variables in figure 7.1; and role enactment representing what is to be explained.

6. One possible way to address duration of impact would be to calibrate how long an event (whatever it might be) produces effects (whatever they might be). Depending on the type of event and the effect of interest, duration of impact can vary quite dramatically.

7. We continue to believe that the best measure of complexity of role differentiation is the total number of roles performed within an organized response. Measurement of role differentiation at the organizational level would make this variable an additional global property of organizing (Barton 1961).

8. The various measures of complexity, knowledge required, and social networking exhibit patterns in the participant sample, which suggest that it may be possible to construct an overall index of complexity, one that has internal (administrative-technical) and external (social networking) components.

9. We say general because the situation is more complicated than implied by this formula. As Dubin notes (1978, 112–13), the number of laws is sensitive not only to how many concepts there are, but also to the character of each one. For example, Kreps's metric is a complex measure because it subsumes four concepts (D, T, R, A), each of which has presence and absence values that are important theoretically. This means that the full specification of the metric requires twenty-four laws of interaction (four for each pair of concepts multiplied by the six possible pairs of concepts). The preferred (and obviously more efficient) way of expressing possible relationships among the concepts is the following derivative law of interaction: their is an underlying continuum of formal organizing (social order) and collective behavior (social action) in the relationships among domains, tasks, resources, and activities as organization is socially constructed. As Mullins notes (1974, 8), the number of laws is also sensitive to whether relationships among concepts are one-way or reciprocal.

10. One might also ask if a case can be made for temporal primacy among the three dimensions. This is certainly not true for two of the three possibilities. We can show that role linkages (continuous or discontinuous) can precede or follow stability or change of role allocation. We can also show that role performance is as likely to expand role linkages as to be influenced by existing ones. On the other hand, a strong argument can be made that role allocation logically precedes the incumbency component of role performance. Recall, however, that our performance measure addresses levels of improvising regardless of whether incumbency is existing or new.

11. A case in point is the application of what logicians call a truth table to Kreps's structural code (Dubin 1978, 129–32). Because the four elements can refer to anything, their various combinations and permutations can be examined as a purely logical exercise. At least one key boundary condition of the theory can be identified through use of a truth table, but we believe that reference to empirical reality is essential. Three related statements are required, with the last one being a logically derived boundary condition of the theory: If D, T, R, and A are individually necessary and collectively sufficient for organization to exist; and if all participants in the sample enact roles in social contexts in which all four elements are present; then only role enactments in organized responses are being considered. The important boundary condition is that role enactments can be analyzed in a wide variety of structural contexts, only some of which are organized.

12. With respect to social networking, for example, the frequency and duration of specific relationships during the emergency period would be important to measure, as would the centrality of participants or organized responses in the networks of which they are parts (Drabek et al. 1981). With respect to disaster experience, at the individual level it would be important to learn more about the precise nature of the experience. If participants were victims, how seriously were they affected. If they were responders, what did they do and how elaborate was their involvement. If they were both victims and responders, how were these roles reconciled. At the community level, it would be important to get measures of physical harm from previous disasters. With respect to disaster preparedness, it would be important to determine the extent to which formal planning and training are routinized in everyday affairs, or actually put to use in an emergency or disaster. With respect to role experience, if postdisaster role incumbency is occupationally based, it would be important to know how long the incumbent has held that occupation.

13. In personal conversations, E. L. Quarantelli and Russell Dynes make a couple of instructive comments: First, if there are cultural universals in human response to disaster, the immediate emergency period is the place to find them. Second, the use of the DRC typology is not necessarily bounded to the immediate emergency period. Social responses related to disaster prevention, mitigation, and long-term recovery can be compared and contrasted using the same analytical tool.

14. For the 423 (organizational) case file, the complete distributions are as follows: need met, organization suspended (N = 245, 58 percent); not suspended at time of interviews (N = 55, 13 percent); suspended due to loss of resources (N = 17, 4 percent); absorbed by another entity (N = 57, 13 percent); and uncertain (N = 49, 12 percent). The relevant distributions for the 257 (participant) case file are as follows: need met, organization suspended (N = 126, 49

percent), not suspended at time of interviews (N = 35, 14 percent); suspended due to loss of resources (N = 9, 3 percent); absorption by another entity (N = 59, 23 percent); and uncertain (N = 28, 11 percent). Categories one and two for each sample are collapsed because Kreps judged that responses still in process had a high probability of reaching the successful end state. Categories three, four, and five are collapsed because Kreps judged that uncertain cases had a high probability of not reaching the successful end state.

15. Similar to the last chapter, the findings for these regression equations have been replicated through discriminant analysis. Using statistically significant Betas for grouping purposes, there is a correct classification of 74 percent of the cases for the participant sample and 73 percent for the organized response sample.

16. There would be an obvious practical concern if or when suspension in process is resisted at the organizational level. But that does not appear to be a frequent problem in the emergency period of natural disasters. It may very well be a problem during other time phases and for other types of disaster events.

17. We say *empirical* advisedly because in reviewing Dubin's discussion of system states, one is never sure whether "system" refers to some empirical entity (a real thing) or the theory itself. This leads to considerable confusion here, and also in Dubin's closing discussion of systems analysis. Respective discussions of system states can involve more than boundary specification, but they cannot involve less. We take the narrow approach because, at least for us, it is more useful.

18. There are two exceptions. First, the existence of emergent responses in the DRC typology is circumscribed by the disaster event. Second, instrumental leadership may or may not be related to predisaster structural arrangements. We continue to believe, however, that the theoretical utility of both variables is maximized when they are treated exogenously.

19. Dubin refers to propositions and predictions interchangeably as truth claims, but he prefers the former term. We think this is because Dubin considers logical as opposed to empirical rules as the sole test of a proposition's (i.e., a prediction's) accuracy. While this is quite consistent with his use of correlation and regression analysis as a metaphor for distinguishing laws of interaction (explanation) from propositions (predictions), the metaphor seems to break down when laws of interaction reach their highest level of efficiency (Dubin 1978, 18–32, 91–93, 106–7, 109–12, 169–70). In any event, we have used correlation and regression analysis as statistical tools to generate empirical generalizations and predictive scenarios (see chapter 6). Thus for us the predictions that can be derived from laws of interaction are matters of evidence as well as formal logic.

20. Dubin would disagree (1978, 19–32). He sees explanation and prediction as separate goals of science, arguing that we can develop powerful explanations with very imprecise predictions and vice versa. We disagree on logical but not empirical grounds. On purely logical grounds the explanation and prediction problems of science are one and the same thing. But when the logical and empirical sides of science are merged—as we think they must be—Dubin's point is very well taken. In constructing our own theory, describing and explaining social process has been the central goal from the beginning.

21. This is particularly important with respect to any subsequent testing with the DRC archives, and its attendant (and chronic) problems of missing data.

Bibliography

Adriaansens, Hans P. M. 1980. *Talcott Parsons and the Conceptual Dilemma.* Boston: Routledge & Kegan Paul.

Aldrich, Howard. 1979. *Organization and Environments.* Englewood Cliffs, N.J.: Prentice-Hall.

Alexander, Jeffrey C. 1982. *Theoretical Logic in Sociology.* Vol. 1: *Positivism, Presuppositions, and Current Controversies.* Berkeley and Los Angeles: University of California Press.

Alihan, Milla A. 1938. *Social Ecology: A Critical Analysis.* New York: Columbia University Press.

Bales, Robert F. 1950. *Interaction Process Analysis.* Reading, Mass.: Addison Wesley.

Barton, Allen H. 1961. *Organizational Measurement.* Princeton: College Entrance Examination Board.

———. 1969. *Communities in Disaster.* Garden City, N.Y.: Anchor, Doubleday.

Bates, Frederick, and Clyde C. Harvey. 1975. *The Structure of Social Systems.* New York: Gardner Press.

Berger, Peter, and Thomas Luckmann. 1966. *The Social Construction of Reality.* Garden City, N.Y.: Doubleday.

Blalock, Hubert M. 1969. *Theory Construction.* Englewood Cliffs, N.J.: Prentice-Hall.

———. 1979. "Measurement and Conceptualization Problems." *American Sociological Review* 44: 881–95.

Blumer, Herbert. 1969. *Symbolic Interactionism: Perspective and Method.* Englewood Cliffs, N.J.: Prentice-Hall.

Bosworth, Susan Lovegren, and Gary A. Kreps. 1984. "Disaster, Organization, and the Concept of Role." Report series no. 4, National Science Foundation, Grant no. CEE-8400486.

———. 1986. "Structure as Process: Organization and Role." *American Sociological Review* 51:699–716.

Carrol, Glenn R. 1984. "Organizational Ecology." *Annual Review of Sociology* 10:71–94.

Collins, Randall. 1981. "On the Micro Foundations of Macro Sociology." *American Journal of Sociology* 86:984–1,015.

———. 1985. *Three Sociological Traditions.* New York: Oxford University Press.

Davis, Kingsley. 1948. *Human Society.* New York: Macmillan.

Denzin, Norman K. 1989. *The Research Act: A Theoretical Introduction to Sociological Methods.* Englewood Cliffs, N.J.: Prentice-Hall.

Drabek, Thomas E. 1970. "Methodology of Studying Disasters: Past Patterns and Future Possibilities." *American Behavioral Scientist* 13:331–43.

———. 1986. *Human System Response to Disaster: An Inventory of Sociological Findings.* New York: Springer-Verlag.

———. 1989. "Taxonomy and Disaster: Theoretical and Applied Issues." In *Social Structure and Disaster,* ed. Gary A. Kreps, 317–45. Newark: University of Delaware Press.

Drabek, Thomas E., et al. 1981. *Managing Multiorganizational Emergency Responses: Emergent Search and Rescue Networks in Natural Disasters and Remote Area Settings.* Boulder: Institute of Behavioral Science, University of Colorado.

Drabek, Thomas E., and Gerard J. Hoetmer, eds. 1991. *Emergency Management: Principles and Practice for Local Government.* Washington, D.C.: International City Management Association.

Drabek, Thomas E., Alvin Mushkatel, and Thomas S. Kilijanek. 1983. *Earthquake Mitigation Policy: The Experience of Two States.* Boulder: Institute of Behavioral Science, University of Colorado.

Dubin, Robert. 1978. *Theory Building.* New York: Free Press.

Durkheim, Emile. 1933. *The Division of Labour in Society.* Toronto: Macmillan.

———. 1938. *The Rules of Sociological Method.* Chicago: University of Chicago Press.

Dynes, Russell R. 1970. *Organized Behavior in Disaster.* Lexington, Mass.: D. C. Heath.

———. 1987. "The Concept of Role in Disaster Research." In *Sociology of Disasters: Contribution of Sociology to Disaster Research,* ed. Russell R. Dynes, Bruna De Marchi, and Carlo Pelanda, 71–102. Milan: Franco Angeli.

Dynes, Russell R., E. L. Quarantelli, and Gary A. Kreps. 1972. *A Perspective on Disaster Planning.* Report series no. 11. Newark: University of Delaware, Disaster Research Center.

Enoch, Joel K. 1988. "Origins, Networks, and Restructuring: An Analysis of Three Methodologies." Master's thesis College of William and Mary.

Faia, Michael A. 1986. *Dynamic Functionalism: Strategy and Tactics.* New York: Cambridge University Press.

Farmer, Elizabeth M. Zeiders. 1989. "Structure, Organization, and Social Movements." In *Social Structure and Disaster,* ed. Gary A. Kreps, 135–65. Newark: University of Delaware Press.

Francis, Patricia R., and Gary A. Kreps. 1984. *Disaster and the Social Order: Organization and Social Network.* Report series no. 2, National Science Foundation, Grant no. CEE-9121135.

Fritz, Charles E. 1961. "Disasters." In *Social Problems,* ed. Robert K. Merton and Robert Nisbet, 651–94. New York: Harcourt Brace & World.

Gamson, William A., Bruce Fireman, and Steven Rytina. 1982. *Encounters with Unjust Authority.* Chicago: Dorsey Press.

Garfinkel, Harold. 1967. *Studies in Ethnomethodology.* Englewood Cliffs, N.J.: Prentice-Hall.

Giddens, Anthony. 1976. *New Rules of Sociological Method: A Positive Critique of Interpretive Sociologies.* New York: Basic Books.

———. 1979. *Central Problems in Social Theory.* Berkeley and Los Angeles: University of California Press.

Glaser, Barney G., and Anselm L. Strauss. 1967. *The Discovery of Grounded Theory: Strategies for Qualitative Research.* Chicago: Aldine.

Goffman, Erving. 1961. "Role Distance." In *Encounters,* ed. Erving Goffman, 83–152. Indianapolis: Bobbs-Merrill.

————. 1981. *Forms of Talk.* Philadelphia: University of Pennsylvania Press.

Haas, J. Eugene, and Thomas E. Drabek. 1970. "Community Disaster and System Stress: A Sociological Perspective." In *Social and Psychological Factors in Stress,* ed. Joseph E. McGrath, 264–86. New York: Holt, Rinehart & Winston.

Hall, Richard H. 1982. *Organizations: Structure and Process.* 3rd ed. Englewood Cliffs, N.J.: Prentice-Hall.

Handel, Warren. 1979. "Normative Expectations and the Emergence of Meaning as Solutions to Problems: Convergence of Structural and Interactionist Views." *American Journal of Sociology* 84:855–81.

Hawley, Amos. 1950. *Human Ecology: A Theory of Community Structure.* New York: Ronald Press.

Hilbert, Richard A. 1981. "Toward an Improved Understanding of Role." *Theory and Society* 10:207–26.

Kalberg, Stephen. 1980. "Max Weber's Types of Rationality: Cornerstone for the Analysis of Rationalization Processes in History." *American Journal of Sociology* 85:1,145–80.

Kimberly, John R., and Robert H. Miles. 1980. *The Organization Life Cycle.* San Francisco: Jossey-Bass.

Kreps, Gary A. 1978. "The Organization of Disaster Response: Some Fundamental Theoretical Issues." In *Disasters: Theory and Research,* ed. E. L. Quarantelli, 65–87. London: Sage Publications.

————. 1981. "The worth of the NAS-NRC (1952–63) and DRC (1963–present) Studies of Individual and Social Responses to Disasters." In *Social Science and Natural Hazards,* ed. James D. Wright and Peter Rossi, 91–122. Cambridge, Mass.: Abt Books.

————. 1983. "The Organization of Disaster Response: Core Concepts and Processes." *International Journal of Mass Emergencies and Disasters* 1:439–67.

————. 1984. "Sociological Inquiry and Disaster Research." *Annual Review of Sociology* 10:309–30.

————. 1985a. "Disaster and the Social Order." *Sociological Theory* 3:49–65.

————. 1985b. *Structural Sociology, Disaster, and Organization.* Final report, National Science Foundation, grant no. CEE-9121135.

————. 1987. "Classical Themes, Structural Sociology, and Disaster Research." In *Sociology of Disasters: Contribution of Sociology to Disaster Research,* ed. Russell R. Dynes, Bruna De Marchi, and Carlo Pelanda, 357–401. Milan: Franco Angeli.

————, ed. 1989a. *Social Structure and Disaster.* Newark: University of Delaware Press.

————. 1989b. "Future Directions in Disaster Research." *International Journal of Mass Emergencies and Disasters* 7:215–41.

————. 1989c. "Description, Taxonomy, and Explanation in Disaster Research." *International Journal of Mass Emergencies and Disasters* 7:277–80.

————. 1991. "Answering Organizational Questions: A Brief for Structural

Codes." In *Studies in Organizational Sociology,* ed. Gale Miller, 143–77. Greenwich, Conn.: JAI Press.

Kreps, Gary A., and Susan Lovegren Bosworth. 1987. *Social Networks and Organizing: Interdependence as Process.* Final report, National Science Foundation, grant no. CEE-8400486.

Kreps, Gary A., John G. Crooks, and John R. Linn. 1987. *Organizational Change: Static and Dynamic Aspects.* Final report, National Science Foundation, grant no. CEE-8400486.

Lenski, Gerhard, and Jean Lenski. 1982. *Human Societies: An Introduction of Macro Sociology.* New York: McGraw-Hill.

Linn, John R., and Gary A. Kreps. 1989. "Disaster and the Restructuring of Organization." In *Social Structure and Disaster,* ed. Gary A. Kreps, 108–34. Newark: University of Delaware Press.

Linton, Ralph. 1936. *The Study of Man.* New York: Appleton-Century.

March, James G., and Herbert A. Simon. 1958. *Organizations.* New York: John Wiley & Sons.

Mayhew, Bruce. 1980. "Structuralism Versus Individualism: Part I, Shadowboxing in the Dark." *Social Forces* 59:335–76.

———. 1981. "Structuralism Versus Individualism: Part II, Ideological and Other Obfuscations." *Social Forces* 59:627–49.

———. 1982. "Structuralism and Ontology." *Social Science Quarterly* 63:635–39.

McCarthy, John D., and Mayer N. Zald. 1977. "Resource Mobilization and Social Movements: A Partial Theory." *American Journal of Sociology* 82:1,212–41.

McKelvey, Bill. 1982. *Organizational Systematics: Taxonomy, Evolution, Classification.* Berkeley and Los Angeles: University of California Press.

Mead, George H. 1934. *Mind, Self, and Society,* ed. Charles W. Morris. Chicago: University of Chicago Press.

Merton, Robert K. 1957. *Social Theory and Social Structure.* New York: Free Press.

Mooney, Jennifer A. 1989. "Organization and Role: Conception and Measurement." Master's thesis. College of William and Mary.

Mullins, Nicholas C. 1971. *The Art of Theory Construction and Use.* New York: Harper & Row.

———. 1974. "Theory Construction from Available Materials: A System for Organizing and Presenting Propositions." *American Journal of Sociology* 80:1–15.

Myers, Kristen. 1990. "A Dialectical Analysis of Role Enactment During the Emergency Period of Natural Disasters." Master's thesis. College of William and Mary.

Parsons, Talcott. 1938. *The Structure of Social Action.* New York: McGraw-Hill.

———. 1950. *The Social System.* Glencoe, Ill.: Free Press.

Perrow, Charles. 1979. *Complex Organizations: A Critical Essay.* 2nd ed. Glenview, Ill.: Scott, Foresman, & Company.

———. 1984. *Normal Accidents: Living with High Risk Technologies.* New York: Basic Books.

Perry, Ronald W. 1982. *The Social Psychology of Civil Defense.* Lexington, Mass.: D. C. Heath.

Perry, Stewart E., Earle Silber, and Donald A. Bloch. 1956. *The Child and his*

Family in Disaster: A Study of the 1935 Vicksburg Tornado. Washington, D.C.: National Academy of Sciences-National Research Council.

Powers, Charles. 1981. "Role-imposition or Role-improvisation: Some Theoretical Principles." *Economic and Social Review* 12:287–99.

Quarantelli, E. L., and Russell R. Dynes. 1977. "Response to Social Crisis and Disaster." *Annual Review of Sociology* 3:23–49.

Rossi, Ino. 1983. *From the Sociology of Symbols to the Sociology of Signs: Toward a Dialectical Sociology.* New York: Columbia University Press.

Rossi, Peter H., James D. Wright, and Eleanor Weber-Burdin. 1982. *Natural Hazards and Public Choice: The State and Local Politics of Hazards Mitigation.* New York: Academic Press.

Russell, Stephen T. 1989. "Role Enactment and Disaster Response: A Methodological Exploration." Master's thesis. College of William and Mary.

Saunders, Sarah L., and Gary A. Kreps. 1987. "The Life History of Emergent Organization in Disaster." *Journal of Applied Behavioral Science* 23:443–62.

Shalin, Dmitri N. 1986. "Pragmatism and Social Interactionism." *American Sociological Review* 51:9–29.

Short, James F. 1984. "Toward the Social Transformation of Risk Analysis." *American Sociological Review* 49:711–26.

Smelser, Neil J. 1962. *Theory of Collective Behavior.* New York: Free Press.

Stallings, Robert A. 1978. "The Structural Patterns of Four Types of Organizations in Disaster." In *Disasters: Theory and Research,* ed. E. L. Quarantelli, 87–103. Beverly Hills, Calif.: Sage.

Starbuck, William H. 1983. "Organizations as Action Generators." *American Sociological Review* 48:91–103.

Stinchcombe, Arthur L. 1968. *Constructing Social Theories.* New York: Harcourt, Brace & World.

———. 1978. *Theoretical Methods in Social History.* New York: Academic Press.

Strauss, Anselm. 1978. *Negotiations: Varieties, Contexts, Processes and Social Order.* San Francisco: Jossey-Bass.

Stryker, Sheldon. 1980. *Symbolic Interactionism: A Social Structural Version.* Menlo Park, Calif.: Benjamin/Cummings.

Stryker, Sheldon, and Anne Statham. 1985. "Symbolic Interaction and Role Theory." In *Handbook of Social Psychology,* vol. 1, ed. Gardner Lindzey and Elliot Aronson, 311–79. New York: Random House.

Sylvan, David, and Barry Glassner. 1985. *A Rationalist Methodology for the Social Sciences.* New York: Basil Blackwell.

Taylor, James B., Louis A. Zurcher, and William H. Key. 1970. *Tornado.* Seattle: University of Washington Press.

Thompson, James D. 1967. *Organizations in Action.* New York: McGraw-Hill.

Turner, Jonathan. 1978. *The Structure of Sociological Theory.* Rev. ed. Homewood, Ill.: Dorsey.

Turner, Ralph H. 1962. "Role-taking: Process Versus Conformity." In *Human Behavior and Social Processes,* ed. Arnold Rose, 20–40. Boston: Houghton-Mifflin.

———. 1964. "Collective Behavior." In *Handbook of Modern Sociology,* ed. Robert E. L. Faris, 382–425. Chicago: Rand McNally.

————. 1968. "Role: II. Sociological Aspects." In *International Encyclopedia of the Social Sciences* 3:552–57. New York: Macmillan and Free Press.

————. 1976. "The Real Self: From Institution to Impulse." *American Journal of Sociology* 81:989–1,016.

————. 1978. "The Role and the Person." *American Journal of Sociology* 84:1–23.

————. 1980. "Strategy for Developing an Integrated Role Theory." *Humboldt Journal of Social Relations* 7:123–39.

————. 1985. "Unanswered Questions in the Convergence Between Structuralist and Interactionist Role Theories." In *Micro-sociological Theory: Perspectives on Sociological Theory,* ed. H. J. Helle and S. N. Eisenstadt, 22–36. London and Beverly Hills, Calif.: Sage.

————. 1989. "Aspects of Role Improvisation." In *Social Structure and Disaster,* ed. Gary A. Kreps, 207–13. Newark: University of Delaware Press.

Turner, Ralph H., and Lewis M. Killian. [1957] 1972. *Collective Behavior.* Englewood Cliffs, N.J.: Prentice-Hall.

Wallace, Walter L. 1971. *The Logic of Science in Sociology.* Chicago: Aldine.

————. 1983. *Principles of Scientific Sociology.* Chicago: Aldine.

————. 1989. "Comments on 'Life History of Organization.'" In *Social Structure and Disaster,* ed. Gary A. Kreps, 219–28. Newark: University of Delaware Press.

Warriner, Charles K. 1956. "Groups Are Real: A Reaffirmation." *American Sociological Review* 21:549–54.

————. 1970. *The Emergence of Society.* Homewood, Ill.: Dorsey Press.

————. 1989. "The Heavy Hand of Culture." In *Social Structure and Disaster,* ed. Gary A. Kreps, 295–305. Newark: University of Delaware Press.

Weber, Max. 1949. *The Methodology of the Social Sciences.* New York: Free Press.

————. 1968. *Economy and Society.* Eds. Guenther Roth and Claus Wittich. New York: Bedminster Press.

Weinstein, Eugene A. 1977. "The Self and Social Structure From a Symbolic Interactionist Perspective." Paper presented to the Section on Social Psychology, American Sociological Association, Chicago.

Weinstein, Eugene A., and Judith M. Tanur. 1976. "Meanings, Purposes, and Structural Resources in Social Interaction." *Cornell Journal of Social Relations* 11:105–10.

Weller, Jack M. 1969. "The Social Organization of Disaster Response." Master's thesis, Ohio State University.

Weller, Jack M., and E. L. Quarantelli. 1973. "Neglected Characteristics of Collective Behavior." *American Journal of Sociology* 79:665–85.

Wenger, Dennis E. 1989. "Appendix to Part One: The Role of Archives for Comparative Studies of Social Structure and Disaster." In *Social Structure and Disaster,* ed. Gary A. Kreps, 238–50. Newark: University of Delaware Press.

White, Harrison C., S. A. Boorman, and R. L. Breiger. 1976. "Social Structure from Multiple Networks. I. Blockmodels of Role and Positions." *American Journal of Sociology* 81:730–80.

Wolff, Kurt, ed. 1950. *The Sociology of Georg Simmel.* Glencoe, Ill.: Free Press.

Wright, James D., and Peter H. Rossi, eds. 1981. *Social Science and Natural Hazards.* Cambridge, Mass.: Abt Books.

Zurcher, Louis A. 1983. "Filling a Role Void: Volunteers in a Disaster Work Crew." In *Social Roles: Conformity and Conflict,* 113–34. Beverly Hills, Calif.: Sage.

———. 1989. "Disaster Taxonomies: Service to Whom?" In *Social Structure and Disaster,* ed. Gary A. Kreps, 238–50. Newark: University of Delaware Press.

Index

Action, social, 31, 34, 38, 43–44, 47, 57, 64–66, 72, 76–77, 79, 198–200. *See also* Dialectical reasoning; Order, social

Activities (A), 24–26, 200; definition of, 25, 40, 64; methodological issues of, 29–30, 67–68, 73–76, 80. *See also* Case materials; Structural code (D,T,R,A)

Adriaansen, Hans P., 39

Alexander, Jeffrey C., 38, 48, 65, 77, 94, 198

Analytical induction, 30–31, 138–39

Archives, 19–22, 28–29, 31–33, 35, 41, 52, 55, 57, 87–96, 100, 102, 109, 112, 114–15, 120, 139, 145, 150, 165, 168, 190, 198–99, 208. *See also* Case Materials

Bales, Robert F., 117, 148, 195

Barton, Allen H., 46, 49, 57, 115, 123, 139, 160, 173, 195, 204, 206

Bates, Frederick, and Clyde C. Harvey, 82–84

Blalock, Hubert M., 64, 95, 206

Blumer, Herbert, 48, 73

Bosworth, Susan L., and Gary A. Kreps, 31, 36, 66, 72, 86, 90, 198, 200–201

Case materials: on organizing, 24, 42–46, 96–97, 102–3, 118; on role enactment, 24, 50–52, 97–109, 118–20

Catalyst, disaster as, 28, 44, 169–70

Change, 33, 189–91; and role enactment, 33, 52, 70–71, 78–79, 82, 85–86, 97, 109–12, 114, 124, 126–34, 141–43, 150–64, 174–89

Classification, 22, 68. *See also* DRC Typology; Taxonomy

Collective behavior, 20, 22, 24–27, 28–29, 33–35, 42–43, 67–69, 74–77, 84, 108, 153–54, 156, 165, 190–91; and the structural code (D,T,R,A), 24–28, 108–9, 124, 135, 154, 163, 190–91, 198

Collective representations, 71–72, 75, 79; and organizing, 25, 39–40, 43, 55, 57, 75–76; and role enactment, 48, 55. *See* Structural code (D,T,R,A)

Collins, Randall, 38, 40, 85

Conflict, 65, 117, 123, 148, 173, 195, 197, 200, 203

Conjoined versus interdependence action, 25, 30, 40, 46, 74, 103

Counterfactuals, 31, 80

Culture, 71, 75–76, 156, 159–60, 163, 178, 193–97

Data protocol, 19–20, 37, 90, 190, 193–97

Denzin, Norman K., 20–21, 30, 33, 102

Description, 29–30, 33, 65, 78, 138, 145, 165, 188–89, 208. *See also* Explanation; Prediction

Dialectical reasoning, 31–32, 38–39, 42–43, 65, 72–73, 76–77, 80, 198

Disaster, 36, 143, 181, 207; definition of, 169–70, 175–78, 203; experience, 58, 61, 63, 147–48, 151, 153–56, 158–61, 163–64, 172, 178, 194; impact ratios, 58, 60, 62, 94, 100, 112, 143, 180; mitigation, 170, 207; as nonroutine social problem, 169–70; planning and preparedness, 20, 29–30, 43, 57, 60–61, 63–64, 159–61, 178, 205; properties of, 167, 193, 199; subcultures, 194; time phases of, 19–24, 33, 38–39, 48, 53, 84, 128, 153, 160, 163, 166, 169, 173, 175, 178, 181–82, 193, 199. *See also* Catalyst, disaster as

Disaster research and general sociology, 160, 186, 189, 206

Disorganization, 68–69, 73–74

217